Come a-Waltzing Matilda

Previously published under Ure Smith Imprint

UNIQUE TO AUSTRALIA

'Come a-Waltzing Matilda'

AUSTRALIAN FOLK-LORE AND FORGOTTEN TALES

by Bill Beatty

WITH DECORATIONS BY E. J. MUNDAY

SEAL
BOOKS

A Seal Book Publication
Seal Books
A division of
Lansdowne Publishing Pty Ltd
Level 5, 70 George Street
Sydney, New South Wales 2000, Australia

This edition published 1995 for
Hinkler Book Distributors Pty Ltd
20–24 Redwood Drive
Dingley, Victoria 3172, Australia

First published by Ure Smith Pty Ltd

Printed in Australia by McPherson's Printing Group, Victoria

Cover illustration:
Eugene von Guerard
The Barwon River, Geelong 1854
Oil on canvas
Gift of W. Max Bell and Norman Belcher, 1923
Copyright: Geelong Art Gallery

Contents

Author's Foreword

'COME A-WALTZING MATILDA' is a selection from an extensive compilation of Australian folk-lore and forgotten tales I have gathered over the years, and which, I hope, will eventually be published in full.

Australia's history is such a short one that it is taken for granted we have little or no folk-lore. It is time for this erroneous impression to be corrected. A country without tradition and without regard to its past is a country without a soul.

That Australia has a fascinating field of traditional customs and stories refreshingly different from those of other lands will be seen even in the compass of this modest volume.

I am grateful to the proprietors of *the Sydney Morning Herald* for permission to reprint some of my newspaper articles and to Angus & Robertson Limited for allowing the inclusion of the words of 'Waltzing Matilda'. My sincere thanks also go to Kylie Tennant, Ernestine Hill, Dame Mary Gilmore, Ion Idriess and other well known Australian writers for their appreciation and encouragement of my attempts to rescue this material from oblivion, and to put it on record.

Bill Beatty.

Waltzing Matilda

By A. B. PATERSON

Once a jolly swagman camped beside a billabong,
  Under the shade of a coolibah tree,
And he sang as he sat and waited while his billy boiled,
  'Who'll come a-waltzing Matilda with me—
Waltzing Matilda, waltzing Matilda, who'll come a-waltzing
      Matilda with me?'
And he sang as he sat and waited while his billy boiled,
  'Who'll come a-waltzing Matilda with me?'

Down came a jumbuck to drink at the billabong,
  Up jumped the swagman and grabbed him with glee,
And he sang, as he stowed it away in his tucker-bag,
  'Who'll come a-waltzing Matilda with me?
Waltzing Matilda, waltzing Matilda, who'll come a-waltzing
      Matilda with me?'
And he sang as he stowed it away in his tucker-bag,
  'Who'll come a-waltzing Matilda with me?'

Up came the squatter, riding on his thoroughbred,
  Down came the troopers – one, two, three –
'Whose is the jumbuck, you've got in your tucker-bag?
  You'll come a-waltzing Matilda with me.
Waltzing Matilda, waltzing Matilda, who'll come a-waltzing
      Matilda with me?
Whose is the jumbuck you've got in your tucker-bag?
  You'll come a-waltzing Matilda with me.'

Up jumped the swagman, and sprang into the billabong,
  'You'll never take me alive!' said he.
And his ghost can be heard, as we pass beside the billabong,
  'Who'll come a-waltzing Matilda with me?
Waltzing Matilda, waltzing Matilda,
  Who'll come a-waltzing Matilda with me?
And his ghost can be heard as we pass beside the billabong,
  'Who'll come a-waltzing Matilda with me?'

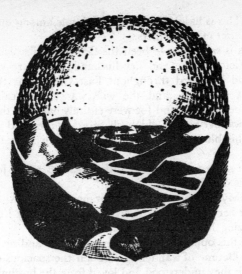

Once a Jolly Swagman

Origin of 'Waltzing Matilda' – Swaggie Joe and Matilda – Banjo Paterson and Christina McPherson – The swagman – Swagmen's Unions – Christina McPherson and bushranger Morgan.

> *'Once a jolly swagman camped beside a billabong,*
> *Under the shade of a coolibah tree,*
> *And he sang as he sat and waited while his billy boiled,*
> *Who'll come a-waltzing Matilda with me—'*

IF YOU ASKED almost any non-Australian what is Australia's national song, the chances are that he would reply, 'Waltzing Matilda'. This ballad with its haunting tune and homely words is known wherever Australians are found – and that covers practically the whole wide world.

Many versions are given of the origin of the term, 'Waltzing Matilda'; there are also many accounts of the inspiration for the words and the source of the tune. The most authentic story concerning the term seems to come from East Gippsland,

Victoria. This is handed down as a folk tale among the settlers in that district of tall timbers.

Matilda is said to have been the first woman swaggie to be seen in Victoria. She and her husband, Joe, were very well known and respected throughout East Gippsland; their surname was unknown, and the wife was always called Mrs Swaggie Joe. Matilda and Joe were entirely happy in their care-free life, wandering the old bush tracks winter and summer, Joe with his bluey on his back, Matilda with a smaller swag on hers.

Matilda often told how her father reacted when Joe asked him for his daughter's hand:

'What! My daughter marry a common swaggie A man who can't offer her even a shack to live in! Do you think I'd let you go a-waltzing Matilda all over the countryside?'

Despite this opposition the girl married Joe and set off with him on a lifetime of wandering through the spacious countryside, which they understood and loved from the bottom of their hearts.

Eventually the day came when they grew infirm, their youthful strength and vigour sapped by the years. They were offered a home by a kindly couple living at Bruthen, but they refused it, saying that they could never live indoors like other folks, and they would go on until they came to the end of the track.

Then one sad day Matilda was taken ill in the morning and died at midday. Swaggie Joe dug her grave at the foot of an old gum tree and sat with his arms about her until it grew dark. Then he buried her.

Next morning as he prepared to fasten on his bluey he muttered, 'Oh well, Bluey, you'll have to be Matilda to me now, and we'll waltz along together 'til the end.'

Swaggie Joe's name for his bluey was soon adopted by other sundowners. 'Waltzing the bluey' was already their idiom for tramping with their swag, so it was not long before it evolved into 'Waltzing Matilda.' It is said that Joe developed the habit of talking to his swag when alone in the bush. He was sometimes seen with it propped against a tree while he talked to it, addressing it as 'Matilda.'

Now for the origin of the words and tune of the song. The verses were written by the Australian poet, A. B. ('Banjo') Paterson in 1896, when he was staying at the home of his fiancee, Miss Sarah Riley, at Winton, Queensland. One day they visited Mr Robert McPherson, owner of Dagworth, one of the largest sheep stations in the district. McPherson and his sister, Christina, were driving Paterson and Miss Riley home when, in a paddock, they saw an old swagman trying to catch a sheep for his tuckerbox. McPherson stopped the buggy, exclaiming, 'He's after a jumbuck!' And jumping down he chased the swaggie away. (Jumbuck was the name coined for a sheep by the aborigines.)

This incident caught Paterson's imagination and he softly spoke the first lines of 'Waltzing Matilda.'

Miss McPherson was intrigued with the words and told the poet that some time previously she had heard a brass band playing a tune that she thought would suit them. When they reached Miss Riley's home Paterson and Miss McPherson sat down at the harmonium and adapted the tune to the words. The tune is an old Rochester (Kent) marching air of the Marlborough Wars. In 1903 Marie Cowan set the music in its present arrangement.

Incidentally, as a baby, Christina McPherson, who was responsible for the music of 'Waltzing Matilda', figured in the capture of Daniel Morgan.

When that bushranger held up the McPherson homestead, then at Peechelba, Victoria, he ordered food to be brought to him while he kept the family in range of his gun. Then he 'requested' Mrs McPherson to play the harmonium to him while he ate. As the baby, Christina, kept crying in the next room, he angrily told a maid to 'go out and keep that brat quiet.'

The maid did so, but having calmed the child, she climbed through the window, raced to an adjoining property, gave the alarm, came back through the window and walked into the main room as though nothing had happened. As a result Morgan was captured. In endeavouring to escape he was shot dead by a station hand.

The Australian swagman must not be confused with the hobo of America or the English tramp. These latter two classes consisted mainly of vagrants who subsisted by begging, stealing or living off the country, and had no intention of working if it could be avoided.

The Australian swagman was the product of conditions in the days of expanding settlement. A continent was being developed and, in fertile areas, farming was being added to sheep grazing on large holdings of pastoralists, who were known as squatters, because in the early days of settlement large areas of land were secured by 'squatting rights'. Labour was a fluid force following seasonal needs to a large extent.

Sheep shearing began in Queensland about July and the shearers followed the job southward for over a thousand miles as spring spread down through New South Wales and Victoria. Each man made his own way from 'shed to shed', as the jobs were called.

Railways were non-existent in the back country, so the sundowner, or swagman, evolved a minimum pack of his necessities and went 'waltzing his bluey' along the track. 'Waltzing' came from the habit of some of the swagmen of moving round a circle of stations, generally completing the journey in about six months. The route he travelled was called 'the racecourse'.

At the sheep stations he could draw free rations of tea, sugar and flour as a traveller passing through. This issue was not regarded as a charity, but partly as a means of maintaining a mobile force of labour and partly in recognition of the vast distances between settlements and normal supply sources.

The swagman was usually a versatile worker, skilled in the rural handicrafts which were the daily portion of the pioneer. If not shearing he might be harvesting grain, picking fruit, building fences, sinking dams or clearing scrub, often on a contract basis rather than wages. Many of the swaggies were young men taking a look at the country; they covered thousands of miles before deciding on a bit of land to start on their own account. Meanwhile they banked the proceeds of their various contracts.

Some of the older men loved the free, wandering life and

merely accumulated enough money for a spell of gregarious conviviality at some bush pub. When the cash was done they took their headaches and a last bottle of firewater back on the 'wallaby track'.

When a man took to the track he was 'on the wallaby', because a wallaby makes many small tracks through the bush. His swag was his 'bluey', so called after the grey-blue blanket which was always rolled round the outside; it is not very often seen nowadays.

THE SWAGMEN'S UNION

Maybe it was an example of typical bush humour but according to old residents of Forbes, New South Wales, a union of swagmen was once formed on the banks of the Lachlan River. It seems that the meeting was largely attended by the best tucker cadgers in the Commonwealth. Officers were elected and the following rules drawn up:—

1. No member to be over one hundred years of age.

2. Each member to pay one pannikin of flour entrance fee. Members who don't care about paying will be admitted free.

3. No member to carry swags weighing over ten pounds.

4. Each member to possess three complete sets of tucker-bags, each set to consist of nine bags.

5. No member to pass any station, farm, boundary-rider's hut, camp or homestead without tapping and obtaining rations or handouts.

6. No member to allow himself to be bitten by a sheep. If a sheep bites a member he must immediately turn it into mutton.

7. Members who defame a 'good' cook, or pay a fine when run in, shall be expelled from the union.

8. No member is allowed to solicit baking-powder, tea, flour, sugar or tobacco from a fellow unionist.

9. Any member found without at least two sets of bags filled with tucker will be fined.

10. No member to look for or accept work of any description. Members found working will be expelled.

11. No member to walk more than five miles per day if rations can be obtained.

12. No member to tramp on Sunday at any price.

A rival organization was the Bagmen's Union of Australia. Its self-appointed president was a man named Kemp. There were no other office-bearers, the head office being just wherever the president happened to be camped. Kemp had a book of rules printed which stipulated the regulations for accepting tucker, lifts on the road, opening and shutting of gates, treatment of dogs, sharing fires, correct method of carrying swags and billycans. A member was allowed to have two straps on his swag, but after five years on the track he was entitled to add a third strap which elevated him to the rank of sergeant.

Bush Characters and Bush Customs

Bush Characters

GONE ARE THE SWAGMEN of yesterday and with them has gone most of the colour associated with carrying the swag.

'Hollow-log Jack' frequented the Monaro country. He reckoned he never slept anywhere but in a hollow log, and swore that there wasn't a camping-place to equal it. He knew every hollow log along the routes he travelled and cleaned out many of them. When he moved on he plugged the ends so that snakes and rabbits would not take possession. According to Hollow-log Jack a man needed only one blanket on the very coldest of nights in these bunks. One end was plugged to stop draughts. Sometimes he walked late into the night to reach a log. His dog went in first and cleared out any wild intruders; then the dog crawled out and the swagman crawled in. Appropriately enough, Jack was found dead in a hollow log.

'Doggy Tom' was known to every man and woman on the

South Coast of New South Wales. He always had at least a dozen dogs with him, and he camped with them at night and tramped the roads with them by day. Doggy Tom was found dead one day with his dogs guar ling his body.

Some of the sundowners used to sow pumpkin, marrow, melon and other seeds near camping-places to ensure supplies of vegetables when they worked round that way months afterwards. 'Pumpkin Paddy' had over one hundred such gardens around the Condamine and Warrego Rivers. He liked potatoes and carried small ones, and thick peel, in a billy for sowing.

Lemon-trees growing in unexpected places along the Richmond River are known as the Parson's Lemons after the Rev A. C. Selwyn, who used to ride on horseback to stations and selections, carrying pocketfuls of citrus seeds to be sown by the river as 'comfort for future travellers'.

'Quandong Joe' was known all over the west of New South Wales. He had quandong seeds on his clothes for buttons, and quandong seeds suspended from his hat to keep the flies from his face. From these seeds he made necklaces, rosary beads, and all kinds of novelties. He also made jam from quandongs and invariably feted a visitor to his camp with one of his quandong pies, in which he specialized.

'Charcoal Annie' was a woman sundowner in the Riverina district who burnt charcoal in river bends and sold it to blacksmiths. She seemed always middle-aged, always carried a sack on her back, and had great, deep, haunted eyes. She lived alone, did no wrong, and died a mystery.

'Billy Patches', a Queensland character, was so-called because of the many neat ptaches on his clothes. On his death a bank-note was found sewn under each patch.

'Old Bob' deserves inclusion in any list of bush characters. He was a boundary-rider who spent most of his spare time with paints and brushes. In any picture he painted it was a certainty that there would be a fence of some sort. Old Bob had a mania for painting fences, whether his picture was of a horse, cow, hut or cottage. He had pictures of such fences as the dog-leg, chock-and-block, post-and-rail, the lazy cocky's, and those varied bush fences that are nameless. A collection of Old Bob's paintings would surely be a complete record of all the types of fences that have been erected in outback Australia.

'Nangus Jack' was a famous whip-maker. His whips were used all over the country. He would spend a week or two making whips for any station he visited; stockwhip, buggy whip, and other kinds. The job finished, he would move on to another station. If things were slack he plaited whips and took them to saddlers in the townships, where they were sold for him. He never turned out a shoddy article. Everything he plaited was a first-class job. When not making whips he plaited bridles, halters, belts, braces and leather watch-chains. Nangus Jack was found dead on Old Man Plains, between Hay and Deniliquin, with one of his whips in his hand, as he would have wished to pass on.

One of the queerest characters ever to roam the outback was Paddy Lenny, known as 'The Horse King of the Northern Territory'. Although he did not own one acre of country, Lenny had at one time over eight hundred horses. With the assistance of a couple of native boys he used to travel his horses from one waterhole to another seeking the best feed. Threats by irate station managers never worried Lenny, and though he hardly ever had enough to eat in his camp, the old Horse King refused to sell one of his horses. Upon his death in Darwin, the Public Curator employed stockmen to muster Lenny's horses so that they could be sold, but drovers and others in the Territory had got in early, as soon as they heard of his death, and purloined many of the animals. One year a buyer offered Lenny £8 a head for all the horses he could muster – at that time he had nearly seven hundred – but the old fellow refused. He preferred to keep his horses and roam the Territory in poverty.

A picturesque character was a woman known all over western Queensland as 'Red Jack'. Her real name was Annie Doyle. For more than twenty years she wandered the west, never remaining long in any locality. Red Jack was a rough character, a slim, wiry woman crowned with a thatch of long red hair, usually bundled up and sometimes skewered with a stick. She dossed at a campfire like the ordinary battler on the road, and knew the wide spaces better than most men. She was a first-class drover, but would tackle any kind of work at a pinch. Dressed like a man on the overland, and with her fiery locks under a wide-brimmed hat, she passed easily for a man and was always addressed as Jack. She owned two smart horses, riding one and leading the other. With these horses she attended every bush race meeting, training them and riding them in the various events. Her most memorable race was at Cloncurry, a match for £10 with a Chinese, who thought he owned the champion of the west. The race – a mile – was held on a Sunday, and all Cloncurry turned out to see it. The Chinese was a splendid rider, but he lacked Annie's experience. After a desperate neck and neck race in which the celestial's pigtail came down and Red Jack's bundle of hair followed suit, Annie won by half a head. Her racings and her wanderings ended at Mareeba, North Queensland, where she died in 1902.

SHINPLASTERS

Currency theorists may be interested in a practice which, for good or ill, has fallen into disuse. At one time printed notes of various denominations were issued by storekeepers over most of north-west Queensland. They could be cashed anywhere in that vast area just the same as banknotes. They were nicknamed 'shinplasters'. As might be expected, there was a certain amount of abuse. Although forgeries were uncommon, there was another way by which the public could be cheated. Unscrupulous store-keepers issuing these notes would often bake them in a hot oven and slightly dampen them. As a result, after a certain period, they would crumble to bits. Many a bushman taking change in these notes would find on arrival at another town that the shin-plasters had turned into powder and were utterly useless.

THE STOCKWHIP

'And he raced his stockhorse past them
And he made the ranges ring
With the stockwhip, as he met them face to face.'

'Banjo' Paterson's song of the stockwhip recalls the fact that the stockwhip is a symbol of the Australian outback; the constant

18

companion of the stockman who handles cattle, wild horses and sheep.

The Australian stockman rides a different kind of horse, wears different clothes, uses different gear from men who handle stock in other parts of the world. One of the things that sets him apart is his stockwhip. Like him it is unique. What the lariat is to the North American cowboy, the bolas to the South American gaucho, and the zhambok is to the South African, the whip is to the Australian stockman. When a whip is used in other countries it is short-handled and made for striking rather than cracking.

Australian whips have been sent all over the world, but mainly as curiosities, for it takes an Australian stockman to handle them. A whip plaited by an expert is a beautiful piece of work. It is really two whips – one is plaited and another plaited over the top of the first. Eight feet is the average length of the stockwhip, though some are made up to twenty feet long. 'Saltbush' Bill Mills – one of the first bushmen to win international fame for his prowess with the stockwhip – used a 55-foot whip.

Kangaroo hide is the main reason why Australian whips are so good. For its weight it is much stronger than any other hide, and it works up into a fine finish. Plaited leather is used on the handle, which is just as important as the rest of the whip. A handle too long or too short can destroy the balance of the whip. The handle, and the way the whip is fixed by an interlocking keeper to the handle, is where the Australian whip differs most from others.

A man who uses a stockwhip all day becomes extremely accurate with it. No wonder it is called the stockman's 'third arm'. Cattlemen have been known to cut a brand on a beast's hide with a whip. Some of the fancy and trick cracks of the experts are remarkable. They can, to all appearances, flog a man unmercifully, yet they are not hurting him in the least, for they crack the whip about a foot to the side of the body and let it curl around harmlessly.

If you have ever tasted a cake made with an emu egg you will really know the meaning of the word 'rich'. One emu egg is equal to twelve hen eggs, and a cake made with one is just food for the Gods. They are delicious, too, scrambled. But if you like your eggs boiled you must cook them for nearly half an hour and keep turning them in the water.

Many and varied are the methods adopted by bushmen to tell if the eggs are fresh. Emu eggs will keep fresh for nine months, or more, and if you smear some fat or wax over them they will last for years. To test their freshness bushmen often use the spinning method. You take three eggs and place them end to end on top of each other, holding the top and bottom ones in each hand. The pressure holds the egg in the centre. That centre egg, if it is fresh, will start to spin round and round. If it stays still, you will know it has had its day.

Should you have but one emu egg to test, you place a straw on top of it. If the egg is fresh the straw will start spinning round.

A medium-sized egg weighs about one and a half pounds. If a horseman comes across a nest, and has no means of carrying them, he usually takes off his shirt, ties the ends of the sleeves and fills the latter with the eggs. Then he puts a sleeve on each side of his saddle and rides home.

Outback folks regard the emu as an excellent weather prophet. The birds will lay their eggs only if they know there will be rain soon, with plenty of juicy green feed for the chicks when they hatch out. If eggs are not found in the months when the birds usually lay, a dry season is indicated.

Of Bush Origin

The name 'billy' seems to be a purely Australian word. Legend says that it was first used in Western Australia on the goldfields.

In the early days France used to export quantities of tinned meat to the miners there. It was labelled 'Boeuf Bouilli' (boiled beef). As cooking utensils were extremely scarce on the gold-fields the miners put the empty tins to good use. Some they used as drinking cups, others they put handles on to make pots for boiling water and cooking purposes. They called them 'bouilli' cans. It was only a matter of time before the name became billy can and was later shortened to billy.

The billy is one of the most widely used articles in outdoor Australia, popular among rich and poor alike. Swagmen sometimes carry sets of billies of graduated size that fit inside each other. Rarely, though, will you see a swaggie with a new or bright-looking billy, It brands him as a new chum, so he blackens it as quickly as possible, boiling it over smoky fires until it becomes a 'respectable' black.

Years ago, billy-boiling contests were popular pastimes at bush carnivals, especially in the districts where drovers used to meet. Some of the entrants carried special billies for these contests. They were as thin as tissue paper. No black or soot stained them, for the cleaner the billy the quicker it boils. Also the fire needs to be a small, compact one, kept directly under the billy.

From Western Australia also came the invention of the Coolgardie safe. It was on the goldfields, too, that this had its origin. Ice was unknown in those parts, but the miners soon solved the problem of keeping food cool and fresh with this safe. The principle was sound but simple. A tray of water on the top of the food container was connected with a drip tray underneath, by means of strips of hessian. The water kept the hessian sides damp, and, as the safe was placed in a current of air, the process of evaporation lowered the temperature inside the safe. It was only necessary to keep water in the top tray in order to keep food in the safe cool and fresh. Today, lots of people prefer the Coolgardie safe to the modern ice chest.

From somewhere in the outback came the idea of the tucker-box. Every bushman who travelled in any kind of vehicle carried a box as a food receptacle. An ideal one was made from a gin case. Small holes were cut in the ends, and these were covered with fine guaze wire to allow air to circulate in the tucker-box, and also to keep out the flies. Whilst the food was being eaten in front of the camp-fire the tucker-box served as a seat.

Apart from the invention of such makeshift masterpieces as the Murrumbidgee blanket and the Wagga rug, it is claimed that the wire mattress was the invention of an Australian bushman. The Wagga rug is made from old sacks. The Murrumbidgee blanket is also made from old sacks with the addition of strips of paper-bark sewn inside it. The first bush wire mattress was merely a frame of saplings. Holes were bored into the wood so that fencing-wire could be interlaced to form a platform on which gum leaves or dry grass were placed. It formed a snug and comfortable bed. Later on netting wire was substituted for the fencing-wire. It is said that the first bush telephone was invented in the early nineties by Edward Argyle, manager of Gunbower sheep station, Victoria. He bought at a Melbourne shop a toy-like telephone gadget, which he tried out to practical use on his fence. To his surprise it worked, and it was not long before the fences were wired to communicate with outlying stations. The scheme was widely adopted, not only in Australia, but on the ranches of Texas and Arizona. American papers, including the *Scientific American*, published the story of the Australian origin of the outback 'phone service.

DAMPER

Most people take it for granted that Australian damper originated in the bush. According to the historian Bonwick, the inventor was a First Fleeter named William Bond, Australia's first baker, who had his place of business in Pitt Street, Sydney. This pioneer died in 1838, at the reputed age of a hundred and ten.

Probably through lack of facilities for making the common bread loaf, much of the bread he made at first was 'damper'.

The name 'damper' was derived from his custom of 'damping' the fire – covering it with ashes, so as to preserve the red coals with which to make a blaze in the morning. The bush damper is still covered in much the same manner.

There are many ways of making damper. Here is one recipe of pioneer days:

Take 1 lb. of flour, water, and pinch of salt. Mix into a stiff dough and knead for at least one hour, not continuously, but the longer it is kneaded the better the damper. Press with the hands into a flat cake, and cook it in at least a foot of hot ashes.

When the pioneers trail-blazed the bush there were no self-raising flours, baking-powders or yeast. Nevertheless, bushmen and women had many substitutes for baking-powder, the most popular being a handful of white wood-ashes. In the artesian bore country, bore-water was sufficient to make the damper rise.

Damper has always retained its popularity with swagmen. At Christmas time, when these wandering gentlemen foregather in celebration, they sometimes put threepenny-bits in the damper!

The man outback seldom had a pair of scales, and even if he had a foot-rule he rarely used it. He measured corn, bran or anything else on his farm, with a kerosene-tin, and he was generally pretty accurate. By looking at a beast for a few moments he could judge within a pound or two its correct weight, and guessing the weight of a bullock is still popular at country shows. Timber could be measured with the hands. Bushmen knew exactly the width of their hands, how far they could span, and how many steps they took to a hundred yards. On the south coast of New South Wales a story is told of a woman who was famed for always winning the 'stepping the hundred yards' event at all country sports carnivals. However, an event at Wyndham was the last one she won. Just before she finished stepping the hundred yards a dog ran in front of her and she tripped and fell. Her dress flew up and revealed a piece of cord fastened from one leg to another so that by stepping the full extent of this cord she was able to measure her paces exactly.

Children of the great outback rarely saw sweets, and they knew nothing of cinemas and radio, but they made their own fun and entertainment. They roasted cobs of young corn at the fire, baked potatoes, quinces and apples in the hot ashes, gathered bunya-nuts and roasted them like chestnuts, used quandong seeds for marbles, after eating the fruit, and where bush-nuts were plentiful up north they had no need to buy peanuts. They used to eat the thick red mass from briar pips before experts knew it was rich in vitamin C. They made their own sporting material. Bush timber made cricket bats, and a fungus known as blackfellow's bread provided the balls. When dad killed a bullock they inflated the bladder and made a football. And then there were the joys of swimming in the creek, or billabong, or at least some kind of waterhole.

The prickly pear has been a costly menace to Australia, nevertheless it was a boon to the old-timers. Many have pulped the pear and used it as a cattle fodder with good results. Bush women have found that the fruit made delicious jam and jelly; indeed, where ordinary fruit was scarce many children have known no other jam. Bushmen in the outback, and even children doing their homework for the correspondence schools, have written with prickly-pear juice as a substitute for ink. It has even been used as a paint. There are many people who swear by prickly pear as a remedy for diabetes. They boil some of the green leaves and drink the juice. And here's a tip regarding the spikes on the plant. They are an excellent substitute for gramophone needles, giving a mellow tone which is not obtainable from the usual steel needles.

Some Australian Ghosts

Quinn's Light – Fisher's Ghost – Ghost Glen – The Martinet Major –
Black Horse of Sutton – Ghost of Glengallan Gates – Light that Fails –
Ghost of Yarralumla – Morgan's Ghost – The Bunyip.

AUSTRALIA'S GHOSTS seem to have died out in recent years. Perhaps the country has been opened up too much for them.

There were the Headless Horseman that caused cattle to stampede; the Tinonee ghost which appeared on a marshy flat near the Manning River; the Phantom Mail – a light which appeared to be on a mail-coach in the One Tree Plain district, near Hay, and which travelled rapidly across the plain. Men have galloped after it, but have never caught it.

QUINN'S LIGHT

No ghost can be altogether satisfactory unless it makes repeated and somewhat regular appearances. One spectre that endeavours to uphold a good ghostly tradition is Quinn's Light.

The strange phenomenon is well attested. It has chosen as

25

its locale the Daudaman Valley in the Go-Go-Billi Ranges down by the Lachlan River, and it takes its name from one John Quinn, who for very many years was a judge at the New South Wales sheepdog trials and a man of sound common sense.

Quinn claimed that on numerous occasions he saw a strange light of extraordinary brilliance which came floating down the valley among the tall timbers, circled his homestead, then made back to its hills.

Quinn described it as resembling a large, yellow, crested eagle with outstretched wings, and said that it illuminated the trees as it passed with a phosphorescent glow. He showed it to others – in case his own testimony should not be believed – and he organized night riders who pursued it, and hunters who shot at the apparition but to no purpose.

GHOSTS OF THE GLEN

In the town of Kiama, on the South Coast of New South Wales, the old folks tell a ghostly tale of the early days there. The story is as old almost as the town itself.

The drama occurred in the days when ticket-of-leave men roamed the countryside – when Kiama was thickly timbered, and most of the men in the district were engaged in timber-cutting.

Many an old resident will recall for you the vivid verse that tells of Kiama's blood-curdling ghosts :

'Over a pitfall, the moon dew is thawing,
And with never a body two shadows stand sawing,
The wraiths of two sawyers (step under and under),
Who did a foul murder, and were blackened with thunder;
An whenever a storm wind comes driving and driving,
Through the blood-spattered timber you may see the saw striving,
You may see the saw heaving and falling and heaving,
Whenever the sea-creek is chafing and grieving.'

In the convict days many of the ticket-of-leave men were to be feared, especially those found amongst the Illawarra sawyers. They were a cut-throat crew who would stop at no evil deed.

One late night a young English immigrant, with a sheep-dog at his side, entered the inn at Kiama. He strolled over to the bar, calling out:

'Good evening, gentlemen! I'm a stranger to the district, but I hope you don't mind me joining the company. Have a drink, everybody! Come on – all of you! The drinks are on me!'

In 'shouting' for the crowd the young man foolishly displayed a purseful of money.

The evening passed, and then, slightly drunk, he decided to continue his journey.

Up spoke one of the few remaining drinkers: 'Now look here, new chum, me and me mate wouldn't think of letting you go out in the bush alone. Anyway, you'd never find your way on a pitch dark night like this. And, what's more, young feller-me-lad, if you're going south we can put you on the right track.'

And so the three men and the dog went into the darkness. They never returned.

It was some months later that a man well known in the district became lost in the thick bush near the present township of Gerringong. When night came he made a rough shelter in a glen and lay down and went to sleep. He awoke to the rumble of thunder. Suddenly he felt his eyes being drawn to an object a few yards away. To his horror he saw it was the doubled-up body of a man. A wasted sheep-dog was licking the dead face – gashed, bloody and terrible to see.

Then he heard the rasping sound of a cross-cut saw and, looking farther into the darkness, he perceived the silhouetted figures of two men working in a saw-pit, complete with logs and crosspieces. A burst of thunder came and, as it died away, one of the men spoke:

'He's still got fifty golden sovereigns left. That's twenty-five apiece. A nice little nest-egg for us. We'll pitch the swine into the fire! But mind the dog – we'd better cut its throat.'

There was a flash of lightning and the apparition vanished.

Next day a search party found the lost man. He told his rescuers of the vision in the glen. Afterwards another search was made where the lost settler was discovered. At the spot he indicated, the burnt bones of a man were found – near by was the skeleton of a dog.

Years later, in the 1830's, a man walked into the same inn at Kiama. His name was Jem Hicks, and he had the drawn features of a haunted soul. Someone remarked that they hadn't seen him for a matter of years – in fact not since the time the new chum had 'shouted' for everyone and then disappeared.

All of a sudden a clap of thunder and lightning rent the air. A dog that was stretched out before the fire began to howl. Hicks started to tremble, and cried out:

'Curse the money! Curse the dog! Am I never to get peace?'

In a stumbling rush he went into the night and was never seen again.

So ends the story of the ghosts of the glen. But not so the spectres themselves, for, as old-timers in the district will inform you, the ghostly tableau has appeared on several occasions to wanderers in the glen.

FISHER'S GHOST

Most historic of Australia's ghosts is Fisher's, at Campbelltown, New South Wales. Near Sydney, on the main highway through Campbelltown, the road crosses a small creek on which is a neat sign marked FISHER'S GHOST CREEK.

Of the thousands of motorists who have read that notice few have failed to wonder as to the origin of the name. Is there a story? There certainly is.

On the 17th of June, 1826 John Farley, a ticket-of-leave man, burst into the crowded parlour of the Plough Inn at Campbelltown. His face was pallid, his eyes staring, and he was shaking as if with the palsy. He cried out:

'A ghost! I've seen a ghost!'

An uproar of laughter greeted this dramatic announcement. Farley was bombarded from all sides by derisive questions and ribald interjections. The pub patrons agreed that he had been the victim of a practical joker, or else was suffering from hallucinations. But he stuck to his story.

'I was passing Fisher's farm and, as you know, there's a full moon outside. Leaning over the slip-rails I saw a man with a pipe in his mouth. But he wasn't smoking, and, when I got a bit nearer I saw it was Fred Fisher himself. Then I got panicky, for I could see right through him, as if he wasn't solid. I knew then that it wasn't Fred Fisher himself. It was his ghost!'

'How did you know it was Fred Fisher's ghost? How do you know he's dead?' someone called out.

True, Fred Fisher had simply disappeared from the district, and there had been no cause to believe other than that he'd gone elsewhere in the country.

'What was the ghost doing?' came another question.

Farley continued his story. 'He was just leaning over the slip-rails. Then, as I went nearer, he began to point. I was too scared to move. Still, he kept on pointing down the paddock towards the creek. Then he just wasn't there – sort of faded away!'

Next morning Fisher's ghost was the one topic of conversation in the township. The news reached the local sergeant of police, who had already been making inquiries about Fisher's disappearance, and had notified the police headquarters in Sydney about the matter.

The sergeant decided to act on Farley's story. He sent a trooper and two native trackers to examine Fisher's property, remarking with a laugh not to expect to find footprints of a ghost.

No sooner had the party reached the slip-rails than Gilbert, one of the trackers, pointed to certain marks. There, smeared on the rails of the fence, in the exact position described by Farley, were traces of dried blood.

Soon, Gilbert gave a little cry of triumph. The whites of his eyes gleamed excitedly as he followed a trail towards the creek. There, at a particular spot, he directed the party to dig. In a few moments they came upon the body of Fisher dressed in the clothes described by Farley, and in the place he said the ghost had indicated.

Who was the murderer? Police investigations resulted in Fisher's partner, a man named Worrall, who was then living in Sydney, being charged with the crime. Though he protested his innocence he was found guilty and sentenced to death. On the day of his execution he confessed to the crime.

And to this day, in Campbelltown, the oldest inhabitants will tell you that if you care to wander, unaccompanied as did John Farley, round Fisher's farm about midnight on the night of the 17th of June you will see a dim figure leaning over the slip-rails, pointing in the direction of the creek that runs at the bottom of the farm.

There is a sequel to this story. Mr. J. K. Chisholm of Gledswood knew Farley well. When the latter was on his death-bed Mr. Chisholm went to see him.

'I want to ask you a question, Farley,' he said. 'Will you tell me the truth?'

Farley answered: 'I am a dying man, Mr. Chisholm. I'll speak only the truth.'

'Well, it's only one question, Farley, and this it it: Did you really see Fisher's ghost, or did you make up that story because you had suspicions and wanted the matter investigated?'

Farley raised himself on his elbows painfully and looked straight at his visitor.

'Mr. Chisholm, I saw that ghost as plainly as I see you now.'

GHOST OF GLENGALLAN GATES

This apparition was a gate opener in the Allora district of Queensland. Riders would feel their horses trembling and sweating with fear as they approached the gates. Then a grey, billowy form would fly from a post, and the gates would spring open. As soon as the horseman passed through, generally at a frenzied gallop, the gates would swing to again.

The haunting continued for many years, and seemed to defy explanation. Unbelievers claimed that the ghost was merely a large, whitish owl, which made the gate-post its nightly perch. When the bird rose at the approach of a horseman the sudden movement caused the finely-balanced gates to swing open, and then, having reached the limit of their movement, they swung back again.

The gates were removed some years ago, when the old track was transformed into a main road, but it is said that horses still betray terror when passing the crumbling gate stumps at night.

Records of the Monaro district of New South Wales abound in stories of wayside ghosts, shades of bushrangers who returned to the scenes of their crimes, sudden apparitions of the long since dead. Here are some picturesque tales of these spooks:

THE MARTINET MAJOR

More than a century ago a certain major acquired large tracts of land in the Monaro district. A bachelor, he was a martinet of the worst kind. He had a number of convicts working for him, including an unruly member sent out as a political rebel. The latter resented the fact that he was 'a lag' along with the pickpockets and cut-throats working on the station and, as a result, always exasperated the peppery major.

One day the major abused this convict, who picked up a stone and threw it at him.

The major, who was also a magistrate, immediately sentenced the man to death, and the hanging took place on the property that same evening.

But, so the story goes, the convict had his revenge. He haunted the place in a most annoying fashion, singing ribald songs at the foot of the major's four-poster bedstead; hunting the cattle out of the barns at night; kicking over buckets of milk left on the dairy floor by the milkmaids; rattling tins and tolling bells in the dead of night until the major could no longer stand it. Thoroughly exasperated, though he never admitted to being scared, he sold his property and returned to England.

The present owner of the property (it seems a pity to have to record) has never seen the ghost.

BLACK HORSE OF SUTTON

Also in the Monaro district operated a famous spectre known as the Black Horse of Sutton. This apparition was seen at intervals by a certain family, but only when disaster befell their house. The first visitation took place when the father of the house went to Goulburn to arrange a land deal to extend his large property. As he was returning home he was thrown from his horse and killed.

It was a mild summer night and the man's wife was seated on the broad-flagged verandah of the homestead when she heard the faint echo of galloping hoofs along the dusty home road. There was silence; then the sound of a gate being opened; the wheeling of a horse as though a man had turned to close the gate; the clanging sound as it shut fast; then the sound of galloping hoofs again.

The woman stood up and walked to the top of the verandah steps to welcome her husband. . . .

'It must be John. Strange – I wonder why he didn't cooee as he always does? Why – I'm trembling! Perhaps it's just – oh! – his horse! John! John! Where are you? . . .

A riderless horse had come into view, its hoofs drumming on the drive. It crossed the lawn at breakneck speed straight towards the house. The sound was muffled, only to be taken up again at the back of the house. The riderless horse had passed through the house and disappeared into the ranges beyond.

The woman watched it in the dusk petrified. She hoped it was a trick of her imagination in the fast-falling evening shadows. But she knew she would wait in vain for the return of her husband. When a search was made he was found dead – his horse grazing near by.

Old identities in the district will tell you that when disaster came to that family the riderless horse was seen galloping swiftly – a messenger of death. It made its appearance when the woman's eldest son was killed at the Boer War. Again when the youngest son met his death in an accident.

The house has long been demolished and sheep graze across the country where the riderless horse comes no more.

BLACK GHOST OF YARRALUMLA

Yarralumla House, the beautiful Canberra residence of Australia's Governor-General, possesses a mystery of its own that is most intriguing. According to more or less conflicting versions of the story, a ghost – a real Australian blackfellow ghost – has been known to walk there.

The wanderer is popularly supposed to be an aborigine searching for a lost diamond. But he is a very modest ghost who knows his place, never entering the house, but wandering about the lawns at Yarralumla, harmless and self-effacing.

It is said he has been seen from the dining-room on cold dreary nights when the breezes whistle down on Canberra from the snowbound Monaro ranges.

On summer nights he has been seen digging under a deodar tree, where a diamond of great value, for which he is ever searching, is said to be hidden.

The tale is told in an unsigned manuscript dated 1881, 'written near Yarralumla'. The letter was found in this historic home after it had been handed over to the Commonwealth Government by its former owners. It states:

'In 1826, a large diamond was stolen from James Cobbity, on an obscure station in Queensland. The theft was traced to one of the convicts who had run away, probably to New South Wales. The convict was captured in 1858, but the diamond could not be traced; neither would the convict (name unknown) give any information, in spite of frequent floggings.

'During 1842 he left a statement to a groom, and a map of the hiding-place of the hidden diamond.

'The groom, for a minor offence, was sent to Berrima gaol. He was clever with horses, and one day, when left to his duties, plaited a rope of straw and then escaped by throwing it over the wall, where he caught an iron bar. Passing it over, he swung himself down and escaped. He and his family lived out west for several years, according to the Rev James Hassall who, seeing him live honestly, did not think it necessary to inform against him. I have no reason to think he tried to sell the diamond. Probably the ownership of a thing so valuable would bring suspicion and lead to his re-arrest.

'After his death his son took possession of the jewel, and with a trusty blackfellow set off for Sydney. After leaving Cooma for Queanbeyan they met with, it was afterwards ascertained, a bushranging gang. The blackfellow and his companion became separated, and finally the former was captured and searched, to no avail, for he had swallowed the jewel.

c

'The gang, in anger, shot him. He was buried in a piece of land belonging to Colonel Gibbes, and later Mr. Campbell. I believe the diamond to be among his bones. It is of great value. My hand is enfeebled with age, or I should describe the trouble through which I have passed. My life has been wasted, my money expended, I die almost destitute, and in sight of my goal.

'I believe the grave to be under the large deodar-tree. Being buried by blacks, it would be in a round hole.

'Believe and receive a fortune. Scoff and leave the jewel in its hiding-place.

'Written near Yarralumla.'

If the story is untrue, the deodar is not. The tree is considered to be the finest of its kind in the Commonwealth. No attempt has been made to uproot it, for the owners of Yarralumla have always thought more of this grand old tree than the chance of treasure among its roots, and they have left the jewel – if any – in its hiding-place. Many thousands of deodars growing throughout the country have been planted from the seeds of this famous old-timer with its absorbing tale of mystery.

LIGHT THAT FAILS

Broome, the pearling port of Western Australia, provides a ghostly manifestation that has been in evidence for many years.

There is a beacon on the foreshore that, for some unaccountable reason, sometimes becomes dim. Complaints have been made by skippers in those waters, and time and again the light has been completely overhauled and cleaned, but all to no avail. Without any known cause the light continues to grow dim at certain times. The coloured divers firmly believe that ghosts of drowned pearlers, on certain memorial nights, flit and roam round the beacon. That, they declare, is the explanation for the light dimming, as if enveloped by mist, even on the clearest of nights. Moreover, say the coloured seamen, it will always be so, for no effort of the white man can clear the ghosts of the dead away.

MORGAN'S GHOST

Old hands around Woodend, Victoria, will tell you that the ghost of bushranger Dan Morgan still rides over the mountains in the vicinity at night. Not far from Woodend is Hanging Rock, claimed to be Morgan's hideout. There is an underground stream which emerges near the foot of the rock and runs over the cliff. The water in this stream is always rust-coloured, and a deposit of red rust is left on the rocks. Because of this and the link with Morgan the water has long been referred to locally as 'Morgan's Blood.'

When Morgan was shot dead at Peechelba his head was cut off and sent to Melbourne to be examined for scientific purposes, which no doubt accounts for the story that the ghost riding about the hills is a headless ghost.

BEHOLD THE BUNYIP

Mention of the bunyip will perhaps mean little to the present generation of young Australians. But there are many older folk who can vividly recall the fears inspired by lonely parts of the bush where they wandered as youngsters – fears arising from alleged association of the localities with this mysterious beast. A flourishing Victorian country newspaper still circulates under the name of *The Bunyip*, and Australia's fairy-tale creature is known to both black folk and white, though nobody knows what it looks like. Oddly enough, this truly fabulous creature has never been represented in any definite form in art or literature.

Despite some local variations, the story of the bunyip has so much in common throughout a considerable part of Australia that it is fair to assume that the myth had a basis in some common act of natural history.

The bunyip of the aborigines was a large, dark-coloured, furred animal, with glowing eyes and a bellowing call, a haunter of swamps and billabongs.

It did not take the white man long to get interested in the bunyip. Indicating a pre-knowledge, the first official reference appeared in the minutes of the Geographical Society of Australia, on the 19th December, 1821. The suggestion was recorded, following the report by the explorer Hamilton Hume of the existence of a strange animal in Lake Bathurst, supposedly a manatee, hippopotamus, or bunyip, that Hume be reimbursed for expenditure incurred in any further attempt to obtain hide, teeth or other tangible evidence of the existence of this creature.

In the early days of Victoria, before it became a separate colony, Governor Latrobe wrote that there were 'two kinds' of bunyip. He sent drawings of the 'southern' kind to Tasmania, but they have been lost.

It may be that the 'northern' kind of bunyip was in part inspired by swamp-feeding cows, truants from the infant settlement of Parramatta. Early Sydney records of the marsh monster introduce horns and tasselled tails, which must have added special terror to the age-old stories of the local aborigines. It is a pity that no copies remain of Latrobe's drawings of the bunyip. Contemporary Victorian writers called it the 'bunyip or kianpraty'.

There are records of alleged eyewitnesses. The year 1872 was the date of the Narrandera (New South Wales) bunyip, which was seen by many observers. It was described as: 'About half as long again as an ordinary retriever dog. Hair all over its body, jet black and shining. Its coat very long.' The following year one was recorded and described from Dalby, Queensland: 'It had a head like a seal, and a tail consisting of two fins, a larger and a smaller one'.

The Great Lake in Tasmania is supposed to have been inhabited by several bunyips. One bumped a boat in 1873. Francis McPartland, in 1870, saw three or four together. Seven observers in this locality, within ten years, all agree in describing the creature as like a huge sheep-dog about the head, and from three to five feet long.

There are many observers who steadfastly believe, and with much reason, that the actual origin of the widespread bunyip myth lies in the fact that from time to time seals have made their way up the winding waters of the Murray and Darling rivers and the vast network of associated streams, to live there for a time in the billabongs and lagoons.

More than ninety years ago a seal was actually shot in a lagoon near Conargo, New South Wales; it was stuffed and remained over the chimney-place at the Conargo Hotel for many years. This animal had penetrated over nine hundred miles inland along the streams of the Murray basin.

The mysterious booming sound made by the bittern, a very shy bird, has become associated with the bunyip, but actual observers have usually described the sound of the latter as a roar or bellow.

The imagination of the Port Phillip natives pictured the bunyip as a fearsome booming beast, as big as a bullock, with an emu's neck, the mane and tail of a horse, and a seal's flippers. It had a cuckoo's instinct, and laid turtle's eggs in the nest of a platypus. Strangely enough the description fits very closely that extinct marine reptile the plesiosaurus. But the bunyip, unlike the plesiosaurus, when it tired of crayfish, ate blacks!

In any case it seems that the fabled bunyip has at least some slight substratum of fact.

Treasure Trove

From Spanish Shores – Dog God Idol – Ship with a Silver Keel – Mystery Trees – One Chance in a Million – Stolen Gold – The £10,000 pearl.

THE ISLANDS OF North Australia, especially in the Torres Strait, are a fascinating field for treasure trove. Some of the old Spanish shipwrecks have been seen by the pearl divers and a fair amount of their treasures recovered. Most of it, however, now lies smothered beneath coral.

Some years ago Frank Jardine, a well-known pearler, found beneath the rusty anchor of one of these wrecks a small fortune in ancient Spanish gold coins. On Stephens Island a fisherman found a native idol which was decorated with valuable old Castilian jewellery. Then again, on Prince of Wales Island a crumbling skeleton was found, alongside of which was a huge rusty sword of ancient Spanish design. Near by was a valuable gold goblet.

Quite a number of gold coins have been found on Booby Island. In the early days Booby Island was the headquarters of the only real pirates that Australia has ever known. They were a band of Asiatic cut-throats who plundered the Spanish treasure ships as they sailed to and from the Philippines. The buccaneers were finally wiped out in a sea battle with a Spanish man-o'-war, but their valuable loot is thought to be buried somewhere on Booby. That lonely island is riddled with caves, some of which have never been explored. Maybe the pirates' hoard is hidden in one of them.

Sixty odd years ago Booby Island was a regular calling-place for all the sailing vessels plying to and from Australia via Torres Strait. There is very little to be seen today on the island to remind one of its importance, save one curiosity – a cave that was used as a post-office. It was an arrangement between the captains and crews whereby they used to drop their letters into a box that was kept in the cave. When a ship called the captain would open the box and, if there were any letters for his run, collect them. Alongside the seamen's letter-box was a big diary. In this the captains signed and entered the dates their ships called. The letter-box is still there but the diary has vanished. The only records to be seen are hundreds of names of seamen and their ships scratched on the walls of the cave. At one time the Queensland Government always kept in this unattended post-office food, water and clothing for shipwrecked sailors.

Dog God Idol

Not all the hidden treasures of Torres Strait are from the old Spanish wrecks. Secreted somewhere on Moa Island is an ancient and valuable tortoise-shell idol that was once worshipped by the former savage warriors there. The idol was the famous Dog God of Moa. It was a huge and remarkable figure of a dog. About 20 feet long and 12 feet high; modelled in thick tortoise-shell; more than two hundred of the finest tortoise-shells were used in its construction. At present-day values the shell alone would be worth more than £2000.

The missionaries began their work in the Torres Strait about eighty years ago. When rumours reached the natives of Moa about these strange white men who destroyed the old gods and idols, the chiefs determined to safeguard the Dog God. They carried the great idol to a secret cave and sealed up the entrance to it. Then they made a pledge never to reveal its whereabouts to any white man. Those who knew of its hiding-place are now dead, and they have taken the secret with them to the grave.

It is now believed that a landslide in past years must have covered the entrance to the Dog God's home, hiding the idol forever from the prying eyes of man.

SHIP WITH A SILVER KEEL

The natives of Murray Island tell a tale of a ship with a silver keel which was wrecked off the island a long time ago. They say that every person aboard the ship was massacred by the fierce natives of those days. The legend is emphatic that the keel of the vessel was of solid silver – a rich prize to the finder. Unfortunately the natives have a deep, superstitious dread of the wreck and refuse to guide treasure seekers to its whereabouts. Some years ago a white official found a group of native children on Murray Island using large Spanish gold pieces as counters in a game in which flat beans usually serve as this medium.

Among the natives, apart from the stories they tell of white men who came in ships, there is definite evidence that large groups of white men have spent much time among them. Some of the island tribes have a strangely light skin with pronounced Latin features. Moreover, Spanish words are included in their dialects.

ONE CHANCE IN A MILLION

One of the strangest tales of the Torres Strait – and literally true – concerns the schooner *Lancashire Lass* that struck a reef on one of the Barrier Reef islands in 1890.

The vessel laden with pearl-shell was returning to a Queensland port from the pearling grounds east of Cape York. A gale blew up, but the schooner flew before it and made fast time on the homeward course, for she was a good sea boat and skilfully handled. And then, with startling suddenness, there loomed, immediately ahead, great surges piling up and breaking in walls of foam – a sure indication of the weather side of a coral-reef.

It was a terrifying sight, and to change course was quite impossible.

All the skipper could do was to look for a gap in the reef through which he might attempt a passage. But there was no gap; look as he might, he could see nothing but a wall of surf stretching right across the course from one extreme to the other of the limited horizon. There was nothing to be done except to keep the plunging schooner at it, in the desperate hope that some great wave might lift the vessel over the wall.

The one chance in a million came off; as the little craft approached the reef and almost inevitable destruction, a huge comber roared up behind her and carried her over the obstruction into the calmness of the lagoon on the other side. The sails were lowered, and the anchor let go. The schooner rode in safety, while all hands thanked their lucky stars for such unexpected good fortune.

Next day, wind and sea were fairly normal. It now became necessary to find a way out, but, after exploring all round the coral barrier, no gap could be discovered through which the schooner might pass to the open sea. The only hope of escape lay in putting the cargo of pearlshell overboard, so that the ship might be sufficiently lightened to be floated across the reef at high tide.

This was done; the shell was sewn up in bags and lowered over the side to the bottom of the lagoon, into a depth of about 30 feet of water. The site of the cargo was marked by a buoy, and the geographical position determined. At the next high tide, the schooner managed to scrape over the reef and made the Queensland coast in a few days.

When, on arriving at her home port, the story was told, the owners fitted out another and lighter vessel, and with an experienced diver on board this ship sailed for the spot where the cargo had been jettisoned. The reef was crossed safely, and the buoy found. The anchor dropped, the diver was sent below to begin his job.

A few minutes passed without any signal from him, and

then he came up again, making signs for his helmet to be unscrewed.

His story created a sensation; the bags of shell were there right enough, but, he said, they were lying on top of a great mound piled up above the floor of the lagoon, and this mound was composed entirely, as far as he could make out, of silver coins.

To convince the sceptics, he took from the pocket of his diver's dress a lump of Spanish dollars all cemented together by the coral insects, but quite easily separated into individual coins.

There was no delay in beginning the task of raising the loot. There were thousands of dollars there; the schooner had to make several voyages before all the treasure was salvaged.

Consider the miraculous chance that led to the discovery! How the coin got into the lagoon no one can answer with any certainty. Probably a Spanish ship on her way to the Philippines was wrecked on the outer reef and at some time lifted bodily over the coral wall into the shallow water inside. Then, in the course of long years, the ship disintegrated, until nothing was left but the most valuable and imperishable part of her lading – the treasure of silver dollars.

MYSTERY TREES

A curiosity at Palm Island, close to Townsville, Queensland, is said to be the location of buried treasure. On the island is growing an avenue of strange trees, not to be found elsewhere in Australia. The trees are large and shady, in two rows. The individual trees are so evenly spaced that the planting of them was obviously the work of man. Though there is no direct evidence to indicate that the Spaniards planted them, they were certainly placed there in the days before Captain Cook came to Australia.

STOLEN GOLD

Somewhere about Mosman heights in suburban Sydney is buried a fortune that will make the finder affluent for life. The amount is said to be more than £20,000.

The money is the proceeds of Australia's first bank robbery when, on 15th September 1826, the Sydney branch of the Bank of Australia was robbed. The money was never recovered, but it was expertly planted in the vicinity of Mosman heights, so it was said.

Midway between Melbourne and Ballarat still lies hidden the secret hoard of Captain Melville. That bushranger reaped a wealth of treasure from the proceeds of his daring robberies, all of which he concealed in a remote hiding-place. When he was captured he openly boasted that his booty was so well planted that it would defy discovery for hundreds of years.

It is doubtless hidden somewhere in the country where Melville operated, and should be a considerable fortune. Included amongst the treasure hunters who have sought in vain to find it was Marcus Clarke, author of the Australian classic, *For the Term of His Natural Life*. He put arduous toil into searching some of the caves in the Grampian Mountains.

Other bushrangers known to have buried the proceeds of their robberies are Ben Hall, Thunderbolt, and Frank Gardiner. Ben Hall's booty is believed to be hidden in the depths of the beautiful Bungonia Caves, about twenty-five miles out of Goulburn. Thunderbolt's spoil is said to be somewhere in the Mudgee ranges.

A strange sequel is told about the loot of Frank Gardiner – 'King of the Bushrangers'. Gardiner is the only bushranger buried outside Australia. When he was freed from prison he decided to go to America. There, in the United States, he became quite a respected citizen.

He had operated as a bushranger in the Forbes district. A few years after his death in America there came to Forbes three husky young Americans. They did not give their names, or mention anything about themselves other than the fact that they were brothers. Soon after their arrival in the district they discovered in the hilly country a hoard of bushrangers' gold. The men then packed up and returned to America.

After their departure some old residents of Forbes recalled the strong resemblance of the young men to Frank Gardiner, and now it is believed that they were his sons. Perhaps he told them where he had hidden the gold and, after his death, they decided to retrieve it.

Presumably the loot was not that of the Eugowra robbery, when Gardiner and his gang bailed up the gold escort and robbed it of £10,000. What became of that plunder is a mystery, but, according t a story, there is good reason for believing that two enterprising Scotsmen 'sprung' the bushrangers' loot, and got away with it to their native land. Some years ago an account was published concerning a man named Percy Faithful who, when in Scotland in 1904, was shown a cottage and told a strange tale about the man living in it.

This Scot, and a friend of his, had emigrated to Australia in their young days. One night, when tramping through the country looking for work, they sought shelter in a hut, whose sole occupant was a woman. The request for a night's lodging was refused, the woman saying that the bushrangers were likely to return at any moment, and they might suspect the travellers of being police spies.

Even as she spoke the gang appeared in the distance and the woman hurriedly locked the two travellers in a small room. The bushrangers, who were in a desperate hurry (police being on their tracks) handed to the woman a bag full of gold, told her to 'plant' it, and then rode away. The Scotsmen, so the story goes, took the gold from the defenceless woman and cleared out. With their doubly illgotten booty, to the value of £10,000, the precious pair boarded at Sydney a vessel bound for the Old Country, which they reached safely, to enjoy the golden fruits of the Eugowra escort robbery. That is the tale.

WARRIOR ISLAND

Much has been written about the great pearling industry of Australia's northern tropical seas, but little has been said of the romantic Torres Strait island that was the birthplace of the industry. Forgotten, too, is the name of Captain Banner, who, in 1868, discovered the first pearls, but whose untimely death prevented him from sharing in the fortunes that were amassed by the majority of the pioneer pearlers. Today the name of that island is Warrier Island.

In the early days, Warrior Island was known by its native name of Tute. It was the home of hostile natives – noted sea warriors whose powerful fleet of huge outrigger canoes was feared throughout Torres Strait and along the coast of New Guinea. All native trading vessels travelling between New Guinea and the mainland had to pay the Warrior Islanders a 'toll' in goods before they were allowed to pass; any vessel that refused to pay was promptly sunk and the natives on board killed.

Strangely enough, the first white men to visit the island received an enthusiastic reception; they were the crew of a French ship, which, in distress, called there in 1790 to repair a damaged rudder. The natives gave the visitors every assistance and treated the sailors like kings. Unfortunately the Frenchmen sailed away without offering the natives anything whatsoever for their services. This unfair treatment incensed the islanders so much that from then on they attacked every white man's boat that neared their territory.

It was not warfare that finally subdued the sea warriors. In the early sixties of last century Captain Moresby of the H.M.S. *Basilisk* managed to make friends with them by giving them presents of tobacco and other trade goods when he encountered them at sea. Later, in 1868, Captain Banner happened to call at the island and was amazed to see all the natives – men, women and children – wearing strings and ornaments of valuable pearls. The children were even using pearls for marbles.

When Captain Banner's story reached civilization, the great pearl rush commenced to the then lonely and little-known seas of Australia's northern coasts. Gradually the pearl-beds of Warrior Island were worked out, and since the year 1900 the island has been forgotten.

In pearl fishing, hardship and endeavour, joys and disappointments, humour and tragedy, go hand in hand. There was one northern pearler who discovered a perfect, round pearl which was valued at £10,000. He gave the gem to his wife to guard for him until the end of the pearling season, when he intended making a special journey to London to sell it. His wife placed the pearl for safe keeping in a small bottle, which she hung on a chain around her neck, inside her dress. Then Fate intervened. On the pearler's last trip to sea for the season, his wife accompanied him, but the boat foundered during a cyclone, and all on board were drowned, with the exception of the pearler himself. His wife, with the bottle containing the pearl still hanging around her neck, went down with the boat, and although divers spent many weeks searching for her body, it was never found. The sea still holds that valuable pearl in its keeping.

Here's a Queer Tale

Wailing at the Wilga Waterhole – Mystery of the Min Min Light – A Tragic Prophecy – Dream and a Rope – Funeral of a Tyrant – The Gilt Dragon – Phantom Ship.

WAILING AT THE WILGA WATERHOLE

VARIOUS THEORIES and conjectures can be offered, but never substantiated, regarding the Wilga Waterhole and the terrifying screams that have come from it for so many years.

The Wilga Waterhole is part of the wandering Barcoo waterway, near Ruthven Station, on the way to Isisford, in central-western Queensland.

It is said that the noises were first heard by white men more than eighty years ago. In any case, the records of this uncanny phenomenon are numerous. Many years ago, when the extraordinary screams and cries that occur at night in this waterhole of the Barcoo River were first heard by a party of bushmen, the story arose that they were made by a bunyip.

As was inevitable, a long controversy began as to whether there ever was such a creature. But even the fabulous bunyip was never credited with emitting such yells and blood-curdling screams as came from the Wilga Waterhole – if the accounts of various people are to be believed.

The story is consistent always: nothing but a series of terrifying, fiendish yells an᷍ screams arising suddenly and dying away mysteriously to silence.

It is on record that more than sixty years ago a couple of shearers, on their way to a station in the Longreach district, camped by this waterhole one fine summer evening. Though it was dry weather, the Wilga Waterhole as usual was well supplied.

After hobbling their horses, and leaving them to graze, the two men made tea over their campfire, ate their damper and salt beef, and smoked and yarned for some hours.

The fire had nearly died down, the men began to yawn, and there was an uncanny stillness.

Suddenly there came a soft, distant wailing that grew rapidly nearer and louder. To the astonished men the cries appeared to be in different keys – devilish, unearthly shrieking, such as no human voices ever uttered. One thing was certain – the screaming, now ringing in their ears at deafening pitch, was coming from the waterhole.

The shearers thought their ear-drums would burst, but they were too terrified to move. Then, to their fervent relief, the shrieking diminished in volume until it was merely a weird wailing. Moments later, it ceased utterly, and once more the bush was deathly silent. Throughout it all, not a ripple or movement marked the surface of the lagoon from whence the noises had emanated.

Without waiting for the dawn the shearers caught their horses and rode off.

When the men told their story at the shearing shed it was received with derision by most, but others mentioned that the Wilga Waterhole was a notorious spot, and that the aborigines always avoided it. Some of the old shearing hands said that horses were scared of it and drovers admitted that they never could get cattle to rest there. There were instances where cattle driven from distant parts had arrived there almost exhausted but had stampeded at sundown.

There is a very old story that a new hand employed at Ruthven Station built a slab and bark hut near the waterhole. He brought his wife to live there. She was a typical bush woman, sensible, practical, accustomed all her life to the loneliness of the outback.

The couple had been there for but a short time when one night the husband arrived home late, having been delayed, to find his wife in a state of collapse. She could tell him of nothing she had seen, but that the most appalling shrieks had come from the waterhole. The station-hand soothed his wife, telling her that it must have been some nocturnal birds nearby, and that her nervous system was probably upset, thereby magnifying the illusion.

The couple had known nothing of the evil reputation of the waterhole. It was taken for granted in the district and had long since ceased to be a matter of comment.

Soon after this episode the station-hand was away for two nights. On his arrival home he found his wife hysterical. Crying and sobbing, she told him of the terrible screaming and wailing at the waterhole that had caused her almost to lose her reason.

Forthwith the man packed up and took his wife away.

At Ruthven Station he told the shearers the reason for his departure. The local hands were not surprised, but shearers from other districts scoffed at the tales told of this terrifying place. There and then a party of the visiting shearers decided to camp by the waterhole and brave the debil-debils, ghosts, bunyips, or whatever the unknown were.

The men took every precaution to see that they would not be the victims of practical jokers or bush humorists. They had scouts posted whilst they sat round a roaring log-fire, swapping yarns and drinking billies of tea. Once midnight had passed the men put away their pipes and, with many a wisecrack about the silent spook, settled themselves in their blankets.

It was a soft, low wailing that first reached their startled ears. But before they were on their feet it had increased to a yelling, screaming pitch such as each man knew was never uttered by bird, beast, or human, The shearers decamped in a body, some not even waiting to pick up their blankets.

Of the many theories that have been formed as to the origin of the unearthly noises, one is that they are caused by a subterranean channel. The channel perhaps connects the Wilga to other waterholes, and, under certain conditions when the water rushes through ,it causes the shrieking and yelling. Nevertheless, an exhaustive examination has failed to prove this theory or, for that matter, any other. So the wailing at the Wilga Waterhole continues to hold its mystery.

MYSTERY OF THE MIN MIN LIGHT

One of Australia's most remarkable ghostly manifestations is the strange wandering light that appears at indefinite periods at Min Min, near Boulia, in western Queensland. Known locally as the ghost light, it is a moon of light suspended in space, darting hither and thither, vanishing ghost-like in the dark recesses of the trees.

The locality in which it appears happens to have been the site of a notorious shanty which was known as the Min Min Hotel.

No haunts on earth were lower than some of these western shanties of the Queensland of eighty odd years ago. The Min Min Hotel was regarded as the worst of these vicious dens. It stood beside the road to Warenda, and other outlying stations, towards the border of Central Australia.

Dispensing adulterated liquor and drugs, the Min Min Hotel derived its profits from the process known as 'lambing down' unwary shearers and station-hands, who arrived there with large cheques and still larger thirsts.

Many of these men remained there. The fierce, doped spirits caused their deaths. Others were killed in wild brawls, or were murdered for their money, and at the rear of the hotel site there is still to be seen the Min Min graveyard, where these victims were buried. It is more than seventy years since the hotel was destroyed by fire.

Shortly after the fire a stockman rode wildly one night to the police station. He was greatly agitated, and it was some minutes before he could pull himself together and tell his story.

'You won't believe me, but it's true – I swear it's the gospel truth! About 10 oclock this evening I was riding not far from the Min Min graveyard when all of a sudden I saw a strange glow appear right in the middle of the cemetery. I looked at it amazed. The glow got bigger, till it was about the size of a watermelon. I couldn't believe my eyes as I saw it hovering over the ground. And then I broke into a cold sweat, for it started to come towards me.

'It was too much for my nerves. I was terror-stricken. I dug the spurs into the horse and headed towards Boulia as fast as I could. But every time I looked back over my shoulder I could see the light following me! It only disappeared when I got to the outskirts of the town.

'Don't smile, sergeant! Can't you see it's the truth I'm telling you?'

But the police made light of the stockman's story, and the whole town ragged the unfortunate man about the spook he had seen.

Then came report after report that substantiated the story. Today the phenomenon is an established fact. Thousands of people have seen and photographed the Min Min light. Many scientists have gone to Boulia in the hope of solving the mystery, but have been completely baffled by it.

True, it has some features in common with the will-o'-the-wisp, that curious light seen in marshlands and church graveyards in northern Europe. But there are vital points of difference between the will-o'-the-wisp and the Min Min light. The former is produced from decaying animal matter in churchyards or marshes, whereas the Australian light not only shines above a graveyard but moves about over hard, rocky plain country totally unlike European marshlands.

The riddle remains unsolved.

A Tragic Prophecy

A railway station and district in Queensland are named in honour of a notable pioneering family in that State – the Petries.

Because of their understanding of the aborigines, John Petrie

51

and his son Tom were beloved by the native tribes who lived near by. Indeed, they regarded John, and later his son, almost as gods.

When John announced his attention of climbing Mount Beerwah, in the Glasshouse Mountains, the natives were terrified. They implored him not to make the ascent, saying that a great Spirit dwelt on the summit of the mountain who would punish by blindness anyone daring to look at him. They assured Petrie that only once had the peak been climbed and that, sure enough the foolish native who had accomplished it had been struck blind.

John laughed at their superstition and said that a white man need have no such fears. He ascended the peak but, by an extraordinary coincidence, shortly afterwards became totally and permanently blind.

FUNERAL OF A TYRANT

In the little country cemetery at Belmont Park, Richmond, in the Hawkesbury district, lies the grave of a certain infamous military captain. Old Hawkesbury residents tell the story of his funeral which they firmly believe.

In life the captain was hated by all. His career in the colony brought a long list of cruel, unjust sentences to the convicts – whippings, tortures, solitary confinements. They called him the cruellest tyrant that ever lived. Even the troops detested him.

He would have been dead long before if he had not built himself a 'fort' to live in. Many men would have risked hanging to get even with him. Not a soul mourned his passing – there was general relief that death had claimed him. Only his regiment attended the funeral, and then not a man went voluntarily.

When the coffin was lifted on to the gun-carriage (so the tale runs) the horses were hitched to it, but they refused to pull. Despite all efforts – whippings, coaxing – the horses could not be persuaded to pull the body.

Eventually they were unhitched. Bullocks were brought along for the task. But again there was no response. The bullocks also refused to pull in spite of every effort to start them.

Four of the soldiers finally carried the coffin on their shoulders but they did so only under compulsion by their commanding officer. Refusal would have meant the death penalty.

As one stands today at the foot of the forgotten grave, in this little country cemetery, the thought arises – what sinister influence did this man exert that reached out even after death, and was communicated to the very animals?

DREAM AND A ROPE

Some Australian crime mysteries have been solved in strange circumstances, but none is stranger than a Maitland murder 100 years ago.

Shaun Cott was a farm hand working for William Hayes on his property in the Maitland district of New South Wales. In the course of time Cott was missed from the township, and people remarked indifferently that his absence appeared to have become permanent.

There had been rumours of gold discoveries, and it was thought that Cott had gone off to see if there was any foundation to those rumours.

His disappearance had no interest for anybody, until the advent of John Anthony, who came to live in the district some months later. One day the newcomer was told casually by a local rustic of Cott's quiet departure. Anthony had met Hayes and remarked on the farmer's hard and cruel face. For some strange reason he could not keep his thoughts from Cott's disappearance.

A week later he called on Sergeant McLean, of the Maitland police force, and told him he had had a vivid dream. In the dream Cott told him that he had been murdered by his employer, Hayes, and revealed the exact spot on the farm where his body lay buried.

At first the sergeant roared with laughter. Then his merriment turned to anger when Anthony insisted that his dream be taken seriously.

An hour later, Anthony, accompanied by a police trooper, arrived at the farm. Though Hayes tried to look composed, it was quite evident that he was ill at ease. The trooper told him that he had authority to dig up a certain small patch of peas.

Within a few minutes the body of Shaun Cott, fully clothed, was unearthed. Hayes was at once arrested and charged with the murder.

At the trial he fought hard, declaring that as the result of an argument he and Cott had come to blows, and that the latter had grasped a piece of timber. He averred that in self-defence he tapped Cott with a shinbone, with no thought of killing him.

Here the police played their trump card. Cott's skull showed that it had been fractured well towards the back, proving that Hayes had taken his unfortunate victim by surprise, smashing him down from the rear.

A man then came forward and swore that a day or two before his disappearance Cott had complained that Hayes was humbugging him about his wages, and that he had received no money for some time. This evidence proved a motive.

Thus it came about that William Hayes went to death – the only man in Australia ever brought to the rope by a dream.

The Phantom Schooner

Australia possesses vast territories in the Southern Ocean surrounding the Antarctic Circle – such places as Queen Mary Land, King George V Land, South Victoria Land, all of which are dependencies of the Commonwealth. In the waters of the south occurred a fantastic sea incident.

On September 22nd, 1860, Captain Brighton, of the whaler *Hope*, opened his log-book and wrote the date, together with this entry: 'Sighted a whale. Followed her for hours, but eventually she gave us the slip. Now close to the ice barrier'.

That was all he had to report. Little did he know that in but an hour's time he was to set down in his log one of the most amazing reports that ever a skipper wrote.

As he made his way to the deck there came from the ice barrier, several hundred yards away, an ominous crack. Another and another followed, detonating like cannon shots in the chill, still night air.

The crew stared across the intervening strip of water to the ice barrier. However, the whaler was far enough away to be safe. Then, with a reverberating roar, the towering walls parted abruptly. Hundreds of tons of ice crashed into the sea, throwing up great spouts of green water.

Suddenly a deck-hand cried out in alarm and pointed with a trembling finger to an apparition. The men gasped in fear, and some began mumbling prayers as The Thing slowly approached them. Even stout-hearted Captain Brighton felt the cold sweat of fear on his forehead. For from the frozen heart of the ice barrier floated a ghost ship!

Its decks were covered with ice and snow. Its sails hung and flapped in tattered frozen shreds. Its rigging was all awry, drooping here and there in a rotting noose like a hangman's rope. The deck and hull were crushed and battered as if by some giant hand. But grim and eerie as was the vessel, it was the sight of the crew of the phantom ship that raised a strangled cry of horror from those on the whaler. For on that ice-strewn deck were seven dead men, statuesque in their frozen whiteness.

'The Flying Dutchman! That's what it is, skipper! The Flying Dutchman!'

Although inwardly trembling, Captain Brighton knew it was essential to calm his panic-stricken crew. In as scornful tones as he could summon he turned to the men:

'Flying Dutchman, my eye! Man me a boat and I'll board your ghost ship myself!'

His coolness had the desired effect. But he required all his courage to set foot on that hoary, silent deck, among the dead men. His footsteps echoed eerily as he made his way to the cabins below.

As he opened a door Brighton started. There, leaning back in a chair, with pen in hand and the ship's log before him, was a fellow captain.

'Your ship – what is the name of your ship? What has happened to you all?'

The man remained silent, unstirring.

The whaling captain was speaking to a dead man. His glance fell on the log-book spread open before the immobile figure. He read the last entry under the dead hand:

'May 4th 1823. No food for 71 days. I am the only one left alive.'

1823 – thirty-seven years before! For that incredible length of time this strange ship had been on her untiring commission of death, locked in the heart of the giant ice barrier.

In another cabin was found the body of a woman – the captain's wife. She, too, like all the others, was in a perfect state of preservation.

The ship was the English schooner, *Jenny*, which had left the port of Lima, Peru, half a human lifetime before.

Reverently the nine bodies discovered on board were buried at sea.

A few months later Captain Brighton, on his return to England handed over to the Admiralty the log-book of the strangely-fated *Jenny*.

MYSTERY OF THE GILT DRAGON

The mystery of the *Gilt Dragon* is one of Australia's strangest tragedies of the sea. Attached to the large fleet of ships owned and operated by the famous old Dutch East India Company, she was one of their finest vessels.

For several years the *Gilt Dragon* sailed between Holland and Java. It was on the 4th of October 1655, that she set out from Holland on what was destined to be her last voyage. On this occasion the stately ship was carrying an unusually rich cargo, including 80,000 golden guilders and a great quantity of silver ingots. There were nearly two hundred people aboard, comprising passengers and crew, and the vessel was under the command of Captain Albertz, one of the company's most popular skippers.

After calling at the Cape of Good Hope she passed a sister ship, also bound for Batavia. That was the last ever seen of the *Gilt Dragon* and, as the months passed without any further news of her, she was given up for lost. It was thought that she must have foundered during a storm.

It was not until the 7th of June 1656, that the truth about the ship was learned in a dramatic fashion. Early that morning a long-boat containing seven men, almost dead, crept into Batavia Harbour. It was some time before the starving men were able to speak. Then they revealed the startling news that they were from the *Gilt Dragon*, which had been lost for nearly a year.

The men said that their vessel had been caught in a bad storm one night and, after being driven many miles off her course, had been wrecked on the shores of the Great South Land – as Australia was then known. One hundred and eighteen people had been drowned and the others managed to reach the land. The following morning ten of the men volunteered to try to reach Batavia in the long-boat and bring help for the castaways.

Three of the men died on the perilous journey. The survivors brought a note from their captain giving the exact position where they had landed. It was twenty-five miles south of what is now called Green Head, on the coast of Western Australia. The report also mentioned that every bit of the great treasure had been successfully brought ashore before the vessel broke up and sank.

Immediately several ships were sent to rescue the castaways and collect the treasure, but although they sailed to the spot no trace of either was found, nor even part of the wreck. Since then a number of well-equipped land parties have searched practically the entire coastline of Western Australia, but have discovered nothing.

However, there was a strange sequel not so long ago. A few years back a sensational discovery was made on a lonely part of the coast of Western Australia near where the *Gilt Dragon* was wrecked. A boy came across a small cove, the mouth of which was partly blocked by huge boulders ; inside the cave was a crumbling skeleton, centuries old, alongside of which were several ancient gold and silver coins. The skeleton was that of a white man, and all the coins were Spanish and Dutch, bearing dates between 1618 and 1648. But there was no trace of any treasure.

Here is another angle on the mystery. In 1875 two men named Burt and Ogbourne, members of a Royal Naval expedition which was engaged on a geographical survey of the coast of Western Australia, when working in from the coast about twelve miles north of where the *Gilt Dragon* was wrecked, took a short cut through dense bush to return to their ship. They came across a peculiar ring of stones, about six feet in diameter, each of the stones being of a size that a man might carry with both hands. As stones are very scarce in the district it seems that they must have been carried into the bush from the coast.

The men, who then knew nothing about the *Gilt Dragon* or its missing treasure, took little notice of the circle of stones, except to remark on the curiosity of seeing such a thing in the dense bush.

It was not until about forty years later that one of them – Burt – happened to read about the ill-fated ship in an old Dutch book. He recalled the circle of stones and at once set out to find the spot again. But he failed to locate it.

Since then another man, a Mr. Stokes, a grazier, has stated that he saw the ring of stones when searching for lost sheep, but had made no examination of them. In spite of several searches the mysterious circle of stones has not been found again.

This is not altogether surprising, since it is no easy matter to find a six-foot ring in a vast track of uninhabited bush country, more particularly when it is borne in mind that it was first seen in 1875, and that it is not only possible but probable that, in the intervening years, the stones have been buried beneath sand blown in from the coast during cyclonic gales.

At any rate it is considered that beneath the stones the treasure, or the clue to it, is buried. Some day, perhaps, the strange circle will be rediscovered, and then the mystery of the cast-aways and the treasure from the *Gilt Dragon* will be solved.

Those Were The Days

The Hanging Picnic – Cure for a Common Scold – Pistols for Two – Wheel-barrows for Police – Jugilbar Castle – Holy Snakes.

THE HANGING PICNIC

OF ALL THE happenings in Australia's not so distant past, one of the most extraordinary and yet least-known was the hanging picnic of South Australia. It took place in North Adelaide, in 1839, on the grounds now occupied by one of the city's finest golf links. It is hard to conceive that such a grim event occurred in this serene and sylvan setting.

The first sheriff of Adelaide was a former lawyer from Tasmania – Mr Samuel Smart. He was appointed by Governor Hindmarsh before the capital boasted of a police force. Things were getting rather out of hand about this time. Gangs of toughs were making their presence felt, and in one instance the Governor was forced to order the Marines to open fire on a riotous mob. Robberies began to take place, the Government

Stores were broken into and goods, arms, and ammunition pillaged.

The new sheriff, nevertheless, was by no means sleeping on his job. He had been quietly going about ascertaining the names of the ringleaders of all these disturbances, and as the result of these investigations some of the gangsters were arrested.

As was to be expected, Samuel Smart became a marked man; it was not long before an attempt was made on his life. Three men entered his home one night and a bullet was fired at his head. Though the shot merely grazed him and left but a slight wound, the thugs became alarmed and decamped. Smart recognized the one who had fired the shot, and a reward was offered for his capture. Shortly afterwards the would-be murderer, a youth named Michael Magee, was rounded up, taken to trial, and condemned to death.

This was an epic event indeed for Adelaide – the first execution to take place in South Australia! Such a momentous affair was not to be treated lightly. When the good citizens learned that Magee was to be hanged on Wednesday, 2nd May 1839, on the north bank of the Torrens River, they determined not only to be present, but to do the day full justice. They would make a picnic of it!

Meanwhile, the Governor was having a headache over the whole business. There was no official hangman in the colony, and although a sum of five pounds was offered to anyone who would act, the offer was not accepted. The amount was doubled, but still nobody came forward. In normal circumstances, the sheriff would have acted as hangman, but, because he had figured as the victim in the case, it was thought not to be ethical for him to perform the execution.

When the fateful morning dawned, all Adelaide was agog with speculation as to what exactly was going to happen. Not a shop opened, scarcely a soul remained home; a thousand people, including some hundreds of women and children, made their way merrily to the picnic-execution grounds. The earliest arrivals obtained the best positions around a massive gum tree that had been chosen as the site for the hanging. It possessed one particularly strong horizontal branch, ideal for the grim task. Today the tree is no more, but it was located near the centre of the present golf links.

About nine o'clock the picnickers were thrilled to see a little procession slowly wending its way through the trees. The colony's newly-formed military force of ten mounted men led the cortege. Behind them came sixteen marines, and rumbling along in the rear was a two-horse dray with the condemned man.

But the latter was not the centre of attraction. Excitement ran at fever pitch through the crowd when it was seen that the hangman was also in the dray.

Magee was seated on one end of a crudely built coffin made from rough unvarnished deal wood. His legs were on either side of it, his arms pinioned behind his back. On the other end of the coffin sat the executioner.

Everyone asked the same question – 'Who is he?' There was little chance of identifying him. He wore a hooded mask that completely enveloped his head, and he was taking no risk that he would be recognized in any other way. His clothes had been padded so heavily that he looked horribly disfigured, with a huge hump on both his chest and back. A more terrifying and grotesque object would have been hard to conceive.

The procession halted beside the tree, the members dismounted, and the Colonial Chaplain, the Rev. C. B. Howard, began reading aloud the prayer before death.

His words were drowned by excited whispers from a crowd still preoccupied with the identity of the hangman.

When the brief service finished, the executioner stepped forward. He greased the rope, flung it over the bough after a couple of vain attempts, and adjusted the noose at the required height. His hands, however, and all his movements betrayed his extreme nervousness. So badly did he tie the noose around Magee's neck that the knot slid under the poor wretch's chin, leaving him dangling in mid-air, cursing and shrieking in agony. Panic-stricken at having bungled the job, the hangman took to his heels and fled, while the onlookers yelled in derision.

A mounted policeman galloped in pursuit of the runaway

executioner and brought him back to finish his work. Finish
it he did, but in a shocking fashion. Beside himself now with
terror, he leaped on to the suspended victim and clung to him
for thirteen minutes, by the sheriff's watch, before life was
pronounced extinct.

It is recorded that a few of the women spectators showed
their gentle upbringing by fainting at the gruesome spectacle,
or by having recourse to their smelling salts. But a good time
was had by all, and, in the jolly picnic that followed everyone
agreed that this, South Australia's first hanging and first
holiday, had indeed been a gala occasion.

CURE FOR A COMMON SCOLD

More than a century has passed since a 'Public Petition Against
a Common Scold' was presented to the magistrates in Geelong,
Victoria. The petition was signed by 26 'respectable householders' in Little Scotland, which is now incorporated in the
City of Geelong West.

On 26th October 1849 Mrs Peggy X, of Little Scotland,
was brought before the Bench to answer for her misdemeanours.
She was described as a veritable vixen before whom the inhabitants quailed.

Peggy was by no means a stranger to the court; she had just
emerged from gaol where she had spent eight days for 'threaten-
ings of a most deadly nature' against Mrs Y. It appears that
immediately after regaining her freedom she made a bee line
to the home of Mrs Y and continued to harangue that lady in
even more vigorous terms.

Fearful of her threats, Mrs Y straightway applied to the
magistrates to have Peggy bound to keep the peace. So a
warrant was immediately issued for her apprehension.

Simultaneously a number of householders in Little Scotland
called a meeting for the purpose of considering means to
restrain Peggy in her termagantic career'. It resulted in this
petition to the magistrates:

'We, the undersigned inhabitants of the township of Little
Scotland, hereby petition your Worships in the case of Peggy
X, lately imprisoned by your Worships for breaking the peace

f the township and now at large. Your petitioners humbly
eg that your Worships will cause the said Peggy X to be
rought before you to be dealt with as in your judgment may
em fit, the said Peggy X being a common nuisance to the
id township, putting its inhabitants in continual bodily
ar.'

It is on record that Peggy made an able defence. She begged
e magistrates to send a constable for the Archdeacon of
eelong, who could prove that she had run into his house
nly the night before to save her life from the vengeance of
ose who would have 'masecrated' her if they had been
llowed.

The court deemed such a course unnecessary, and ordered
eggy to be removed to the lock-up, there to be confined for
ne month, unless she found sufficient security for her good
ehaviour, 'which, being a thing altogether out of nature unless
eggy X was found down literally and not legally'.

The Bench had finished with the virago, but the 'respectable
ouseholders' of Little Scotland had not.

That night a large number of people gathered outside her
ome to witness the burning of a monster effigy.

PISTOLS FOR TWO

arly Australian society often favoured the duello as a means
f vindicating honour. Sir Thomas Mitchell, the Surveyor-
General and explorer, and Sir Stuart Donaldson, first Premier
f New South Wales, fought a duel in Centennial Park in
851.

Donaldson had commented sharply on the statement of
xpenses issued by Mitchell's Department. Mitchell declared
Donaldson's allegations to be a pack of lies.

A duel followed, in which three shots by each party were
xchanged, Mitchell drilling a hole through Donaldson's top-
at. The seconds then separated their principals. However, no
pology was tendered, and there was no reconciliation.

Other notable encounters included the meeting near Parra-
natta, in 1801, between Captain John MacArthur and Colonel
atterson, in which the latter was wounded, and an exchange

of shots between Robert Wardell, editor of *The Australian*, and Attorney-General Bannister at Pyrmont in 1826.

Duels sometimes changed from drama to comedy, as when in 1845 the principals were two gentlemen named Synnot and Griffin. The former was so nervous that he pressed his trigger prematurely and set fire to his own trousers. Amid much mirth it was at once declared that honour had been satisfied.

Australia's oddest and funniest pistol duel took place in Victoria in 1843. The site chosen for it was an open space at the corner of Lonsdale and Spencer Streets, Melbourne. The duellists were the Hon. Gilbert Kennedy and Mr George Demoulin.

Accompanied by their seconds and an excited group of spectators, they arrived at the rendezvous and prepared for the fray.

When Demoulin saw that he was to stand within a few paces of his opponent he was disagreeably impressed. He knew Kennedy to be a good shot, and he was himself no novice.

After a tense moment came the command, 'Fire!'

The pistols cracked and a cloud of smoke rolled away to reveal poor George holding a hand to his head.

'I'm killed,' he groaned, as he brought down his hand smeared with a dreadful-looking scarlet mess. 'He's blown my brains out . . . they're blinding me. Don't just stand there . . . ye gods . . . have you no pity for a dying man? Why – you're you're laughing"

No longer able to control themselves, the spectators were rocking with merriment. The truth was that the quarrel had been engineered as a practical joke by the Honourable Gilbert and his friends, and Demoulin's pistol had been given a blank charge.

The shot which had exposed his brains was a dab of raspberry jam that had been substituted for a bullet.

WHEELBARROWS FOR POLICE

There was a time when wheelbarrows were part of the equipment of the Sydney Police for the discharge of their duties. In 1837 wheelbarrows were issued to the various watchhouses for use by the police. Their purpose was to convey drunken persons to the lock-ups. In the case of restive prisoners, their legs could be fastened to the barrow by means of buckles and straps. The *Sydney Gazette*, of November 1837, tells us that the policemen appointed for wheelbarrow duty resembled a muster of coachmen on a street stand. In a later issue, the newspaper had this reference to the subject:

'On Tuesday afternoon a constable in a state of intoxication was observed wheeling a man in a barrow to the watchhouse who was also drunk. Instead of taking the man to the nearest watchhouse, the intoxicated policeman wheeled him over half Sydney, every now and then capsizing him into the road, to the mirth of the citizens and the gratification of his own drunken propensities.'

YULGILBAR CASTLE

A well-known landmark on the banks of the Clarence River, in New South Wales, is Yulgilbar Castle. Gone, however, are its glories and its former importance, and only romantic memories remain of the good old days.

The castle has more than forty rooms, all of them large. The main building has an inner court, and the walls of the towers are three feet thick. Workmen were brought out from England specially to build it. One expert, a man named Farquhar, was engaged to build a secret chamber in the castle. He must have done a very excellent job because nobody seems to know just where that secret chamber is.

Yulgilbar Castle was the home of the Honourable Edward Ogilvie, who lived there with his father, Lieutenant William Ogilvie. The latter fought with Nelson at the Battle of Trafalgar.

In the old days a big staff of liveried servants was kept. Mr Ogilvie had everything in keeping with his castle – butler, coachmen, gardeners. The whole atmosphere was very formal and correct. No one was ever allowed to come to dinner unless in dinner-dress. Considering the difficulties of travelling in the country in those days, it must have been quite a problem for guests to provide themselves with a suitable wardrobe, but

E

65

Mr Ogilvie knew no obstacles. He always had a large stock of dinner-suits and dress wear in the castle ready for anyone who had come unprepared.

Many were the distinguished visitors who stayed there – the Earl of Belmore, Sir John Robertson, State governors, politicians, and social leaders. It was Mr Ogilvie's intention that the castle should be occupied by his descendants for all time, and that the estate should be kept intact and controlled by the head of the family, whose seat it was to be – in the manner of the English aristocracy. Alas, he could not forsee that the modes and outlook on life of his day would vanish, never to return.

Holy Snakes!

Well known is the story of Vaucluse House, or, as it is sometimes called, Wentworth House, at Vaucluse, Sydney.

The original owner was Sir Henry Brown Hayes, who was sent to Australia as a convict for abducting an Irish heiress. Sir Henry built Vaucluse House six years after the Judge had sentenced him to death – a sentence which was later commuted to transportation. After serving six years hard labour, and earning his freedom, Sir Henry decided to remain in the land to which he had been banished.

Before his conviction he had been a captain of the South Cork militia and a sheriff of County Cork. He was a widower, forty years of age, when there came to Cork on a visit the beautiful Mary Pike, heiress to a fortune left her by her father, a famous banker.

The Irish heart of Sir Henry was smitten the moment he saw the girl. Unfortunately, his love was not reciprocated, and to all his pleadings she remained indifferent.

In desperation Sir Henry abducted her and kept her a prisoner for eight hours, thinking that surely the idea of being kidnapped under such romantic circumstances would soften the lady's heart. But it was not so. When he produced a minister and a wedding-ring she flung the ring at him and had a warrant issued for his arrest.

And so we find the gallant Sir Henry Brown Hayes, after gaining his freedom, deciding to make his home in the district he called Vaucluse. He named it so because it reminded him of the beautiful closed-up valley in France known as Vaucluse, which he had often visited. On his new estate Sir Henry built his home, which years afterwards was purchased and improved by that famous Australian, William Charles Wentworth.

Sir Henry was not long in his new home before he discovered that the district was overrun with snakes. The reptiles not only invaded the house but even made themselves at home in the owner's bed. Well, he was just the boy to put a stop to that sort of thing.

He had plenty of money so he sent to Ireland for five hundred barrels of soil. After all, hadn't Saint Patrick driven all the varmints from the Emerald Isle so that never more would they dare show themselves on such sacred soil? When the turf arrived he waited for the next Saint Patrick's Day and, on that auspicious occasion, had a trench six feet wide and two feet deep dug right round the house. A gang of convicts, Irish to a man, shovelled the blessed soil into it. Curiously enough, although snakes were plentiful in the district for years afterwards, Sir Henry was never troubled with them again. Not one ever attempted to cross the magical circle of the Irish earth.

There is definite proof of the arrival in Sydney of the soil from Ireland, and when excavations were necessary recently in the grounds of Vaucluse House, workmen unearthed part of the trench of Irish sods that had been laid round this historic mansion.

Sporting Life

Hawkesbury Hill Rollers – Ratting and Cock Fighting – Picnic Races – Tub Races – Early Water Wizards – Two-up Tradition.

HAWKESBURY HILL ROLLERS

PIONEERS OF THE fertile valley of the Hawkesbury – he-men all – worshipped sport with a zest now legendary. No matter what the game, money was freely staked on the contingencies, whatever they might be.

That was in the days before railway communication between the Hawkesbury district and the metropolis, when money was plentiful, spent improvidently, and never mourned when once lost.

Apart from recognized sport, such as horse-racing, cricket, rowing, and pugilism, there were many curious contests. Competitors would run races carrying pumpkins on their heads or men or boys (as the case might be) on their backs. The game of 'chalking' was very popular, too. Strong men would undertake to carry cornsacks full of wet sand certain defined distances for heavy bets. They would swing from horizontal bars, the one afterwards jumping the greatest distance winning the stake. Another fad was to see who could hang longest by the toes.

By way of variety, they jumped from bottles. Two bottles would be laid on their sides on the ground with a board across them. The bottles, of course, had a tendency to roll from under the feet, and it required great agility to leap from this unstable starting-point.

Not only this, but they would take a sledge hammer, holding it by a nail driven into the end of the handle and try who could carry it the greatest distance in a given time.

One of the most popular of these queer sports was hill-rolling. From the top of a hill competitors rolled either lying prone upon the ground or ensconced in an empty cask, to the bottom. The first to reach this destination was the winner. Two famous hill-rolling champions at Windsor a century ago were 'Mad Arthur' and 'Kurrajong Sawyer'. A poster of 1845 reads: 'Come along and witness Mad Arthur and Kurrajong Sawyer roll from the Freemason's Hotel to Blanchard's Hotel'.

The two champions got away to a smart start, but Kurrajong Sawyer was an easy victor, his time being nine minutes. Among the onlookers was a local gentleman called Black Bobby, who openly scoffed at the exhibition. To prove that he could do better, he rolled himself down the long hill in the record time of five minutes.

The crowd showed its approval by adjourning to the pub and rolling out the beer barrel, the contents of which were copiously shared with the champion.

RATTING AND COCK-FIGHTING

Among the cruder sports of our ancestors were ratting and cock-fighting. Contests were arranged in the first half of the 19th century between birds representing two towns such as Windsor and Richmond – often for high stakes.

An advertisement in *Bell's Life* of 2/12/65 states that the new arena at the Butcher's Arms, in Elizabeth Street, Melbourne, has been 'built specially for ratting, sparring, and other sports'.

Note that 'other sports'. The advertisement continues: 'During the past week the killing at the Butchers' Arms has been of first-rate description. Gentlemen desirous of trying their terriers will always find a plentiful supply of rats and native cats. A good stock of ferrets on hand for sale. The building has been erected in consequence of the inefficiency of the old rat pit, where 20,000 rats have been killed every year for the last six years. The new building is provided with a glass pit, has two galleries with cushioned seats, is lighted with gas according to the latest and most improved principle, and has everything conducive to the comfort and enjoyment of patrons.'

Elsewhere in the same newspaper, under Sporting Information, is this entry: 'Match at the Butchers' Arms. The match between Mr Urquhart's and Mr Dodd's dogs for £10 – rats for weight, came off last Monday night in the presence of a good muster of the Fancy. Mr Urquhart's killed her 16 rats in 1 minute 54 seconds, and Mr Dodd's dog her 10 in 1 minute 58 seconds. The former, therefore, won by 4 seconds. Pip, the winner, had previously won the Gold Collar. Rosy, a white bull-terrier, killed 200 rats in 20 minutes.'

The game-cocks were trained to fight to the death by strict dieting, sparring and running exercises. The practice-sparring between two cocks was made possible by sheathing their spurs in 'hots' – soft rolls of leather – and muzzling their beaks with pads. At eighteen months a bird was in its prime. Before the match each cock had its tail docked by two-thirds, its wings trimmed, its hackle and rump feathers close-clipped and its comb cut. For the fight it could be 'heeled along' with keen two-inch steel spurs, or 'heeled short' with spurs of one and a-half inches, as agreed by the owners. The match might be between a pair, or a 'battle-royal' might be substituted in which a number of birds were put into the ring, the sole survivor to be the winner.

PICNIC RACES

Picnic races are part of Australia's bush tradition. One of the most popular features of Australian country life, they evolved in the days when country people were cut off from each other y great distances. Picnic race meetings were a means of fore-gathering, and they are an historical part of Australia's early social life. Nowadays streamlined motorcars and private aero-planes have replaced bullock waggons and sulkies for the conveyance of guests, but the old atmosphere and lavish hospitality remain.

Origin of the picnic race meetings is believed to have been the outcome of a schoolboy pastime when the Gibson and Chisholm boys built themselves a racetrack during their school holidays in 1830 and raced their ponies over the rough bush course. Sons of Dr Andrew Lucian Gibson and the John Chisholm family from *Wallagarang*, Goulburn, the boys built their racetrack on the Gibson property, *Tirranna*, five miles from Goulburn, when they were home from their school in Sydney. As the boys grew up Mrs Gibson set special days aside for 'picnic races', and issued invitations to her neighbours and friends in other districts. Guests arrived for lunch, and after the races were entertained at dinner and a ball at the homestead.

The picnic day was a picnic in name only. The meal menus were in the nature of banquets, with champagne flowing, and the women guests wore their finest imported model gowns.

During heavy rains one year, just before the picnic races, the *Tirranna* property was flooded, and one of their most promising mounts was housed in the big drawing-room in case the animal was swept away by the flood.

By 1871 the *Tirranna* race meeting had become so popular, with city visitors as well as country guests, that it was decided by a committee to thank Mrs Gibson for her arduous task of entertaining so many people and to make a ruling that in future guests would bring their own lunches and dinners. The ball, which had outgrown the *Tirranna* drawing-room, was to be held in the township of Goulburn.

In the meantime picnic race meetings had been established on other country properties in New South Wales. One of the most notable was the Bong Bong races held at Throsby Park, Moss Vale, property of Pat Hill Throsby. The custom spread to other States, but they were picnics in the true meaning of the word.

At Rockhampton, Queensland, visitors came from near and far in carriages, buggies and bullock-waggons, to camp out for a week alongside the bush racecourse. Social functions, including the ball, were held in tents. Each horse was ridden by its owner, and, of course, there were no bookmakers on the course although friends took bets between themselves.

At all these picnic race meetings the usual week's festivities embraced racing, pigeon shoots, kangaroo shoots, and a day set aside for children's sports. Each day's activities would be followed by a dance at night, which went on well into the early hours of the next day. The guests brought their own camping equipment and provisions – all except meat, which was supplied by the station-owner host.

A feature of picnic races which seems to have remained the same throughout the years is the fun of the accommodation problem. At the annual meetings country pubs take the overflow of guests from the homesteads. As many as six visitors often have to share one bedroom, and a method of solving hanging space for clothes is to tie a rope from wall to wall. Elegant race frocks and glamorous evening gowns hanging on a rope among the homely furnishings of a small bush pub make an incongruous picture.

THE TUB RACES

The 'Tub Races' were a highlight of Sydney's aquatic sporting events in the sixties and seventies of last century. They were held by the fishermen who lived on the east side of Woolloomooloo Bay.

The tubs were made by cutting large hogsheads in halves. Low stools were fixed into them and on these the competitors sat as they sculled from the Bay wharf around Pinchgut Island and back. The champions could make remarkably fast times and sometimes the 'photo-finish' results would end up in a fight with sculls.

Considerable skill was needed to handle the tubs. A novice would get nowhere in one of them, and indeed would simply revolve on the one spot. The champion sculler was a fisherman named Hastie, who could send a tub at great speed and on a dead-straight course.

The Woolloomooloo fishermen were mostly Australian-born (in those days the Southern European fish merchants had not migrated to these shores), and they sold their catches at the old Woolloomooloo Municipal Market. The fish were dumped on the floor in fifty or sixty lots and bought by hawkers who carried them around Sydney suburbs in baskets.

EARLY WATER WIZARDS

Woolloomooloo Bay was the scene of the first swimming championship to be held in Australia; Saturday, 14th February 1846, was the memorable day for the sporting fraternity of Sydney Town.

Few people nowadays are aware that Australia was the first country to hold a world's swimming championship. It was held on Saturday, 9th January 1858, during the days of the great Victorian gold rush. The venue was St. Kilda, Melbourne, where Captain Kenney had established his bathing ship on similar lines to Robinson's Domain Baths in Sydney. The latter was an enclosure formed by mooring an old colonial trader, the *Cornwallis*, some 50 yards offshore and connecting bow and stern to the shore by means of wooden paling fences.

The world championship was won by Joe Bennett, a Sydney-sider and outstanding swimmer of his day, from Charles Steedman, ex-champion of England, and Bennett's brother John. A record crowd of over 1000 witnessed the contest.

For nearly 100 years since then Australian swimmers have contributed greatly to the improvement of swimming technique.

In the early fifties, G. W. Wallis, a Sydney lad, was taught the aboriginal side-stroke by a full-blooded native at Woolloomooloo Bay. In 1855 the boy visited England with his father and while there swam in baths owned by Professor Beckwith, who, impressed by the lad's speed and unusual style, induced him to teach him his stroke. Beckwith, in turn, imparted it to H. Gardiner, who, employing it, became champion of England soon afterwards.

The Australian 'crawl' stroke was first swum by a 12-year-old lad, Alick Wickham, in a 66⅔ yards handicap at Bronte Baths, Sydney; he completed the distance in the then remarkable time for a junior of 44 seconds. So astonished was George Farmer that he shouted: 'Look at that kid crawling!' and the old-time coach's remark was r'sponsible for the stroke being dubbed 'the crawl'.

Like the aboriginal stroke, the 'crawl' was modified and improved and later superseded by other styles until the golden age of Australian swimming began in 1897 with such world champions as the Cavills and F. C. Lane, followed by an astonishing array of record-holders.

It was the early water wizards, however, who pioneered modern speed, and who set high standards of sportsmanship for the swimmers of the future.

TWO-UP TRADITION

In spite of the penalties attached to playing the game, Two-up remains an Australian tradition; all the king's horses and all the king's men would find extreme difficulty in stamping it out.

Two-up is a gambling game that is as Australian as a wool-shed and as sudden in its outcome as the crack of a drover's stockwhip. It is played well-screened from the eyes of the law in back-rooms, laneways, secluded paddocks.

The Great Australian Game finds its roots well-sunk into the tradition and heritage of the nation. It was a game born of the monotony and boredom of colonizing – an escape from the tiresome job of digging postholes or mine shafts. It was played on the goldfields of Victoria and the West; in the shearing sheds and the drovers' camps; in Europe, the Middle East and the Far East, wherever Australian troops landed and battled, the two pennies rose from the kip, spun in the air and landed, accompanied by mixed language and suppressed elation.

An old yarn worth repeating concerns the Frenchman who saw the game played for the first time when the Aussies landed in France during World War I. 'Never have I seen a people so devout! They gather in small groups along the waterfront.

Then at a signal from their leader they raise their faces to heaven only to humble themselves immediately by bending in the dust. Mon Dieu! Such devotion!'

The game can be played in low denominations and requires no elaborate equipment. There is no limit to the number of players. According to those who play it, Two-up is the fairest gambling game in the world. It is impossible to corrupt a ring, indicative of the rise of the game's popularity throughout the low income groups which placed the sport on a national basis.

Its history is confused, but according to some authorities it is an offshoot of the English game, Chuck-farthing. Other investigators give it a Chinese origin. Certainly, in its hundred years and more of playing, the game has not altered. It's still the same old toss and spin that attracted gold miners and drovers to the ring, and its language is as individual as the game itself.

The players assemble in a ring and one man, chosen or voluntary, takes the centre of the floor where he is given a kip – the small, flat piece of board on which the pennies are placed for spinning.

The spinner hands to the boxer (one of the organizers) the sum for which he wishes to spin and then goes about attempting to spin three heads in a row. Some schools place two pennies on the kip, others three. When three pennies are used it is considered 'sudden death', meaning that there is no possibility of having to repeat the throw.

Before spinning is commenced, side bets by the watchers are taken. When 'all is set on the side', there is a call from the ring-keeper, 'Up and do 'em, Spinner!' or 'Come in, Spinner!' and the spinner tosses the coins into the air.

Should any member of the school consider the toss to be a foul he is at liberty to shout 'bar' and the spinner is compelled to respin. The boxer and the ringy are in complete control of the school and any disputes are within their office. They call the results of the spin and fill the centre with bets. (Among the many phrases most confusing to the newly initiated is 'another swy in the guts', meaning another two pounds is wanted in the centre before the spinner is able to go.)

It is a hard game to beat. Years of thought have been given to the possibility of cheating and the only logical method is the application of a double-headed penny or a 'nob', or a double-tailed penny, which is a 'grey'. But this is fairly impossible as a 'Picker-up', a man nominated from the watching crowd, picks up and checks the coins. Some of the more skilled players have learnt to 'butterfly' the coin in which case the coins give the illusion of spinning but are merely fluttering. Such a malpractice is, however, easily spotted by the players and spins of that nature are barred.

Many Australian novels have featured Two-up in some way or other, but C. J. Dennis with his language of the digger captured the true spirit of the game. In his *Songs of a Sentimental Bloke* and the *Moods of Ginger Mick* he makes the casual, unpointed reference to the game which is exactly how it is treated by Australians. It will never die out as a game. No matter how you look at it, Two-up is tradition.

Bobbies and Bushies

First Bushrangers – Ned Kelly – Thunderbolt – Matthew Brady – Captain Melville – A Chinaman's Shirt-tail – Captain Moonlight – Jackey-Jackey.

FIRST BUSHRANGERS

THE NAME 'BUSHRANGER' explains itself and was the term given by the authorities to those who engaged in robbery under arms. From the desperate exploits of Michael Howe in the early days of Tasmania, to the reign of terror by the Kelly gang in the late seventies of last century bushranging was a disreputable phase of Australian history which has long since been relegated to the past.

The first bushrangers were escaped convicts who had to rob to live. Starvation or robbery was their choice and they would rather die than return to manacles and chains. Later, when the goldfields were yielding their rich treasures, free men of the more adventurous type were tempted by the opportunities offered by attacking and robbing the gold convoys on their way from the diggings to the coast.

Mention bushrangers to most Australians anywhere, and they will talk of the Kelly gang. Ned Kelly has become almost a legendary figure: certainly many legends concerning him are widely believed, while very many people regard him as a hero who took to bushranging only because he was wronged, and persecuted by the police. Books, articles, plays, even a ballet have been devoted to Ned Kelly and his gang. Fiction has been liberally mingled with fact by many writers.

In his introduction to *Ned Kelly: Being His Own Story of His Life and Crimes*, Clive Turnbull describes the notorious outlaw as our only folk hero; truly observing that the phrase 'Game as Ned Kelly' has become part of the national idiom.

Other writers consider (and with much justification on the evidence of contemporary accounts), that the most notorious of all bushrangers was a hardened scoundrel, neither chivalrous nor brave.

Glenrowan and neighbouring districts will always be known as the 'Kelly Country'. When their daring, swift, mysterious movements and their ruthlessness kept the residents of Glenrowan and other little Victorian townships in a state of alarm, Ned Kelly and his companions in crime had many friends besides their own near relatives. Indeed, their sympathizers were legion throughout Australia. After the gang had been broken up, certain papers and documents were found which indicated that Ned went close to altering the whole political history of Victoria. It is said that Ned intended proclaiming north-eastern Victoria a Republic with Benalla the capital city and himself as the first President.

Around the campfire, in the old colonial days, yarns of bushranging exploits were favourite topics of the drovers, shearers and station hands. Here are some of these stories:

THUNDERBOLT

Fred Ward, better known as 'Thunderbolt', was the last of the bushrangers in New South Wales. He commenced his reign in

1863, holding up coach after coach. But he never used violence. Many were his daring robberies, and always this handsome outlaw would ride away with his plunder, singing at the top of his voice. Although wanted dead or alive (and he was finally shot down in 1870) the troubadour bushranger inspired none of the terror as did some of the early outlaws. Indeed his exploits were taken good-humouredly by most people, for he had lots of friends and admirers.

A tale is told that Thunderbolt held up a German brass band while the musicians were rehearsing in the district of Goonoo Goonoo, on their way to the town of Tenterfield. When the conductor of the band protested that they would be stranded without the few pounds that they possessed, Thunderbolt said he was sorry but that he wanted to put the money on a 'dead cert' at the Tenterfield races the following day. He added, however, that if the horse won he would return the money in care of the Tenterfield post-office. Thunderbolt's horse won his race, and the money was returned to the German band.

On one occasion Thunderbolt rode up to Tabulam Station, on the Clarence River. He was picturesquely dressed in a cabbage-tree hat, moleskins, and a blue shirt. Nearing the homestead he dismounted and tied up his magnificent horse. The lady of the household was not unduly alarmed at the sight of the handsome stranger, who flourished his hat and asked politely, 'May I crave a glass of water?' She fetched him the water and, as he drank, he remarked casually, 'You are alone, I presume?' 'Yes', she answered, guilelessly. The gallant stranger then blew a whistle and two other men appeared from nowhere. The lady was wearing a beautiful enamelled watch suspended round her neck. (This watch was given at her death to the Sydney Art Gallery.) When Tunderbolt demanded it she said that it had belonged to her dear mother and was the only keepsake she had of her. 'You can keep it,' Thunderbolt replied, 'but lead us over the house. We want all the money and valuables you have.'

As the owner of the house had taken everything of value into Casino that morning, the lady did not mind showing them over the place, where they found nothing to their purpose. As they passed one of the bedrooms she turned to Thunderbolt, saying, 'Will you ɪ ease tell them to walk on tiptoe past this door? My sister is ill and must not be disturbed.' Then followed the strange sight of the crinolined lady with three bushrangers in her wake all walking on tiptoe.

MATTHEW BRADY

The Tasmanian outlaw, Matthew Brady, was a spirited youth of good education who was transported to Van Diemen's Land for forgery. When he turned bushranger he soon earned the nickname of 'Gentleman Brady.' On one occasion, when he held up the Duke of York Inn, he saw an officer whom he mistook for Colonel Balfour, notorious for his ill-treatment of convicts. Brady knocked the man down, but on learning that it was not Colonel Balfour he offered a flowery apology and tried to console his victim.

With three of his gang Brady raided the residence of the Rev Dr Browne, of Launceston. The minister was sitting with his wife, who had been confined only a few hours before. He begged them not to make a disturbance that might alarm Mrs Browne. The bushrangers appeared greatly concerned, apologized for coming at such a time, and promised to be very quiet. The promise was so faithfully kept that Mrs Browne's sister, in a nearby room, was not aware of the visit until next morning. The gentlemen of the road took all available cash and goods!

It seems that Matthew Brady was always considerate to women. One time when he raided a house, and was surprised by the troopers, he took great pains to see that the ladies there would not be injured by the firing. Then there was the instance concerning Mrs Beckford, wife of the organist of St. John's Church, Launceston. Their home was on the banks of the Tamar, thirteen miles from the township. One day Mrs Beckford was alone, hanging out the washing, when she was startled by the report of a gun. Brady walked over to her, saying: 'Forgive me, my dear lady, for frightening you, but I just killed that native in time. I happened to be passing through the bush when I caught sight of him with poised spear. As you were working, unconscious of your peril, he was just about to throw the spear at you.'

Mrs Beckford, grateful beyond measure, although she knew her deliverer was the notorious outlaw, invited him to her home and replenished his stores with provisions and food-stuffs from her well-stocked pantry. This, despite the fact that it was a very serious crime to assist a bushranger in any way.

Another daring episode was the raiding of the home of Mr Cruttenden in the district of Sorrell by Brady and his gang. They made the owner a prisoner, together with his servants. Now it happened that Mr Cruttenden was expecting a party of friends from Hobart to dine with him. When these people arrived, later in the day, they were received at the door by Brady, who they did not know, and naturally thought was a friend of their host. Imagine their consternation when they were shown into the room and saw Mr Cruttenden and his servants tied up! Before they could do a thing the bushrangers had them trussed up, also. Then the outlaws sat down to the table and feasted themselves on the grand dinner prepared for the guests, whilst those poor people could only look on helplessly.

But that was not all. When it was getting dusk, Brady and his gang left the house, leaving their prisoners still tied up. The bushrangers then made their way into the township of Sorrell and went straight to the jail. Arriving there they found a group of soldiers cleaning their muskets. In a jiffy they had the soldiers secured, and, taking them into the jail, locked them up, at the same time releasing all the prisoners. Then they made off to their mountain hide-out.

When Governor Sir George Arthur dispatched all his forces to capture Brady dead or alive, the daring outlaw showed his contempt by posting large notices in Hobart reading as follows:

'Mountain Home. April 25. It has caused Matthew Brady much concern that such a person known as Sir George Arthur is at large. Twenty gallons of rum will be given to any one that will deliver his person to me.

(Signed) MATTHEW BRADY.'

Nevertheless Brady's brave days were drawing to a close. Constantly harassed by pursuing troopers, he was separated from his fellow rogues by a shot in his ankle. No longer the proud and chivalrous 'Prince of Bushrangers', Brady was now the anxious and suffering fugitive.

The man who finally ran him to earth was John Batman, who was later to win much greater fame as the founder of the Port Phillip colony. Batman, who migrated from New South Wales to Tasmania, was an expert bushman and experienced explorer. Hearing that Brady had made his retreat in the Western Tier, Batman set out for that wild and rugged country.

On the greenstone slopes of Dry's Bluff, which rises abruptly from the surrounding terrain to some 4,000 feet, Batman eventually glimpsed his quarry limping slowly, and evidently in pain. At the same moment Brady saw his pursuer. Instantly his dejected look vanished; the gun was at his shoulder, a finger on the trigger. In a firm voice he called out, 'Stand, soldier!'

'I'm no soldier, Brady,' was the reply. 'I'm John Batman; surrender – there is no chance for you.'

The bushranger waited a few moments before replying, 'You are right, Batman; my time is come. I yield to you because you're a brave man.'

Petitions poured in to the governor to save Brady from the gallows. Settlers told of his forbearance and women of his kindness. His cell table was loaded with presents of wine, fruit, flowers and cakes sent by his admirers. A dense mass of spectators watched his execution in Hobart; the men cheered him for his courage and women wept for the man who died more like a martyr than a felon.

CAPTAIN MELVILLE

Worthy of a Hollywood movie is the episode of Captain Melville – the Beau Brummel of bushrangers – paying his unexpected visit to the homestead of the wealthy Victorian squatter, McKinnon.

Young and handsome, and extremely fond of dress, Melville surprised the household just as Mr McKinnon and his two attractive daughters were leaving for a country ball. He ordered everyone into the drawing-room:

'Sit down, everybody! My deepest apologies to you Mr McKinnon, and your household, for this unusual intrusion, but I feel in the mood for a little musical relaxation.

'I understand that you and your two charming daughters are very excellent musicians. I, myself, am an ardent music-lover but, unfortunately, my occupation gives me little opportunity to indulge in such luxury. Hence this visit.

'My "desires" are usually fulfilled, and I have no doubt they will be on this occasion.

'Come, now! Don't look so uncomfortable! Let's spend a pleasant musical evening . . . .'

Too helpless to do otherwise, Mr McKinnon 'obliged'. His daughters played the piano and sang duets. The bushranger later went to the grand piano and placing his gun on the music-stand sang a group of Moore's Irish melodies. He also revealed himself as a talented solo pianist.

The evening went on in this amazing fashion when suddenly, in answer to a call for help from one of the servants, mounted police arrived. But Melville got away. Leaping through a window the bushranger made good his escape.

A CHINAMAN'S SHIRT TALE

The year 1851 saw the advent of the 'Vandemonians'. The term was applied to bushranging graduates from the penal settlements of Van Diemen's Land. Australia's bushranging records of the years 1851 to 1865 are full of the exploits of these time-expired or runaway convicts.

One of these gentry was Tommy Ryan. His career as a highwayman was brief, mainly because of the proverbial luck of a Chinese shepherd, Ya Yu, who worked in the New South Wales district of Carcoar, on the property of a Mr Lawson. One morning Ya Yu was sitting on a log, quietly watching the mob of sheep entrusted to his care, when Tommy Ryan came up and addressed him:

'Good-day, John Chinaman!'

'Me no John Chinaman. Me Ya Yu.'

'Well then, good-day to you, Ya Yu! Mind if I sit on the log with you and have a smoke?'

'Me no mind. Welly lonely watchum sheep.'

Been, working here long?'

'Three-four years. Mister Lawson give Ya Yu job when he no find gold. Welly good man, Mister Lawson. Ya Yu come all way from China to get plenty gold. Work welly, welly hard, but me no find gold. Me welly worried. Money all gone. But Mister Lawson give Ya Yu job watchum sheep.'

'Does he pay you good wages?'

'Welly good wages. Ya Yu no worried now.'

'I bet you're saving all your money – socking it away to take back to China.'

'Me savee money all li. Welly soon Ya Yu go back to China. Me go. . . . Whaffor!'

The visitor had whipped out a revolver and was pointing it threateningly at the Chinaman:

'Give me that money, Ya Yu!'

'Whaffor! Whaffor! Me no savvy! Me no gotum money!'

Bang! A bullet whizzed through Ya Yu's hat.

'If you don't do what I tell you I'll make the next hole in your yellow skull!'

'You welly bad man. You – '

'Shut up! Take your pants off. Take *all* your clothes off and give them to me. I know you Chinks always carry your money on you.'

'Me – me – give you tlousers all li, but me wantum shirt.'

'Oh you do? And I bet that's where your money's hidden! Give me that shirt . . . Ah, a patch on the tail – just as I thought. I can feel the sovereigns and the banknotes inside! Get going, Ya Yu! Run home to your 'welly good boss' and tell him a 'welly bad' bushranger stripped you!

Sewn up in the shirt Tommy Ryan found all the worldly wealth of the pastoral Celestial. Four sovereigns, twenty-eight pounds in banknotes, and two cheques of a total value of £23 signed by a Mr Iceley, storekeeper of Coombing Park, and easily negotiable in the district.

The naked Chinaman lost no time in getting back to his

boss to tell him of the hold-up. Meanwhile, Ryan made his way towards Bathurst. Not far from the town he bailed up a man named Lewis, a disillusioned digger returning after six months pick and shovel work with only a few pennyweights of gold dust, a pound note and a bit of silver. The bushranger took these paltry possessions, at the same time warning his victim that if he reported the robbery he'd be a marked man.

Lane disregarded the warning and informed the mounted police in Bathurst. Three days later Captain Battye picked up the tracks of Ryan and arrested him in the bush, about 15 miles out of Bathurst. When he was searched he was found to have on him all the money stolen from Ya Yu, Lane's possessions, and a loaded revolver.

Ryan was tried at the ensuing Circuit Court at Bathurst before Chief Justice Sir Alfred Stephen. The jury found him guilty on the two counts of robbery under arms.

Sir Alfred addressed the Vandemonian as follows:

'You are a hardened ruffian, a villain of the deepest dye. I will make it my business to put you out of the way of decent people for a very considerable length of time.

'For robbing the inoffensive Chinese shepherd, Ya Yu, your sentence will be ten years penal servitude upon the public roads of the colony of New South Wales. For the robbery of Lane you will do a further fifteen years. A total sentence of twenty-five years' imprisonment. Furthermore, by order of the Court, the money that you have taken from your two victims will be handed back to them.

'Before concluding I would like to address our Chinese friend. Are you fully satisfied with British justice, Ya Yu? Judging by your smile of extreme contentment, it would appear so.'

'You welly good man – welly good man! But whaffor no shirt? Whaffor no tlousers? Ya Yu wantum all li! Him bad man wearum!'

'Oh – oh, of course! We'll see that you get back your shirt and your trousers. But we can't disrobe the prisoner in the dock. That will have to be attended to later.

'This Court hereby orders that the shirt and trousers on the prisoner Thomas Ryan be removed from his person and returned to the rightful owner, Ya Yu.'

Captain Moonlight

Beneath the garb of a clergyman beat the heart of a rogue who became one of Australia's legendary bushrangers – Captain Moonlight.

George Scott was a lay preacher in Victoria who deserted the path of Holy Writ and took to the pathless bush. He came from New Zealand, and being a man of good education found employment as a lay reader in the Anglican church at Egerton, a small town between Geelong and Ballarat. It was not long before he became the darling of the parish and the white-haired boy of the Melbourne diocese.

One night, Mr Prothero, the manager of the Union Bank at Egerton, was stretched out in an easy chair in his comfortable room on the bank premises, warming his feet. A glass of whisky, convenient to his hand, showed that he was warming himself within as well as without.

Hearing the door open, Prothero looked around. What he saw surprised and amused him: no other than the Reverend George Scott, clerically garbed, reversed collar and all. But for some extraordinary reason he was masked.

'What's the joke, man?' exclaimed Prothero, 'Good gracious, what's the joke? Are you going to a masked ball? Hey! What are you doing at that drawer? My – my revolver! Confound you, Scott, don't you dare point that revolver at me! It's loaded! What the devil's the matter with you? Have you lost your reason?'

'The mistake you're making, Prothero,' said Scott, 'is that you think I'm joking. I'm not! You're well aware that there's a bullet in the barrel of this gun. Step over to this table – now write on this sheet of paper what I dictate – "CAPTAIN MOONLIGHT HAS STUCK ME UP AND ROBBED THE BANK." Now sign it – "WILLIAM PROTHERO." Leave the note in the middle of the desk – there. Now, Prothero, you will walk in front of me to the bank chamber. And remember – if you make one false move it will be your last move!'

Had Prothero turned round whilst he was writing he would have seen his captor flick open the lid protecting the face of the eight-day clock on the mantel-shelf and push the minute hand on thirty minutes. As they left the room he heard the clock strike ten.

In the bank chamber notes and gold to the value of a couple of thousand pounds were handed over to the menacing visitor who then quickly bound and gagged his captor.

That same night in the parlour of the local pub a number of the townspeople were gathered as was their custom after the day's work. The Rev Mr Scott strolled in and with a cheery greeting to all in general said that he was looking for old Danny Richards as he was anxious for him to do a small repair job in the church. Richards not being around he bade them all good night. As an afterthought he asked the time, and being told that it was a quarter-to-ten remarked that he did not realize the hour was so late.

Shortly afterwards a man named Thomas, a friend of the bank manager, came rushing into the parlour, waving the note from Prothero's desk and calling loudly for the police.

Next day Prothero was interrogated by a police inspector:

'I tell you, Inspector, it was Scott – the '*Reverend*' Mr Scott! There was NO Captain Moonlight, or any other such person! Scott forced me to write the name 'Captain Moonlight'

'Mr Prothero, I can well understand you being robbed by a masked man dressed as a clergyman, but surely you must be mistaken in thinking it was the Reverend George Scott! It's fantastic!'

When Prothero maintained that the robber was Scott the inspector demanded, 'Then answer me this! You say that he marched you to the bank chamber at ten o'clock – that you heard the hour strike and that your clock is a reliable one. There are witnesses to swear that at a quarter to ten the Reverend Scott was in the parlour of the hotel looking for old Mr Richards. Indeed, he had just left there when your friend, Thomas – I repeat *your friend* – came running there with the news of the alleged hold-up!'

Needless to say, Parson Scott professed to be appalled by

the terrible charge laid against him. What is more, he had everybody's sympathy. Prothero and his friend were not believed. They were both arrested. £2,000 had disappeared from the bank and both men were called upon to find sureties and personal guarantees to come up for trial if called.

Soon afterwards Mr Scott discreetly left the district. A few years later the city of Sydney was graced with the presence of a distinguished visitor who was entertained by high society until he gave a bad cheque for the purchase of a luxury yacht. It was his turn now to be arrested. The police discovered that this elegant trickster had once been a preacher in the Victorian town of Egerton, where he was known by the name of Scott.

Messrs Prothero and Thomas were immediately cleared of the charges laid against them, and Scott was given ten years imprisonment.

From then onwards, George Scott, reverend or not, was known colloquially as Captain Moonlight. As such, after graduation from prison, he took to the road and with his gang led the famous raid on Wantabadgery, vieing for notoriety with Ned Kelly. The clerical Captain made his final bow to the world on the gallows at Darlinghurst.

JACKEY JACKEY

Among Australian bushrangers none struck the public imagination of his day more than William John Westwood, better known as 'Jackey Jackey – the gentleman bushranger'. The nickname 'Jackey Jackey' was given him after a brave and noble Red Indian Chief then in the world's eye.

Westwood had a reputation for good manners, consideration for women and innocence of bloodshed. He was born in 1820, the son of an English farmer in Kent. He was well educated but at the age of sixteen was found guilty of forgery and transported to Botany Bay as a convict. On the farm where he worked the overseer was far too fond of the lash, so, three years later, at the age of twenty, Westwood escaped and took to the bush.

Many colourful tales are told of the escapades of this handsome highwayman. One concerns a Grand Ball in Sydney given by Governor Gipps in 1841. The parliamentary member for Parramatta was on his way to the function when he was bailed up by Westwood:

'You may put your hands down, Mr Gorman. I'm not going to rob you. I merely wish to accompany you to the Governor's Ball this evening. I want you to take me along as your friend.

'Now don't look so astonished. You can see that under my cloak I'm dressed the part – full evening clothes. All you have to do is to introduce me as an English friend, recently arrived here.'

'Are you crazy, man!' exclaimed Gorman. 'Are you trying to stage a hold-up there? You must know that there will be police and a military guard!'

'My dear sir, I'm not going to rob anyone at the Ball, I assure you, though I may steal the heart of some fair damsel. I'll be a thorough gentleman. But mark you this – if you warn anyone of my identity I'll shoot to kill!'

Westwood not only attended the Ball but was introduced to the Governor and members of the Vice-Regal party. Despite the flutter of excitement he caused among the ladies the young stranger disappeared as mysteriously as he came. Even the Honourable Member for Parramatta seemed strangely silent about his vanished friend.

Another of Westwood's escapades was his cool daring in making an appearance at a billiard saloon in the town of Goulburn when all the troopers were after him. Dressed like a shearer, and pretending to be a little drunk, he approached three of the local billiard experts and challenged them to a game. Producing a wad of notes he offered to play all three for £100 stakes. After beating them hands down he collected the money, shouted drinks all round, announced his identity and withdrew unmolested.

Eventually when captured, Westwood was imprisoned on Cockatoo Island. Here he organized a mass escape, and led it by swimming from the island to the Balmain shore – a distance of about 440 yards through shark-infested waters. Recaptured again, he was sent to the dreaded Port Arthur penal settlement in Tasmania. He was only twenty-two, and so far had not inflicted bodily harm on anyone. Here he witnessed for the first time the torturing of prisoners and the inhuman treatment by many of the warders. His only friend was the chaplain who was powerless to help him.

Finally, unable to stand the treatment any longer, he decided to end it all. Calling together some of the other convicts he addressed them as follows:

'I've made up my mind to stand this oppression no longer. I'm making an escape – though I'm certain to be caught. And that means the gallows. Yet death will be preferable to this hell. If any of you wish to follow me – you know what your fate will be!'

Led by Westwood a number of the convicts made the break. All were caught and sentenced to death. Just before his execution Westwood wrote a letter to the prison chaplain at Port Arthur. That letter is still preserved. In it he thanks the chaplain for his many acts of kindness, but it concludes with these words:

My grave will be a haven. Flogged, goaded and tantalized, I have been reduced to a lunatic and savage. Out of my bitter cup of sorrow the sweetest draught is that which takes away the misery of living death.

Famous and Infamous Characters

The King of the Hawkesbury – A Picturesque Pioneer – Queen of Scotland Island – Margaret Catchpole – One of the Old Breed – Francis Morgan – Good King Joe – Quong Tart – Amazon of the Manning River – A Mass-Murderer – A Woman Pirate.

THE KING OF THE HAWKESBURY

THERE ARE NOT MANY more beautiful places in New South Wales than the spot where the old Northern Road crosses the Hawkesbury River at Wiseman's Ferry, some fifty-two miles from Sydney. For many years it was an important station on the land route between the capital and the Hunter Valley.

Solomon Wiseman, the man who gave his name to the ferry, must have possessed some remarkable qualities. He came to the colony because he could not see eye-to-eye with certain customs men in the Isle of Wight regarding the nocturnal landing of dutiable goods. After serving his sentence of transportation he settled on the Hawkesbury at this spot, long before the road was made. Here he established the first ferry over the river, and it remained the only one for many years. To construct the road-way up the mountains on either side, large numbers of convicts were sent to the ferry, and Solomon Wiseman was appointed District Superintendent. This was a job of some importance, with much power and glory appertaining to it. There were also perquisites of which the astute Solomon was not slow to avail himself.

He supplied provisions to convicts on the Hawkerbury, thereby netting £4000 a year, and he ruled the whole district. There is a cave on the northern side of the river, known as the Judgment Cave, where Solomon is supposed to have sat and delivered judgment.

There are about twenty houses today in the village of Wiseman's Ferry – or Wiseman's, as it is called locally. The homestead of the King of the Hawkesbury is now an hotel. The original portion of this fine old building has walls about three feet thick. He built his house – as all pioneers did – with a view to its lasting. It is two-storeyed with magnificent circular steps leading up to the front verandah.

Legend has it that Solomon used to throw his wives over the balcony on to those steps. Legend gives him three wives, but does not say just how many times he threw each of the ladies over.

But he was a remarkable old man. To quote Judge Therry's reminiscences: 'He was quite a character – a person of great natural shrewdness and of considerable prosperity. He was very hospitable, walking round with a telescope under his arm so that he could see his visitors coming from afar. At the time I visited Solomon Wiseman (it was about 1830) he was surrounded by all the substantial comforts that a farmer with a like income enjoys in England. His household consisted of his wife, an amiable Englishwoman, and four sons, remarkably fine youths, varying from thirteen to eighteen years of age. Being inquisitive how these youths were brought up, and how he provided for their education, I found his notions on the subject of education curious and original. He said education was a point on which he was not particular; and asked me what was the good of it? adding the observation that the acquisition of wealth was the main lesson of life. I told him that, amongst other things, "Education aided in the acquirement of property". "Oh," he said, "my views are quite different. I have four sons, and I say to Richard, 'There's a herd of cattle for you', and to Tom 'There's a flock of sheep – look after them.' So, in five years' time they become rich, each the owner of large herds of cattle and flocks of sheep. Now that's what I call education, for by it they acquire means to live." It was idle to reason with mine host on the advantage of the observance of duties, and the restraints that education was designed to confer. He looked only to the one point of material gain, and discarded every other consideration. In literary attainments of any kind Solomon was sadly deficient, and took unmerciful liberties with the English language and English history.'

The story goes that Solomon flogged a convict, who died as a result of it. As he expired he cursed Wiseman. 'You will never rest!' he cried.

Years later the vault in which Solomon was buried was broken open. His coffin was smashed and his bones were scattered. Hoodlums kicked the skull of the King of the Hawkesbury in the dust. Later, what remained of his skeleton was buried in the churchyard. Thus his body did not rest. Nor could his spirit. A traveller from Europe visited the inn in the 'eighties. He was given Solomon Wiseman's bedroom. He woke up with the horrid feeling that someone was in the room. Someone was. Solomon Wiseman was standing by the window. The visitor could see through him, and with a piercing shriek, he fled from the room.

A PICTURESQUE PIONEER

In the Pittwater district, on the way to Palm Beach, New South Wales, is a locality called Stokes Point. It is named after a fine old pioneer who lived a secluded life on a little promontory across the bay.

Mr Stokes had been transported to this country for being found with a stolen handkerchief in his possession. But to the end of his days he protested his innonence. Often he told the story:

'It was a lovely Spring day in London, and off I went to Hyde Park to enjoy the sunshine. While I was making my way through the crowd at Piccadilly a pickpocket must have planted the handkerchief on me. Maybe he thought he was being watched, and wanted to get rid of it.

'Fortunately the handkerchief was worth only elevenpence. Had it been valued at a shilling or more I would have been hanged. As it was I was sentenced and transported to New South Wales as a convict.'

The conduct of Mr Stokes certainly bore witness to his good character. In London he had been a ladies' shoemaker, and his neatness and tidiness were in keeping with the refinement of his early employment.

On Sundays he was a resplendent sight. Always on the Sabbath he came from Pittwater to Mona Vale attired in all his magnificence. He wore a tightly fitting bottle-green coat with large pearl buttons, an amazing tall hat, and carried a walking-stick that Beau Brummel might have envied. Fashions came and fashions went, but the colourful Sunday garb of Mr Stokes continued to dazzle the district.

THE QUEEN OF SCOTLAND ISLAND

There is very little about Scotland Island to suggest that once it was of considerable importance in the affairs of the young colony of New South Wales. Situated in the southern portion of Pittwater, not far from Sydney, its heavily timbered slopes to-day, save for the cleared spaces around the week-end cottages, would seem to be in almost the same condition as they were more than a century ago.

In the early years of the last century the island was the scene of considerable shipbuilding activity, in addition to being the site of extensive salt-works. Andrew Thompson, a stalwart pioneer of the Windsor district, was the first owner of the island. He gave it its name, in honour of his native Scotland. In the churchyard at Windsor is the grave of Andrew Thompson; the tombstone bears a long eulogy by Governor Macquarie. Thompson had been transported to Australia for setting fire to a hay-stack when he was but fifteen years old, thus displaying, perhaps, a singular initiative in revenging himself upon some nasty Farmer Giles. At any rate he proved an honourable and worthy addition to the land to which he was banished.

On the island he built himself his home, established a farm, and carried on a prosperous business for some years, combining ship-building with other interests. When he died in 1810 the *Sydney Gazette* made mention of the launching of a vessel at Scotland Island 'one of the finest ever built in the colony', and named by Andrew Thompson at the laying-down of the keel as the *Geordy*.

After the death of Thompson many attempts were made to sell the island, but for some considerable time no buyer could be found, for its isolated position rendered farming there an unprofitable venture.

For many years the island remained uninhabited; then came a romantic and mysterious person, one Arnbrof Diersknecht, a Belgian. In company with his wife he rebuilt Thomson's cottage and established himself on the island. The pair were better known as Mr and Mrs Benns, but the latter, throughout the district, was referred to as the 'Queen of Scotland Island'. She was a little dark woman of gentle manners and great kindness of heart, but with a certain regal bearing. Her jewellery befitted her 'royal' title. She wore ornate golden earrings hanging to her shoulders, bracelets, and a magnificent necklet. Very little was known of the 'Queen' or her consort, but many picturesque tales were told of their past. There is a story that, before Mrs Benn's death, she buried her collection of valuable jewellery somewhere on the island.

Nor is this the only legendary treasure buried on the island. In Governor Macquarie's term of office there was a scarcity of coined money in the colony. To meet the difficulty the governor gave orders that the five-shilling Spanish dollar, the coin then most in use, should be punched. The small central piece so removed (called the 'dump') was made a coin worth fifteen-pence; while the remaining portion, known as the 'holey dollar', was made current at the old value of five shillings. A three-legged pot full of holey dollars is said to have been hidden on Scotland Island by two men in a stolen boat full of stolen treasure in Andrew Thompson's time.

'I wonder,' the descendant of an early settler remarked, 'if any of the present generation of Australians know how the very early settlers of Sydney interpreted the musical notes of the butcher-bird? My grandfather used to tell many tales about Margaret Catchpole. One was that so many men asked her to marry them that even the butcher-birds began to mock them. If you listen to one of these birds, especially in the early morning in autumn – it is then that the butcher-bird sings his sweetest songs – it requires no stretch of imagination to hear him say:

' "Pretty Margie Catchpole, won't you marry me?"

'My children are so sure that this is what the butcher-birds say that they always call them "Pretty Margie Catchpoles".'

The legends that linger round Margaret Catchpole are many and varied. It is a fact that she gained local fame in her native English village when, as a young girl, she rode bareback one stormy night to fetch a doctor, some miles distant, for the wife of one of the villagers. On another occasion she jumped fully dressed into a river to save the life of a drowning child.

Margaret Catchpole was born in Seven Hills, near Ipswich, Suffolk, in 1762. She became a domestic at £6 a year and keep in the services of a family named Cobbold, in which there were twenty-two children.

She had a young man named Will Laud, a sailor who later turned down his job for the more profitable one of smuggling.

When Will was caught in the act Margaret determined to be near him. Dressing herself in male attire, she took a horse from the stables of her employer and rode to London, a distance of seventy miles, in eight and a-half hours – no mean achievement. On her arrival she tried to sell the horse, but was arrested and sentenced to seven years in Ipswich jail.

Margaret had served about three years of her sentence when news came to her through the jail grape vine intelligence that her lover, Will Laud, had managed to escape from prison and was in hiding, waiting for her to join him. She waited the opportunity and soon afterwards made a break. Her lover kept her in hiding but the soldiers found her whereabouts and came to arrest her. Will Laud, in attempting to shield her, was killed, and Margaret was sentenced to death – a sentence later commuted to transportation for life.

And so we find her in Australia. There is some doubt as to the exact year she reached here, but Henry Fulton, a former rector of Windsor and Richmond, says that she came out in the transport *Nile*, which arrived in December 1801. Because of the shortage of domestics in the colony Margaret was not sent to the Female Penitentiary at Parramatta but was assigned as cook and laundress to the Commissary Palmer.

Strangely enough she never married – and this in a community where women were at a premium. Credence is thus given to the story that she had sworn to remain faithful to the memory of her lover, Will Laud. Certain it is that one aspirant for her hand was the brilliant young botanist, George Cayley, sent to Australia as a plant-collector by Sir Joseph Banks.

In her middle-age she worked as a nurse and midwife in the Hawkesbury district. Some of Australia's most noted pioneers were assisted into this world by the very capable hands of Margaret Catchpole. When the terrible floods of 1806 devastated the Hawkesbury flats she was a gallant figure in heroic rescue work.

Today you can see the little slab cottage on a hill at Richmond where she spent the last years of her life. Surely this is worthy of national preservation, or at least a commemorative plaque.

Though she lies buried somewhere in the Richmond Cemetery, her grave is unknown. In the old register of St. Peter's Church, near by, is the last record of Margaret Catchpole – the entry of her death, as inscribed in the year 1819, by the Rev Henry Fulton:

Margaret Catchpole, aged 51 years, came prisoner in the *Nile* in the year 1801. Died may 13th; was buried May 14th, 1819.—Henry Fulton.

FRANCIS MORGAN

Much of the charm of Sydney lies in its beautiful harbour. Peers and poets have proclaimed its glories.

Round the sea-world shine the beacons of a thousand ports o' call,
But the harbour lights of Sydney are the grandest of them all.'

So sang Henry Lawson. A certain British Prime Minister proclaimed Sydney Harbour as 'a paradise of waters'. But one of the first persons who is recorded as having eulogized the beauty of the harbour was a murderer named Francis Morgan. He did so from the foot of the gallows on Pinchgut Island – if tradition be true.

Everyone who has seen Sydney Harbour has noticed Fort Denison, or Pinchgut, as it was called in the early days. For a short while it was used to house refractory convicts, and as these unfortunates were fed on a small weekly ration of bread and water they soon coined for it the title of Pinchgut.

The island has suffered tremendous change in outline since the First Fleet entered the harbour. It was at that time a conical-shaped rocky islet, about eighty feet in height, covered with bushes and stunted trees. Governor Phillip christened it Rock Island, a literal translation of its aboriginal name Mattenwaya. Soon after the inception of the infant colony it was recognized that the shark-infested waters would make Rock Island an ideal spot for the safeguarding of refractory convicts, so accommodation was made there for them.

In 1796 one, Francis Morgan, was condemned to death in connection with the murder of a man on the North Shore. The place chosen for his execution was on this island. At the foot of the gallows he was asked, before the hangman placed the rope over his head, if he had anything to say. The condemned man replied nonchalantly that he did not feel disposed to speak on such a morbid subject as death, nor was he inspired to make a public confession of his sins. He said that the only thing worth mentioning was the superb view of the harbour from his high elevation, and that he was sure there were no waters the world over to compare with it for beauty.

After his execution it was decided to follow the good old British custom of gibbeting malefactors in prominent places as an example of 'Crime does not pay'. Accordingly the body of

Morgan was hung in chains at the top of Pinchgut and dangled there for many months.

In 1840, shortly after the transportation of convicts to Australia had ceased, Sir George Gipps, recognizing the value of Pinchgut as a site for fortification, and realizing that the supply of cheap convict labour must soon cease, began its transformation by razing the rocky formation almost to water-level. The project, however, was not sanctioned by the Home Authorities and the work was abandoned in 1842 when the island had assumed the appearance of a flat area of rubble, only a few feet above the tide, and about an acre in extent. But the position altered in 1854, when Britain and France found themselves at war with Russia, and Governor Denison decided that Pinchgut should be fortified. By 1857 the present Martello tower and guard rooms were finished, and the impregnability of the fortress was assured by the mounting of modern artillery capable of hitting a very large object at a very short range, if the target sat very still. The name was changed from Pinchgut to Fort Denison in honour of the Governor of the day.

The walls of the fort are twelve feet thick at the base and nine feet at the top. The Martello tower – one of the finest of its type still in existence – remains as it was when it formed Sydney's chief defence. The huge blocks of stone are locked together by small coned cross-pieces of granite, revealing true expertness in the stonemason's art. Narrow stairs wind up to the gun-room where, in perfect order, are three of the old eight-inch 32-pounders.

Many people are under the impression that the cells were used for the imprisonment and torture of manacled prisoners. That is not correct. The cells were used for the storage of powder and shot.

In 1900 the island was taken over by the Harbour Trust, under whose control it still remains.

REIGN OF GOOD KING JOE

His name never appeared in *Who's Who* or any directory, but Robert Joel Cooper, better known in the North as King Joe, was one of the most remarkable and colourful of our pioneers, the only white man ever to become the absolute ruler of a tribe of aborigines.

King Joe's kingdom was Melville Island, North Australia, and he ruled his subjects firmly for many years. Physically and mentally he was a fine type of Australian, upright and honourable and of commanding appearance. He stood well over six feet in height and had a remarkably keen pair of blue eyes.

Cooper arrived in the Northern Territory in 1881, having come overland from South Australia, where he was born. Utterly fearless, and straight in all his dealings, he soon won over the fierce Melville Islanders, and before long was proclaimed Chief over the Five Tribes. He was put through all the secret rites of the aborigines, and to the day of his death never revealed them to another white man.

King Joe was a man who would carry out his principles unswervingly. He was a non-smoker and a teetotaller – an exceedingly rare combination in white men who live in North Australian bush country, far removed from civilization.

Before he was chosen chief, trouble was always brewing on Melville Island. The islanders were a warlike race, avoided by both whites and blacks.

When Cooper took charge all this was altered. He ruled with a rod of iron, but always justly. The punishment of evil-doers he attended to personally. Wearing only a loincloth, he would take a spear, wommera and throwing-stick, and hunt down any native who had broken one of the tribal laws and had fled to escape punishment. Being a fine tracker, as well as a first-class bushman, he always returned with the offender.

For a white man to be made a chief of wild aborigines was an honour not easily won. Even when Cooper had been accepted by the tribes, two native pretenders to the 'throne' challenged him to combat. Both were powerful young athletes famed for their prowess as warriors.

Cooper accepted their challenge and prepared for a battle in which he was to fight both men in turn. Surrounded by hundreds of natives, he and his first opponent faced each other. They wore loincloths and carried only spears and a wommera each. They were separated by about 100 yards, and at a given signal each began to creep up on the other. The white man had learned to throw spears when quite a lad and was an expert in the art. However, the native knew all the tricks, too. So agile were the pair that this first test ended in a stalemate; neither drew blood.

The council of the old men of the tribes then decided that, as both were evenly skilled, they should come to grips with waddies. These weapons are about six feet in length, and shaped like a straight sword with two cutting edges. They are made from ironwood. The handle is carved to give a good grip, generally being held by both hands.

The thickness of a native's skull is abnormal; it can withstand a blow which would kill a European. Cooper was well aware of this, but so great was his confidence and fighting skill that he managed to evade the aborigines attacks until he found his opportunity to bring home a tremendous smash on the skull of his opponent. The fight was over. Though the native was not killed, he was knocked unconscious, and the white man was proclaimed victor.

The following day was set aside for the next trial by battle, but the second challenger had lost heart and confidence, and in the first round of the spear-throwing received a wound in his left thigh which put him out of action. King Joe had established himself in the only fashion understood by his subjects. Cooper married a full-blooded native of Melville Island, who proved herself to be an excellent wife and devoted mother. She presented him with a son and two daughters.

There was hardly a dialect between Darwin and the Gulf of Carpentaria with which Robert Joel Cooper was unfamiliar. buffalo-shooting he outclassed even America's famed Buffalo Bill. Altogether, he accounted for 27,000 buffaloes during his reign. In the museum at Adelaide there is a rifle with which he shot 3,000 of them.

King Joe was extremely fond of his son, Reuben. Like his great father, Reuben was tall and well-built, and a wonderful athlete. He was educated at Prince Alfred College, South Australia. Just before World War I the noted Australian athlete,

Snowy Baker, chose Reuben, with some other young, outstanding sportsmen, to tour the world giving exhibitions of physical culture. Cooper senior was justly proud of this, and when the war caused the abandonment of the project he was a very disappointed man.

Before his death, the white ruler was acknowledged by all the people of the North as a man who had done more good for the former fierce Melville Island natives than anybody else who ever entered the Territory. His descendants today have proved themselves worthy children of a notable sire.

QUONG TART

Old Sydneyites often recall that remarkable personality Quong Tart, one of the leading merchants of Sydney in the latter part of the last century.

Though born in China of Chinese parents he became a thorough Australian and even collaborated with the great Australians of his day in art, literature, and politics.

He was a leading light in the Highland Society, of which he was a member, and was an authority on Scottish legend and history. It was his frequent whim to don the kilt, and he loved to call himself MacTart. He spoke with an accent stronger than Harry Lauder's.

How did a Chinese become a member of a Highland Society? The explanation is simple.

In 1859 there came to Sydney a big batch of coolies. Among them a boy aged nine. Little Quong everybody on board called him. Although in the beginning he spoke only his native language, the lad learned a lot from the engineers on the voyage. (In those days, if you called down the ventilator of a steamer's engine-room: 'Are you there Mac?' one or more voices in broad Scots would invariably reply, 'Aye'.) Because of this, Quong's English had a Scottish flavour long before it could develop an Australian twang.

The gang of coolies to which the youngster belonged was sent to the district of Braidwood, New South Wales, to work on alluvial mines at Bell's Creek, owned by a prominent Scot. It was natural that this gentleman should be intrigued by the small Chinese boy who had picked up a few Scottish phrases. Soon Quong Tart was one of the household.

The boy acquired fluent English and acted as interpreter between his patron and the coolies who worked the mines. When it is said his English was fluent, it should be added 'as spoken in the land of the heather'.

Apart from the household of which Quong Tart was now a member, Braidwood was a community of Scots. So it was that from his early formative years this Chinese boy was turned into a Scotsman by his environment. That is why, when he returned to Australia after a visit to China, he greeted newspaper reporters with the remark: 'Ma foot is on ma native heath, ma name is now MacTart'.

There is no need to trace all the steps which led to Quong's accumulation of a great fortune. When he was only 23 years old, just fourteen years after he arrived in Braidwood as a penniless little coolie, the *Sydney Morning Herald* remarked that Mr. Tart enjoyed such amazing popularity in Braidwood that the people were asking him to represent them in Parliament.

Eventually Quong Tart left Braidwood for Sydney. Here is a clipping from the *Sydney Morning Herald*: 'All classes and creeds united in entertaining him at a farewell banquet. Judge McFarland took the chair. The gathering included the leading men of the district.' (There is no need to list their names – most of them were Macs.) The account continues: 'The distinguished guest was eulogized and toasted, and presented with illuminated addresses, together with valuable presents in silver and gold. Mr Tart replied in manly and felicitous terms and sang *Auld Lang Syne*.'

And so to Sydney, to set up as a tea merchant. On to more success and fortune. He pioneered the modern restaurant. In that day Sydney could not boast of even one café where the citizenry could get light refreshments. A meal, yes, and a good meal for sixpence, even fourpence, but a bit rough, needless to say. It took a Chinese, now an educated, wealthy Chinese, to show Australia what a modern restaurant could be.

Quong Tart began with a series of cafés in Pitt and King Streets 'on a scale of splendour never seen in Australia'. In these cafés one could have a cup of tea or a full meal. This type of establishment is familiar and commonplace today. In the 70's and 80's it took Sydney by storm; and Quong Tart increased his wealth.

But money-making was not his main preoccupation. His philanthropy was unlimited. Quong Tart made fortunes and gave back to Australia all he won. In the Braidwood district residents would show with pride a church he had given them, a schoolhouse, sportsground. In Sydney could be pointed out in many directions, the gifts he had bestowed on the community. Apart from these benefactions, dozens of men admitted they owed their start in life to this generous Chinese. His fame spread throughout Australia.

A friend of mine is the proud owner of a collection of photographs of Quong Tart – as a Chinese Mandarin, as an officer in the uniform of the Australian military forces, and in the kilt with bagpipes.

AMAZON OF THE MANNING RIVER

An extraordinary character in Australia's past was a woman named Isabella Mary Kelly who, in the middle of last century, ruled the Manning River district of New South Wales with a rod of iron. Few records of her remain, but it is known she was a sadistic flogger of convicts and a ruthless killer of the aborigines; even darker deeds have been hinted at.

Why Isabella Kelly chose to lose herself in the wilds of a newly-settled outpost will never be known. Along the Manning River old-timers still tell strange stories of this mysterious woman; legends handed down the years – probably embroidered in the process – but, in the main, undoubtedly true and all of them grim.

One day, in the late 1830's, she came into the little township of Dungog and made straight to the office of the police magistrate, Captain Thomas Cook. Without a word of greeting she strode up to the magistrate, who was showing his new assistant his duties, and immediately began to state her business:

'I haven't time to waste, captain. I've come all the way in from Brimbin especially to see you.'

'Pardon me a moment, Miss Kelly,' the magistrate replied, 'I'm showing my new assistant some important work'.

'You have all day and every day to attend to your "important" work! New assistant or old assistant I won't be put off! Now listen to me – '

The assistant asked to be excused to leave the room, but Isabella exclaimed:

'You can stay! This is no tete-a-tete! It matters not who is present when I have anything to say! My business is this, Captain. The blacks are proving troublesome. Some of my cattle at Brimbin are missing – no doubt the blacks have stolen them. I want you to send out an armed expedition to wipe out every native in the district.'

'Miss Kelly,' answered the magistrate, 'your request is too ruthless to consider! Moreover, I object to your overbearing manner. You seem to forget that I — '

'I forget nothing! Don't go beating about the bush! I want no humbugging in the matter. I demand that you send an expedition!'

'And I refuse!'

'Very well. I shall take matters into my own hands in the same way that I'm forced to do everything else. But I'm capable! I run my properties single-handed. I even save your public scourger here the job of punishing my convict servants by flogging them myself.'

'Undoubtedly you do a more thorough job than the public scourger. Your stark brutality to your convicts is known through out the countryside!'

'I treat my convict scum as they deserve to be treated! I know how to conduct my own affairs! And I know how to act now that you've refused my request. There wont' be a black left alive within miles of my properties! I'll exterminate them myself!'

'That won't be surprising! Already you have a grim reputation as a killer of the blacks. Nor does it stop at blacks.'

'So you're referring to the settler who tried to squat on some of may land? If I waited for you fools of magistrates to act, nothing would be done! I am the law on my own property!

Lucky for the wretched knave that I merely wounded him! Let it be a warning! If any trespasser dares to squat on my land again I'll put a bullet through his head!'

'Please leave my office, Miss Kelly! Your insolence is insufferable. I intend sending a full report to the Colonial Secretary informing him of your barbarous conduct to blacks and whites alike!'

'Do your damndest, you incompetent nincompoop! What care I about your reports to the Colonial Secretary? You're an idiot – unfit to hold the post of magistrate!

'I came here, with a request for those cursed blacks to be taught a lesson, though I might have known that I would be wasting my time with you! But by heavens I know how to use a gun, and I'll see to it that my district is free of the wretches for all time!'

As Miss Kelly strode out of the room, slamming the door, the assistant exclaimed:

'A veritable virago, if ever there was one! Who is that amazing woman?'

'You won't be long here before you'll learn all about her,' replied the magistrate. 'She's the uncrowned ruler of the Manning River district.'

'What authority has she?'

'None but her own. It's her stinging tongue, arrogance and vile temper that everyone fears – myself included. But make no mistake about it, her demeanour is not a mere bluff. She knows no mercy. She's womanhood's cruelest creature. She'll kill those natives in cold blood!'

'From where did this amazon come? Apparently she's been well-educated. What's her history?'

'There's not much known about her history. According to reports she was engaged to be married to an army officer in Dublin. It was to be a big social wedding and elaborate preparations were made for it, but on the wedding-day the bridegroom failed to arrive at the church. It's said that her jilted romance so embittered her that she fled from her friends and surroundings and came to this outlandish place.'

'When did she arrive here?'

'Some twenty years ago – nobody knows for certain. It seems that she was in her middle twenties, and she came with some thirty assigned convict servants.'

'Then apparently she was given her district as a land grant?'

'It's all very vague. Nobody knows about her private affairs or legal rights. She certainly lays claim to a tremendous slice of territory. She's divided it up into two huge station properties for cattle and horses.'

'And she runs both properties single handed?'

'Yes. She makes her convict servants work like slaves. The law states that when convicts need punishment they must be dealt with by the public scourger. But Isabella Kelly defies authority. She flogs the convicts herself. Her treatment of them is shocking. To give you an instance of her lack of all human decency: on one occasion she decided to take two of her convicts to Port Macquarie and have them put in the solitary confinement cells in the penal settlement there. Saddling up her horse, and with her pistols round her belt, she marched them off. On the way they were crossing a flooded river when her horse was swept from under her and she was thrown into the swiftly-flowing waters. One of the convicts, risking his own life, swam out after her and saved her from drowning. She showed her gratitude by forcing her saviour and his companion to continue marching to the penal settlement where she had them thrown into the dungeons!'

'What an inhuman monster! But surely you, as magistrate, have sufficient authority to put a stop to her diabolical actions?'

'The power of the magistrates is confined to the punishment of unruly convicts. We have little, if any, authority over their masters.'

'Then surely the Colonial Secretary will heed your report?'

'I've already sent him a report on Isabella Kelly, but nothing has been done in the matter. I can do no more than send in a further report about her. In the meantime, I'm afraid, she'll make short shift of the natives.'

Sure enough, Isabella Kelly returned to Brimbin and, arming herself with gun and pistol, slaughtered the small aborigine population camped there.

Again, nothing was done by the Chief Secretary and this infamous woman continued her reign of terror.

One day, towards the end of 1840, she set off from Brimbin with a consignment of hides and tallow to be sold at Maitland. Two convicts were in charge of the load and she accompanied them on horseback. On the return trip, as they were crossing the range at Wallarobba, they were bailed up by a gang of bushrangers led by Edward Davis – known as the Jewboy. The gang didn't bother the two convicts, but they tied Isabella to a wheel of the dray, took a pistol from her, and stole the £60 she had been paid for the hides and tallow.

When the gang left, Isabella ordered the convicts to set her free. She had another pistol concealed in her saddle-bag, and she set off after the bushrangers. She caught up with them after five-mile chase and opened fire, one bullet striking a bushranger in the shoulder. Not only did she make them return her money but other money they had in their possession. Eventually the members of this gang were rounded up by the troopers and hanged in Sydney.

By the 1860's Isabella Kelly was a wealthy woman. Brimbin and Mount George Stations in the Taree district had greatly prospered. Brimbin was located at the head of the Dawson River on the northern side and was used for cattle and horses. But now there was considerable settlement on the Manning, and newcomers began to squat on portions of the big territory which Miss Kelly claimed was her land. Finding that she could not scare them away, and unwilling to risk the drastic personal action that succeeded in the past when settlers were few, she invoked the aid of law. That settled her.

The Government appointed a Select Committee to inquire into her title. It was then found that she had no proof that any land grants had been made to her. Furthermore, she had taken no steps to record her title to any of the land.

The reign of Isabella Kelly, the woman who had ruled and terrorized the district for nearly thirty years, was over. She moved to Sydney and soon afterwards sailed for England. However, she returned later to end her days in Sydney. She died in 1897, friendless, alone, and almost forgotten. It is said that she compiled her life story for publication, but the manuscript disappeared after her death. It would have been a valuable historic document of the pioneering days, but it is doubtful if Isabella Kelly would have recorded the whole of her life story – there were so many sinister episodes.

The Bad Old Man of Moorebank

The township of Liverpool, New South Wales, had aspirations of becoming a great seaport, like its namesake in England. It was the dream of Governor Lachlan Macquarie that the village he founded would become a metropolis, with a great export trade moving up and down George's River. In days gone by schooners used to sail up the George's River to Liverpool, which had all the appearances of a seaport, complete with inns bearing nautical names. But though Liverpool's ambitions were worthy, they were not found to be seaworthy. Today the river has silted up and carries only row-boats.

On the banks of the river opposite Liverpool is Moorebank. In that district there once dwelt a bad old man – a mass-murderer who got away with it. The old fellow used to coax members of ships' crews to work for him on his farm.

'What about it, sailor? It's a grand life working on a farm. And, after all, you can always go back to the sea when you feel like it. What's more, son, you'll be able to save quite a tidy bit of money.'

The old chap never had any difficulty in persuading a sailor to work for him. In due course the employee would remind him of the matter of wages.

'Oh – your pay? Yes – yes, of course! Let me see – how many weeks' wages are due to you? I'll settle your account this very day. Indeed I will. And let me tell you how pleased I am with your work.'

Then he would lead the unsuspecting seaman to the edge of a projecting cliff near by, and would point to a big eucalyptus-tree.

'I say, sailor, do you think there's a bees' nest in that tree? My eyesight is not as good as it used to be. The wife reckons she sees lots of bees coming from it. You'll have to stand a bit nearer the edge. . . .'

A hearty push from behind, and over the cliff would topple the former employee. At the foot of the cliff the old man's half-caste wife would be waiting with a tomahawk to finish off the victim.

It was a fool-proof system – almost. But the day came when a police spy was sent to work on the farm to investigate rumours. The farmer, becoming suspicious of the supposed sailor, shot him dead.

When the investigator failed to return, a sergeant and eight soldiers were sent to the scene. They ransacked the farm but failed to find the secret tunnel where the farmer and his wife had gone into hiding. They did find, however, the illicit still for making rum, which added further to the farmer's ill-gotten gains.

It was a pity that the troops were not teetotallers. A pity, too that they should find the rum so excellent that they partook of it in most generous quantities. In addition to being good the rum was exceedingly potent, and ere long the military men were oblivious to everything.

Then from out of his hiding-place came the old man. He soaked the soldier's uniforms thoroughly with rum and set fire to the surrounding scrub. It was midsummer's day and a strong wind was blowing. All that was left of the party of troops were a few fire-arms, some brass buttons and bones. Then, to complete his distinguished career, the gentleman farmer killed his wife.

What became of him nobody knows. He and his dogs disappeared into the bush. His tracks were traced as far as the Woronora River, and some of his clothes were found on a rock in that vicinity. But of the man himself, or his dogs, nothing was seen. The good folks of Liverpool maintained (and little wonder) that he'd been carried off by Lucifer. Certainly he was a disciple of the devil, if ever there were one.

CHARLOTTE BADGER – BUCCANEER

Australia had a woman pirate. Many remarkable women have graced or disgraced the pages of our past but surely none so extraordinary as Charlotte Badger. She was born in the slums of London and began her adolescent career as a pickpocket. Quick, intelligent, and endowed with more than her share of good looks, she diligently practised her chosen profession. Before she was out of her teens she was recognized by fellow criminals as one of the best pickpockets in all London. But with all her cleverness the Law eventually caught up with her and in the year 1806 she was convicted at the Old Bailey and sentenced to transportation to New South Wales for the term of her natural life.

On the voyage out to this country the light-fingered lady formed a lasting friendship with another convict woman – Sarah Barnes; a friendship which was to lead them to amazing adventure in the South Seas. It was Charlotte who was the brains of the partnership. Sarah was amiable and placid, without any of the audacity of her friend, but she was willing to follow Charlotte's every direction.

Even on the voyage Charlotte confided to Sarah that she had no intention of ending her days in the convict settlement at Botany Bay and that she would plan an escape for them both.

The colony was only eighteen years old when they arrived and one can well imagine what a depressing place it was to Charlotte after the gaiety of London. More than ever she determined that the permanence of living death was not for her. Dimly at first, but with steadily growing clarity, she began to make her plans.

Some weeks later the colonial brig *Venus* was loading in Sydney Cove for Hobart Town. Superintending its loading was its hard-working, highly-respected mate, John Kelly. Little did Kelly think when he saw Charlotte Badger and Sarah Barnes come aboard with a gang of male convicts that these two women held in their hands his destiny, and that because of them he was to swing high from a gallows' tree a few years later. The two women had been assigned as convict servants in Hobart Town – hence their presence on the boat.

The moment Charlotte saw John Kelly she marked him as the key which was to open freedom for her and Sarah.

The *Venus* sailed and, two days after clearing Sydney Heads, dropped anchor in Twofold Bay. The ship's boat carrying the captain swung away to the shore and Kelly was left in charge of the vessel – and in the hands of the temptress. Charlotte had not been wasting her time. Already she was able to influence Kelly to open a keg of rum and make merry with a foursome comprising herself, Sarah, the mate and a member of the crew.

In the midst of the revelry the captain returned. Infuriated, he had them flogged and put in irons, Kelly included. Nevertheless, Charlotte knew that her plan was working as she intended.

The *Venus* continued her voyage. As the brig rounded Cape Howe for the long run down the south-eastern coast, the captain realised that he needed the mate to help with the navigation. Grudgingly, he released Kelly but made the tactless error of telling him bluntly that on arrival in Hobart Town he intended having him arrested for neglect of duties.

Charlotte saw this as the logical fulfilment of events. She knew that John Kelly was ready for moulding into her momentous plans. She contrived to embitter him against authority, telling him that he would be convicted and sent to the hell of Port Arthur. On the other hand, there was always a south-sea island paradise where they could live happily – if they were free.

Whatever the blandishments Charlotte used, the mate secured all the firearms as the *Venus* neared Van Diemen's Land. He released three of the male convicts Charlotte picked as being suitable for her plans, and with Sarah and Charlotte gave them the guns.

Charlotte took immediate command. The crew was overpowered and with the rest of the convicts forced into the ship's boat and cut adrift. Before the captain entered the boat Charlotte flogged him on the deck of his own ship.

Then came the incredible career of Charlotte Badger, buccaneer. John Kelly remained the navigator, but Charlotte became the captain of the brig. At her command they intercepted another vessel on the high seas, raided it, and removed all food and firearms to their own ship. Then the mutineers sailed for New Zealand. Two trouser-clad women alternated their turns at watch on deck while four men struggled to sail the brig across the stormy Tasman Sea.

At last they reach the Bay of Islands, where they made friends with a Maori tribe. They off-landed their stores, scuttled the *Venus*, and settled down to peace among the reed and flax huts of the natives. In time Sarah migrated inland to Rotorua where she spent the rest of her life as the white wife of a Maori chieftain. Two of the convicts travelled with her and also married into the tribe.

Charlotte, however, remained at the Bay of Islands with Kelly and the other convict, despite the continual danger of a calling warship or a whaler. For eight years the mutineers lived unmolested until one day a man-o'-war sailed into the bay. The natives were bribed into handing over the two white men who were taken to England and hanged. Charlotte was not to be found. By some means she had been warned and had taken to the bush.

Her life for the next twenty years is unknown. According to reports she was next seen in 1818. In that year the American whaling vessel *Lafayette*, bound from San Franscisco to Newcastle, called at the island of Vavau in the Tongan Group. While getting fresh water supplies there the skipper was surprised to be addressed by a white woman. It was our fantastic friend, Charlotte Badger. She had a half-caste youth by her side – the child of herself and the native ruler of the island. She spoke Polynesian fluently and was quite candid with the Yankee skipper, telling him about her astonishing past. Apparently she was still an attractive personality for when the skipper sailed away from the island Charlotte accompanied him.

That is the last known of her. Where she went with her Yankee soul-mate will never be discovered. Nor will anyone ever know whether she dragged him or subsequent lovers down to disaster as she did poor John Kelly.

Old Bush Ballads

The Stockman's Last Bed – Holy Dan – The Wild Colonial Boy – On the
Road to Gundagai – The Bushman's Lullaby – Sweet Alice – The Gig-gun
Shearer – Billy Barlow in Australia.

NOWADAYS, THE OLD bush ballads are heard but rarely; indeed
they seem to be forgotten entirely. A pity, for they have their
rightful place in our history, just as much as our Colonial
architecture and furnishings. Most of the old songs were of the
simple kind – sentimental ballads, dirges, or humorous stories.
Among the most popular ditties were Bold Jack Donohoe,
The Old Bullock Dray, Paddy Malone, The Dying Stockman,
The Old Bark Hut, and The Wild Colonial Boy. Some of these
ballads have been in existence for well over a hundred years.
They were composed at a time when our population was a
curious conglomeration of highly-educated and ignorant
people. Books and papers were luxuries, so ballad-making
came into vogue just as it had done in Europe centuries before.

America preserves with pride her old colonial songs. We could well follow her example.

Here is a small selection of these bush ballads.

THE STOCKMAN'S LAST BED

Whether stockman or not,
For a moment give ear –
Poor Jack, he is dead,
And no more shall we hear,
The crack of his whip,
Or his steed's lively trot,
His clear, 'Go ahead',
*Or his jingling quart-pot.**

For he sleeps where the wattles
Their sweet fragrance shed,
And tall gum-trees shadow
The stockman's last bed.

One day, while out yarding,
He was gored by a steer,
'Alas!' cried poor Jack,
'It's all up with me here;
And never shall I
The saddle regain,
Or bound like a wallaby
Over the plain.'

So they've laid him where wattles
Their sweet fragrance shed,
And tall gum-trees shadow
The stockman's last bed.

His whip at his side,
His dogs they all mourn;
His horse stands awaiting
His master's return;

* A cylindrical tin vessel used by bushmen as a kettle; the lid serving as a drinking-cup.

While he lies neglected –
Unheeded he dies,
Save Australia's dark children,
None knows where he lies.

For he sleeps where the wattles
Their sweet fragrance shed,
And tall gum-trees shadow
The stockman's last bed.

Then, stockmen, if ever,
On some future day,
While following a mob,
You should happen to stray –
Oh! pause by the spot,
Where poor Jack's bones are laid,
Far, far from the home, where
In childhood he played.

And tread softly where wattles
Their sweet fragrance shed,
And tall gum-trees shadow
The stockman's last bed.

HOLY DAN

It was in the Queensland drought,
  And over hill and dell,
No grass – the water far apart,
  All dry and hot as hell.
The wretched bullock teams drew up
  Beside a water-hole –
They'd struggled on through dust and drought,
  For days to reach this goal.

And though the water rendered forth,
  A rank, unholy stench,
The bullocks and the bullockies
  Drank deep, their thirst to quench.

Two of the drivers cursed and swore,
  As only drivers can.
The other one, named Daniel,
  Best known as Holy Dan,
Admonished them and said it was
  The Lord's all-wise decree,
And if they'd only watch and wait,
  A change they'd quickly see.

'Twas strange that of Dan's bullocks,
  Not one had gone aloft,
But this, he said, was due to prayer
  And supplication oft.
At last, one died but Dan was calm,
  He hardly seemed to care.
He knelt beside the bullock's corpse,
  And offered up a prayer.

'One bullock, Thou hast taken, Lord,
  And so it seemeth best.
Thy will be done, but see my need,
  And spare to me the rest!'

A month went by. Dan's bullocks now
  Were dying every day,
But still on each occasion would
  The faithful fellow pray,
'Another Thou hast taken, Lord,
  And so it seemeth best.
Thy will be done, but see my need,
  And spare to me the rest!'

And still they camped beside the hole,
  And still it never rained,
And still Dan's bullocks died and died,
  Till only one remained.
Then Dan broke down – good, Holy Dan –
  The man who never swore.
He knelt beside the latest corpse,
  And here's the prayer he bore.

'That's nineteen Thou hast taken, Lord,
    And now you'll plainly see,
You'd better take the bloody lot,
    One's no damn good to me.'
The other riders laughed so much
    They shook the sky around,
The lightning flashed, the thunder roared,
    And Holy Dan was drowned.

THE WILD COLONIAL BOY

It's of a wild Colonial boy – Jack Dowling was his name:
Of poor but honest parents, he was born in Castlemaine.
He was his father's only son, his mother's pride and joy,
And dearly did they always love their wild Colonial boy.

Chorus:

Then come, all my hearties! We'll roam the mountains high;
Together we will plunder – together we will die!
We'll wander over valleys, and gallop over plains,
For we scorn to live in slavery, bound down with iron chains!

When scarcely sixteen years of age, Jack left his father's home,
And through Australia's sunny clime, a bushranger did roam.
He would rob the lordly squatters: their flocks he would destroy;
A terror to Australia was The Wild Colonial Boy!

In 'thirty-six this daring youth commenced his wild career,
With a heart that knew no danger; no foeman did he fear.
He stuck the Beechworth mail-coach up, and robbed Judge McEvoy,
Who, trembling, gave his gold up to The Wild Colonial Boy.

He bade the Judge 'Good morning', and told him to beware,
That he'd never rob 'an honest' judge who acted on the square.
But you would rob a mother of her son and only joy,
You'd breed a race of outlaws, like the Wild Colonial Boy!

As Jack rode out one morning, to view the scene around,
A-listening to the little birds, with their pleasant laughing sound,
Up rode three mounted troopers, Kelly, Davis and Fitzroy,
With a warrant for the capture of The Wild Colonial Boy.

'Surrender now, John Dowling – you see there's three to one;
Surrender in the Queen's name, you daring highwayman!'
Jack drew a pistol from his belt, and waved the little toy:
'I'll fight, but not surrender,' said The Wild Colonial Boy.

He fired at Trooper Kelly, and brought him to the ground,
But in return from Davis, received a mortal wound;
All shattered through the jaws he lay, still firing at Fitzroy –
And that is how they captured The Wild Colonial Boy.

Chorus:

Then come, all my hearties! We'll roam the mountains high;
Together we will plunder – together we will die!
We'll wander over valleys, and gallop over plains,
For we scorn to live in slavery, bound down with iron chains!

ON THE ROAD TO GUNDAGAI

Oh! we started down from Roto, when the sheds had all cut out.
We'd whips and whips of Rhino, as we meant to push about;
So we humped our blues serenely, and we made for Sydney Town,
With a three-spot cheque between us, as wanted knocking down.

Chorus:

But we camped at Lazy Harry's, on the road to Gundagai,
The road to Gundagai! Not five miles from Gundagai!
Yes, we camped at Lazy Harry's, on the road to Gundagai.

Well, we struck the Murrumbidgee near the Yanko in a week,
And passed through old Narrandera and crossed the Burnet creek;
And we never stopped at Wagga, for we'd Sydney in our eye,
But we camped at Lazy Harry's, on the road to Gundagai.

Chorus: But we camped, etc.

Oh! I've seen a lot of girls, my boys, and drunk a lot of beer,
And I've met with some of both, chaps, as has left me mighty queer;
But for beer to knock you sideways, and for girls to make you sigh,
You must camp at Lazy Harry's, on the road to Gundagai.

Chorus: *But we camped, etc.*

Well, we chucked our bloomin' swags off, and we walked into the bar,
And we called for rum-and-raspb'ry and a shilling each cigar;
But the girl that served the pizen, she winked at us so sly,
That we camped at Lazy Harry's, not five miles from Gundagai.

Chorus: *So we camped, etc.*

In a week the spree was over, and the cheque was all knocked down,
So we shouldered our 'Matildas', and we turned our backs on town;
But the girls they stood a nobbler and we sadly said 'Good-bye',
And we tramped from Lazy Harry's, not five miles from Gundagai.

Chorus: *And we tramped from, etc.*

THE BUSHMAN'S LULLABY

Lift me down to the creek-bank, Jack;
It must be cooler outside;
The long hot day is well-nigh done,
It's a chance if I see another one.
I should like to look on the setting sun,
And the waters cool and wide.

We didn't think it would be like this
Last week as we rode together;
True mates we've been in this far land
For many a day since Devon's strand
We left for these wastes of sun-scorched land,
In the blessed English weather.

We left when the leafy lanes were green,
And the trees met overhead;
The merry brooks ran clear and gay;
The air was sweet with the scent of hay;
How well I remember the very day,
And the words my mother said.

We have striven and toiled and fought it out
Under the hard blue sky,
Where the plains glowed red in termulous light,
Where the haunting mirage mocked the sight
Of desperate men from morn till night,
And the streams had long been dry.

Where we dug for gold on the mountain side,
Where the ice-fed river ran,
Through frost and blast, through fire and snow,
Where an Englishman could live and go,
We've followed our luck for weal or woe,
And never asked help from man.

And now it's over, it's hard to die,
Ere the summer of life is o'er,
Ere time has printed one single mark,
When the pulse beats high, and the limbs are stark,
And, oh God, to see home no more!

No more! No more! Ah! vain the vow,
That, whether rich or poor,
Whatever the years might bring or change,
I would one day stand by the grey old grange
While the children gathered, all shy and strange,
As I entered the well-known door.

You will go home to the old place, Jack;
Tell my mother from me
That I thought of the words she used to say,
Her looks, her tone, as I dying lay;
That I prayed to God as I used to pray
When I knelt beside her knee.

By the lonely water they made their couch,
And the southern night fast fled;
They heard the wild fowl splash and cry,
They heard the mourning reeds low sigh.
Such was the bushman's lullaby;
With the dawn his soul was sped.

SWEET ALICE
(Tune – 'Sweet Alice Ben Bolt')

Oh, don't you remember sweet Alice, Dan Holt,
   The lubra so dusky and dark –
The Warrego gin with a straw through her nose,
   And teeth like a Moreton Bay shark?
The terrible sheep-wash tobacco she smoked,
   In her gunyah down there by the lake.
The grubs that she roasted, the snakes that she grilled,
   And the damper you taught her to bake?

And don't you remember the moon's silver sheen,
   On the Condamine's waters so white,
And don't you remember the big bull-dog ants,
   That we found in the blankets at night?
Do you mind the old wattle-tree flowers, Dan Holt,
   That scattered their fragrance around?
And don't you remember the broken-down colt
   You sold me, and swore he was sound?

And don't you remember the diggings, Dan Holt,
   And your luck at the Sandy Creek rush,
And the poker you played and the bluffs that you made,
   And your habit of holding a flush?
And don't you remember the pastings you got
   From the boys down at Callaghan's store,
When Hooligan found a fifth ace in your hand,
   While he held your pile with his four?

And don't you remember my fiver, Dan Holt,
  That you borrowed so frankly and free,
When the publican landed your fifty pound note
  In Tambo – your very last spree?

Time changes most natures, but yours, Dan Holt,
  Was the firmest I ever did see.
And I fancy I'll whistle a good many tunes
  Ere you think of my fiver and me.
You were not the cleanest potato, Dan Holt,
  And you hadn't the cleanest of fins,
But you made your pile on the 'Towers,'* Dan Holt,
  And that covers most of your sins.

Well, who'd think to see you now, dining in state
  With dukes and the devil knows who.
You were flashing your dover† twelve short months ago
  In a lambing camp on the Paroo.
When's my time coming? Perhaps never, I think,
  And it's likely enough your old mate
Will be humping his drum‡ on the Hughenden Road
  To the end of his chapter of Fate.

THE BIG-GUN SHEARER
(A Song of the Sheep-shearing by Hand Days)

Now, some shearing I have done, and some prizes I have won,
Through my knuckling down so close on the skin;
  But I'd rather 'Tommyhock' every day and shear a flock,
For that's the only way to make some tin!

Chorus:
I am just about to cut out for the Darling:
To turn a hundred out I know the plan;
Give me sufficient cash, and you'll see me make a splash,
For I'm Tomahawking Fred, the ladies' man!

---

* 'Towers' – Charters Towers goldfield, Queensland.
† Flashing your dover:—Using hand-shears, bearing the brand 'Dover'.
‡ Humping his drum:—Carrying his swag.

Put me on a shearing floor, and it's there I'm game to bet,
That I'd give to any ringer ten sheep start;
When on the whipping side, away from them I slide,
Just like a bullet or a dart.

Of me you might have read, for I'm Tomahawking Fred,
My shearing laurels known both near and far;
I'm the Don of River-ine, 'midst the shearers cut a shine;
And the tar-boys say I never call for tar.

Wire in and go ahead, for I'm Tomahawking Fred;
In a shearing shed, my lads, I cut a shine.
What of Roberts and Jack Gunn – shearing laurels they have won,
But my tally's never under ninety-nine.

BILLY BARLOW IN AUSTRALIA

(This bush song appeared on the programme of the Maitland
Amateur Company's Benevolent Society's performance in the
'long room' of the Northumberland Hotel, West Maitland
N.S.W., on 28th August 1843. The story of Billy Barlow is
typical of the times. A convict, after serving part of his sentence
could qualify for a 'ticket-of-leave' pass. This was his protection
when accosted by a trooper. But a free immigrant had no such
protection and was always liable to be arrested on suspicion of
being an escaped convict.)

When I was at Home I was down on my luck,
And earned a poor living by drawing a truck;
But old aunt died, and left me a thousand – 'Oh, Oh! –
I'll start on my travels,' thought Billy Barlow.
        Oh, dear, lack-a-day, oh!
        So off to Australia came Billy Barlow.

When to Sydney I got, there a merchant I met,
Who said he would teach me a fortune to get;
He'd cattle and sheep past the Colony's bounds,
Which he sold with a station for my thousand pounds.
        Oh, dear, lack-a-day, oh!
        He gammoned the cash out of Billy Barlow.

When the bargain was struck, and the money was paid,
He said, 'My dear fellow, your fortune is made;
I can furnish supplies for the station you know,
And your bill is sufficient, dear Mr. Barlow!'
     Oh, dear, lack-a-day, oh!
     A gentleman settler was Billy Barlow.

So I got my supplies, and I gave him my bill,
And for New England started, my pockets to fill;
But by bushrangers met, with my traps they made free,
Took my horse, and left Billy tied up to a tree.
     Oh, dear, lack-a-day, oh!
     "I'll die of starvation,' thought Billy Barlow.

At last I got loose, and I walked on my way;
A trooper came up, and to me did say:
'Are you free?' Says I, 'Yes to be sure; don't you know?'
And I handed my card – 'Mr. William Barlow.'
     Oh, dear, lack-a-day, oh!
     He said, 'That's all gammon,' to Billy Barlow.

Then he put on the handcuffs, and brought me away,
Right back down to Maitland, before Mr Day.
When I said I was free, why the J.P. replied:
'I must send you to Sydney to be identified.'
     Oh, dear, lack-a-day, oh!
     So to Sydney once more went poor Billy Barlow.

They at last let me go, and I then did repair
For my station once more, and at length I got there;
But a few days before, the blacks, you must know,
Had speared all the cattle of Billy Barlow.
     Oh, dear, lack-a-day, oh!
     'It's a beautiful country,' said Billy Barlow.

And for nine months before, no rain there had been,
So the devil a blade of grass could be seen;
And one-third of my wethers the scab they had got,
And the other two-thirds had just died of the rot.
     Oh, dear, lack-a-day, oh!
     'I shall soon be a settler,' said Billy Barlow.

And the matter to mend, now my bill was near due,
So I wrote to my friend, and asked him to renew;
He replied he was sorry he couldn't, because
The bill had passed into a usurer's claws.
    Oh, dear, lack-a-day, oh!
    'But perhaps he'll renew it,' thought Billy Barlow.

I applied; to renew he was oh! so content,
If secured, and allowed just three hundred per cent;
But as I couldn't do, Barr, Rodgers and Co.
Quick sent up a summons for Billy Barlow.
    Oh, dear, lack-a-day, oh!
    They settled the hash of poor Billy Barlow.

For a month or six weeks I stewed over my loss,
When a tall man rode up one day on a black horse;
He asked, 'Don't you know me?' I answered him 'No.'
'Why,' said he, 'My name's Kingsmill. How are you, Barlow?'
    Oh, dear, lack-a-day, oh!
    He'd got a 'Fi. fa.' for poor Billy Barlow.

What I'd left of my sheep and my traps he did seize,
And he said, 'They won't pay all the costs and MY FEES*';*
Then he sold off the lot, and I'm sure 'twas a sin,
At sixpence a head, and the station thrown in.
    Oh, dear, lack-a-day, oh!
    'I'll go back to England,' said Billy Barlow.

My sheep being sold, and my money all gone,
Oh! I wandered about then quite sad and forlorn,
How I managed to live, it would shock you to know,
And as thin as a lath got poor Billy Barlow.
    Oh, dear, lack-a-day, oh!
    Quite down on his luck was poor Billy Barlow.

In a few further weeks, the Sheriff, you see,
Sent a tall man on horseback once more unto me;
Having got all he could by the writ of 'Fi. fa.',
By way of a change he'd brought up a 'Ca. sa.'
    Oh, dear, lack-a-day, oh!
    He seized on the body of Billy Barlow.

He took me to Sydney, and there they did lock
Poor unfortunate Billy fast 'under the clock';
And to get myself out I was forced, you must know,
The schedule to file of poor Billy Barlow.
    Oh, dear, lack-a-day, oh!
    In the list of insolvents was Billy Barlow.

EARLY AUSTRALIA
WITH SHAME
REMEMBERED

BILL BEATTY

SEAL
BOOKS

By the same author

Under the imprint of Cassell & Company Ltd.:

BEYOND AUSTRALIA'S CITIES
THE WHITE ROOF OF AUSTRALIA
HERE IN AUSTRALIA
THE AWAKENING GIANT

Under the imprint of Ure Smith Pty. Ltd.:

COME A-WALTZING MATILDA
A TREASURY OF AUSTRALIAN FOLK TALES
UNIQUE TO AUSTRALIA

A Seal Book Publication
Seal Books
A division of
Lansdowne Publishing Pty Ltd
Level 5, 70 George Street
Sydney, New South Wales 2000, Australia

This edition published 1995 for
Hinkler Book Distributors Pty Ltd
20–24 Redwood Drive
Dingley, Victoria 3172, Australia

First published as *With Shame Remembered: early Australia* by Cassell 1962
First published in Seal books 1978

Printed in Australia by McPherson's Printing Group, Victoria

Contents

Author's Note

I WISH to acknowledge with thanks my indebtedness to the various sources mentioned throughout these pages from which this book has been compiled. Well aware that my treatment is far from exhaustive I am also well aware that it is not original (except perhaps in the manner of presentation), since the facts have been recorded by historians or stated by eye-witnesses. Still, I sincerely hope that the reader will glean some worthwhile information from this approach to the rough and raw days of early settlement in Australia, and feel a sympathetic understanding of the extraordinary problems of the incredible period.

Delving through the writings of well-known Australian historians one finds a deal of conflicting material. For example, the value of Lieutenant Governor Davey's work in Tasmania is much disputed. The general opinion is that he was a dissipated weakling of whom the colony was well rid, but some consider this condemnation unjust. Then again, Andrew Thompson is said by some to have been convicted for house breaking and burglary while others assert that he was sentenced for setting fire to a haystack. Most references state that Mary Reiby's husband came to Australia as an officer on the same convict ship that brought her here, but the *Australian Encyclopaedia* is not in accordance with that statement. That Margaret Catchpole's lover was killed in trying to protect her is the general version of his death, but some sources say that Will Laud was killed while escaping from prison. Mention may be made, too, of the manner of Bennelong's death. The famous aborigine is said to have been killed in a tribal fight in the bush, according to various historians, but others do not agree and say that he was killed in a drunken brawl in a Sydney street. There is also conflicting opinion regarding dates referring to some events.

Few of these things may be of major importance, nevertheless they are rather frustrating. I have accepted the ruling of the *Australian Encyclopaedia* in such matters where mentioned by that authoritative work.

BILL BEATTY

Introduction

Man's inhumanity to man
Makes countless thousands mourn. BURNS

IT has been said that the first chaplains to the convict settlement of New South Wales had more sinners to the square mile than anywhere else in Christendom; even Hogarth might have hesitated to record on canvas the unsavoury scenes that in the beginning were everyday ones. 'Here iniquity abounds', wrote a member of the London Missionary Society from Tahiti on his arrival in Sydney, 'and those outward gross sins which in Europe would render a person contemptible in the public eye, and obnoxious to the civil law, are becoming fashionable and familiar—adultery, fornication, theft, drunkenness, extortion, violence and uncleanness of every kind'.

Eminent authors have presented Australia's history on a large scale or mirrored it in miniature. Since WITH SHAME REMEMBERED deals so much with the seamy side of the Australian story (and one should be prepared to look squarely at the degradation into which human beings can fall), the pages that follow concern a particular angle rather than any balanced picture of this country's extraordinary and intensely interesting early history.

'Australian history is almost always picturesque,' wrote Mark Twain. 'Indeed, it is so curious and strange that it is itself the chiefest novelty the country has to offer, and so it pushes the other novelties into second and third place. It does not read like history, but like the most beautiful lies; and all of a fresh new sort, no mouldy old stale ones. It is full of surprises and adventures, and incongruities, and contradictions and incredibilities; but they are all true, they all happened.'

The appalling details of some of the worst aspects of convictism are not hyperbole but stark fact substantiated by dependable eyewitnesses. Yet harsh and sometimes horrifying as was the convicts' lot there was a silver, and even a golden side to the story. Except those who were confined to the penal settlements at Port Arthur, Norfolk Island, Toongabbie and such places during their grimmest periods, the convicts often had better prospects than they would have had in the country of their birth. In some cases they received full pardons or were granted remissions, even while they were still on ticket-of-leave. Thus they had opportunities for making good.

Free settlers and the snobbish aristocracy led by John Macarthur were a minority small in numbers, so that ex-convicts could scarcely harbour an inferiority complex in a community most of whose members were in various stages of bondage. Compared with life in the slums of Great Britain with their misery, poverty and hopelessness, there was much in favour of this so different land. Above all there was far more opportunity here for their children. The first generation of 'Cornstalks' were a healthy, vigorous offspring and of a higher moral standard than their parents.

Some of the emancipated convicts amassed wealth, rose to positions of importance in the colony and came to be leaders in the community. This was despite the contempt of the 'exclusives' who ignored them and refused to associate with those outside their select circle.

The beginning of the end of transportation (Victoria and South Australia were the only ones to escape it) was the 'assisted' immigration from 1820 to 1850. It was towards the end of Macquarie's Governorship (1809-1822) that the Home Office began to realise the potentiality of the expanding wool industry which would enable Australia to ride on the sheep's back to prosperity and bring profit to British manufacturers through needed exports. Australia deserved encouragement —she could no longer be regarded merely as a penal outpost.

Though we may abhor the wretchedness, perverse cruelty and inhumanity of Australia's beginnings we should bear in mind that such evils were by no means unknown in other countries. As late as 1856 the right of a husband to sell his wife was still maintained in England. And is the world of the twentieth century so much more humane? History cannot forget the horrors of Belsen, the frightfulness of the concentration camps and the atrocities in Poland and Hungary. Consider the infamous Devil's Island penal settlement of so recent years in the wilds of French Guiana with its steaming jungle, poisonous snakes, the man-eating pirai fish in the rivers, and the inhumanity of French authorities. What it meant to be a convict or a liberé, who, his sentence served, was left to rot in despair, was a a cold-blooded diabolical instance of twentieth century criminal punishment. Consider, too, the bitter political retaliations in Algeria today with the senseless killings of innocent civilians.

What of the white man's attitude towards the black? Australia's treatment of the aborigines in the early years is a sorry story (and there are critics of present-day approach), but racial intolerance may be found today the world over. The mob violence in Southern U.S.A., the South African apartheid affrays and killings are not pleasant pictures. Since the year 1900 more than 1800 American negroes of the South have been publicly executed by hanging, stoning, shooting or drowning at the hands of hysterical mobs meting out their own brand of 'Dixie Justice'. Only thirteen American States have anti-lynch laws and whilst numerous Federal anti-lynch draft bills have been introduced in Congress since 1922, no such law has ever been enacted. And this nearly a century after Lincoln's emancipation proclamation.

It may be said that the skeletons in Australia's cupboard have all but crumbled to dust, but this is no cause for pharisaism on our part. The many cruel injustices of the past rather call for contrition and the resolve that never again will we smirch our record with such inhumanity.

CHAPTER 1

In the Beginning

Away with these whimsical bubbles of air
Which only excite a momentary stare;
Attention to plans of utility pay,
Weigh anchor, and steer for Botany Bay.
Let no one think much of a trifling expense,
Who knows what may happen a hundred years hence?
The loss of America what can repay?
New Colonies seek for at Botany Bay.

So wrote a London wit in December, 1786. The world in general and Australians in particular have in the past been conscious of the bar sinister of convict ancestry that figures on this country's escutcheon. It was only in 1938 that the last of the convicts transported to Australia died on these shores; in that year Samuel Speed, the sole survivor, died at the Old Men's Home at Perth. He arrived in Western Australia in 1864 under sentence of seven years for arson, but was released as a good-conduct man after three years.

It was not until 1960 that the first published history of the convict period in Western Australia—1850-1868—made its appearance under the title of *Unwilling Emigrants* (Alexandra Hasluck). In 1931, a small kangaroo-skin pouch containing a bundle of letters was found during the demolition of old police buildings at Toodyay, Western Australia. The letters were handed over to the Western Australian Historical Society. Examination showed that they had been written between 1867 and 1879 to a convict named William Sykes, by members of his family in Yorkshire.

Incredibly, the majority of the members of this *historical* society wanted to destroy the letters. They dismissed them as being 'purely personal and of no historical interest', but when a few members thought otherwise the letter-burners came right out into the open and declared vehemently that the

1

convict history of the State was one best forgotten. Perhaps this astonishing outlook was not altogether surprising since the first official centenary volume, published in 1929 under the editorship of Sir Hal Colebatch, gave the history of Western Australia without any reference to convicts whatsoever! Fortunately the letters were saved partly by the efforts of Mrs. Alexandra Hasluck, the author of *Unwilling Emigrants*, and the only published history of the convict period in Western Australia.

There was a time—fifty years ago and less—when, as a people, Australians were ashamed of their beginnings, but today a more sensible attitude has been adopted; so much so that to have a convict forbear is almost a sign of distinction. Australia itself now honours many ex-convicts with place-naming and in other ways. If Americans study their own history they will see that for many years prior to the establishment of a British settlement in Australia, Britain was sending her convicts to America at the rate of more than 1000 a year. After the American War of Independence, Botany Bay was substituted for Chesapeake Bay and New South Wales received the stream of settlers who formerly went to the plantations of Virginia and Maryland. The British Government had hoped that the Americans, though now independent, would be willing to accept convicts as they had done before, but the hostile reception given to the first post-war shipload sent out clearly proved that they were over-optimistic.

The Australian nation owes its foundation to the convict system. That the British Government's only interest in this country during its first years was as a dumping ground for prisoners is shown by the fact that no definite legal provisions were made for civil government. On August 18, 1786, Lord Sydney, Secretary for Home Affairs and the Colonies in the Government of George III, signed a dispatch to the Lords Commissioners of the Treasury which began: 'The several gaols and places for the confinement of felons in this kingdom being in so crowded a state that the greatest danger is to be apprehended . . . his Majesty . . . has been pleased to signify to me his Royal commands that measures should immediately

2

be pursued for sending out of this kingdom such of the convicts as are under sentence or order of transportation . . .

'His Majesty has thought it advisable to fix upon Botany Bay, situated on the coast of New South Wales . . . which, according to the accounts given by the late Captain Cook, as well as the representations of persons who accompanied him during his last voyage and who have been consulted upon the subject, is looked upon as a place likely to answer the above purposes.

'I am, therefore, commanded to signify to your Lordships his Majesty's pleasure that you do forthwith take such measures as may be necessary for providing a proper number of vessels for the conveyance of 750 convicts to Botany Bay together with such provisions, necessaries and implements for agriculture as may be necessary for their use after their arrival.'

Many Australians seem to be under the impression that the convicts were not criminals in the true sense of the word but merely guilty of trifling misdemeanours and harshly punished by the severe penal laws of their day. Stealing a loaf of bread, poaching a rabbit, or advocating political reform are often quoted as common offences for which great numbers of the prisoners were exiled. Certainly very many were convicted for what would be described today as minor offences, but there are no instances of prisoners transported here for stealing a loaf of bread or poaching a rabbit.[1] Not that details are known of the full nature of the offence of most of the convicts. 'Larceny' was applied to a wide range of thefts which could cover anything from shoplifting to highway robbery. (Details of the offences would be filed in English court records at the town or city where prisoners were tried.) Those guilty of stealing goods to the value of one shilling or more were liable to be hanged, hence values were often 'controlled' to bring them below that dangerous

1 While in Scotland in 1953 the writer was shown an old notice board on a property bearing the warning that anyone found poaching there would be transported to Australia. Despite this, there are no known cases of transportation for that offence. Of course, if several animals were poached the penalty would be applied.

3

level. For example, Simeon Lord[2] was transported for stealing 100 yards of muslin and 100 yards of calico to a total value of ten pence—obviously an under-valuation. William Walker, alias William Swallow, a convict who figured in the piracy of the brig *Cyprus*,[3] was sentenced for stealing clothes and food in 1820 'worth eight pence'—surely another instance of 'controlled' valuation.

As regards political prisoners, the Irish rebels, Scottish Martyrs, Tolpuddle trade-union pioneers and the French-Canadian Patriots combined would form a very small minority among the thousands of transportees. But without any 'white-washing' or bias one can get a fair estimate of the crimes in general of prisoners sent here by examining the criminal laws of those times. And those laws and penalties were severe.

Crimes that brought the penalty of transportation included the advocacy of universal suffrage, trade-unionism even in its mildest form, and parliamentary reform. Such things were classed as the diabolical thinking of anarchists. At the time of Australia's first settlement there were 200 offences in England which carried the death penalty (a boy of eleven years was hanged for stealing a handkerchief), and the English gaols, like their administration, were physically and morally rotten.[4] Many of Australia's 'criminals' were boys and girls not yet in their teens; one of those who had been sentenced to transportation for the term of his natural life was a child of seven. Governor Hunter, in giving evidence before the English House of Commons in 1812, stated that during his regime in New South Wales transportees included boys and girls no older than twelve and men and women of over eighty years.

There were, of course, some desperate characters among the convicts. But very many of the prisoners were offenders whose convictions had their roots in poverty and despair or who could not adjust themselves to society because of ignorance, indolence or lack of self-restraint. Many of the women

2 See *The Emancipists*, Chapter 14.
3 See *Escape*, Chapter 6.
4 *British Imperialism & Australia* (Fitzpatrick).

4

were obviously 'born to be bad', but the inhumanity of social conditions of those times which allowed women naked to the waist to work in the stifling heat of the mines alongside completely naked miners gave them no encouragement to remould their lives. Rather it speeded their downfall.

Beginning as a forlorn, despised, half-forgotten penal settlement whose people had to establish themselves under a violent despotism, neglect and starvation, Australia as a nation was cradled in the Colony of New South Wales when Captain Arthur Phillip sailed into Botany Bay with eleven ships and a personnel of 1000 odd. This was eighteen years after Captain James Cook explored and took possession of the eastern coast in 1770.

Six months before the First Fleet sailed from England the *Sussex Weekly Advertiser* of November 13, 1786, wrote that 'The plan of transporting convicts to Botany Bay is considered as a lunatic scheme'. An eloquent example of the pitfalls of prophecy. The same newspaper, a few weeks beforehand—October 2, 1786—gives an indication of one of the supposed reasons for the First Fleet: 'Whatever expense (and the highest calculation is not immoderate) the plan of sending the convicts may cost government, something must be done in the present alarming state of criminality in this country. A man ignorant of the fact is shocked to hear that in London prisons only there are always above a thousand prisoners for different crimes, and no sooner are fifty or an hundred disposed of than there are as many ready to be committed in their room. The frequency of committments is astonishing.' (Regarding the reference to the expense of dispatching the First Fleet, the cost to Britain has been estimated at £84,000.)

In the same issue of that newspaper is an ominous paragraph: 'Each of the transport ships going to Botany Bay have two guns loaded with grapeshot pointed down the hatchway where the convicts are to be; and which will be fired on them should any riot or mutiny happen'. Not that much publicity was given to the Fleet's departure. Newspapers were not numerous, and at the time most of their news space was given over to the trial of Warren Hastings and the morganatic marriage of the Prince of Wales and Mrs. Fitzherbert. A bare two or three lines stating that the fleet destined for Botany Bay had departed, is the only press mention. But two private references to the sailing are still extant. The minister of a church in the Isle of Wight recorded in his diary that, as the convoy left Spithead, he prayed for its safety and for the souls of the prisoners. And an anonymous officer, writing in the *United Services Journal* for December, 1846, described the embarkation of convicts at Portsmouth:

'I recollect perfectly all the shop-windows and doors of Portsmouth being closed on this occasion, and the streets lined with troops while the waggons—I think 30 in number —passed to Point Beach, where the boats were ready to receive them. As soon as they were embarked, they gave three tremendous cheers, and were rowed off to the transport ready for their reception at Spithead.'

Historians have closely examined the early naval life of Arthur Phillip, and the opinion has often been expressed that he was in many respects an obscure officer. Certainly his appointment to the position of commander-in-chief of the expedition received criticism from Lord Howe of the Admiralty, and it also surprised others. A naval contemporary, Edward Spain, wrote in his memoranda (in the possession of the Mitchell Library, Sydney): 'Fortune smiles when we think of it. Who would have thought it that Captain P—p a man of no great family without any connections should be appointed commodore and governor of the new colony to be established in New Holland.'

Apparently, however, there must have been some people in high authority who knew his worth, even though they were not sure of the spelling of his name. Often it appeared as Phillips, and other variations, even in official documents. The *Sussex Weekly Advertiser*, which spoke of the 'lunatic scheme', printed the following paragraph in its issue of October 16, 1786: 'Mr. Phillips is the officer appointed to superintend the proposed settlement at Botany Bay. This gentleman is a captain in the navy, possessing a spirit of enterprise and an understanding which qualify him for any adventurous undertaking. He is to be stationed at the settlement for three years at an annual salary of £300.'

Arthur Phillip was wisely chosen to be Australia's first Governor. A man more suitable for the task of controlling the motley crowd of soldiers, civilians and convicts which he had to rule could hardly have been found. He possessed the courage and patience to overcome the many obstacles, human and material, that confronted him, and right up to the time of his retirement from ill-health in 1792 he constantly urged the British Government to send out civilian settlers. 'We shall want some good characters', said he, 'to which these people might look up.'

Let us face facts. There was never any glorious empire-building idea of colonising this country. England merely ridded herself of many occupants of her embarrassingly over-crowded prisons. There was a pressing need to 'effectually dispose of convicts' to this far-away land 'the remoteness of its situation from whence it is hardly possible for persons to return without permission' to quote Lord Sydney. The vicious repressions of the poor by the English upper class—perhaps born of the fear of an English equivalent to the French revolution—resulted in an increase of thefts. An example of how the wrong-doers were punished is shown in a copy of the Kent Gaol Register for the Lenten Assizes held at Maidstone on Monday, March 15, 1830. It states that the Court was held before the Right Honorable Sir Nicholas Conyngham, Chief Justice of His Majesty's Court of Common Pleas, and the Honorable Sir John Bayley, Justice of His Majesty's Court of King's Bench. Here are a few of the sentences:

James Price, aged 22, chimney-sweep. Charged on suspicion of stealing 10 feet of lead pipe, value 6/-.
SENTENCE: Transportation to Botany Bay for 14 years.
Roger Cutler, labourer. Stealing 15 lbs. of beef.
SENTENCE: Death.
John Prentice, aged 15 years. Stealing three boxes of caps for guns.
SENTENCE: Transportation to Botany Bay for 7 years.
Thomas Royston, aged 22. Stealing horse and cart.
SENTENCE: Death.

John Broughton, aged 20. Stealing 4 bushels of meal and 4 bushels of flour.
SENTENCE: Death.
James Carey, aged 15. Stealing from a house one sovereign and other articles.
SENTENCE: Death.
Terence Selby, fisherman, aged 23. Charged on suspicion of stealing one pair of boots, value 5/-.
SENTENCE: Transportation to Botany Bay for life.

And so the grim list goes on, covering 91 sentences.

There is ample evidence to show that if Britain had not decided to establish a convict settlement at Botany Bay, Australia would have been colonised by France or some other nation. But whatever the offence that may have led to some unfortunate being sentenced to transportation, the fact remains that the first shiploads to come to this country suffered sufficiently on the voyage itself to expiate anything but the most horrible of crimes. Many of the convicts of the Second Fleet, for instance, were guilty of no more serious an offence than would today be dismissed under the First Offenders' Act. They were shipped to Australia in crazy hulks, spent eight months at sea chained in the holds often waist deep in water, and when disease attacked them were allowed to die like flies. Miserable wretches, denied even the common necessities of sufficient food and water, searched their dead and dying comrades for the paltry possessions they might have managed to retain, even stealing the tobacco quids from the mouths of the dead. As convicts died, the deaths were not reported until nature could no longer endure the presence of the corpses in the stinking holds; for undisclosed deaths meant extra rations to share between the semi-starved wretches who remained.

Thanks to Phillip, conditions on the First Fleet were fairly satisfactory, but 267 convicts died in the Second Fleet, and 199 in the third. A military officer of the day, Captain Hill, wrote: 'The slave traffic is merciful compared with what I have seen in this (second) fleet; in that it is in the interests of the masters to preserve the healths and lives of their captives, they have a joint benefit with the owners; in this, the more they can withold from the unhappy wretches, the more

8

provisions they have to dispose of at a foreign market, and the earlier in the voyage they die, the longer they can draw the deceased's allowance to themselves'.

When the Second Fleet arrived in Sydney Cove the remnants of that pitiful human cargo were mustered on deck one drizzling morning. The living were herded into rain-filled boats to be taken ashore; the dead thrown naked—their clothing being more valuable than their emaciated bodies—into Sydney Harbour, to be washed up for days afterwards on the rocks around the Cove. Of the 486 convicts who were landed sick from the three vessels of the Second Fleet—*Neptune, Surprise,* and *Scarborough*—124 died shortly after their arrival.

So shockingly overcrowded was the *Neptune* that 200 members of the crew deserted before she left England, and even while she was still in the river many of the convicts died, their bodies being dumped overboard. Throughout the entire voyage the male convicts were kept in chains as a precaution against any possibility of an uprising. Death took its heaviest toll in the tropics and sometimes a living prisoner would find himself chained to a dead companion for days before the putrefying corpse was removed. The women convicts were given a fair amount of freedom and were regarded more as concubines of the ship's company who at night selected their favourites and carried them off to their quarters.

On board the *Scarborough* were two passengers destined for fame in Australian history—John and Elizabeth Macarthur. They began the voyage on the *Neptune* but before that vessel's departure from Gravesend John Macarthur and the captain, John Gilbert, were at loggerheads, their violent quarrelling leading to blows. Macarthur's complaints centred around conditions aboard the vessel, 'the stench of the buckets belonging to the convict women', and the location of his cabin. Mrs. Macarthur has much to say about all this in her diary. For a while there was a truce between the two men but during the trip round the coast to Plymouth tempers flared anew. On arrival at Plymouth Docks they fought a duel, although a bloodless one. The wrangling

9

continued, even more violently, and the port authorities arranged for a transfer of masters with Captain Donald Traill as the new skipper of the *Neptune.* Traill, a Master of the Navy, who fought under Nelson, was an inhuman monster and the Macarthurs wisely changed over to the *Scarborough.*

When the three ships comprising the Second Fleet arrived in Sydney Cove, the Reverend Richard Johnson could not steel his nerves to go aboard the *Neptune,* so horrifying was the scene, so intolerable the stench from the vessel. He went on board the *Scarborough* and proposed to go down the hold among the convicts but was dissuaded from it by the captain. His account of what he witnessed on the *Surprise,* the less appalling of the three ships, is bad enough: '. . . a sight truly shocking to the feelings of humanity . . . a great number of them lying nearly naked, without either bed or bedding, unable to turn or help themselves . . . the smell was so offensive I could scarcely bear it . . . the landing of these people was truly affecting and shocking, great numbers were not able to walk, nor to move hand or foot. Such were slung over the ship's side in the same manner as they would sling a cask or box, or anything of that nature. Upon their being brought up to the open air, some fainted, some died upon deck, and others in the boat before they reached the shore.

'When come on shore, many were not able to walk, to stand, or to stir themselves in the least. Hence some were led by others while some crept upon their hands and knees, and some were carried on the backs of others.'

They were taken to tent hospitals, to quote Rev. Johnson again: 'In each of these tents there were about four sick people, where they lay in a most deplorable situation. At first, they had nothing to lie upon but the damp ground, many scarcely a rag to cover them. Grass was got for them to lie upon and a blanket given amongst four of them. The misery I saw amongst them is inexpressible. Their heads, bodies, clothes all full of filth and lice. Scurvy was not the only or worst disease that prevailed amongst them. Some were exercised with violent fevers, and others a no less violent purging or flux . . .'

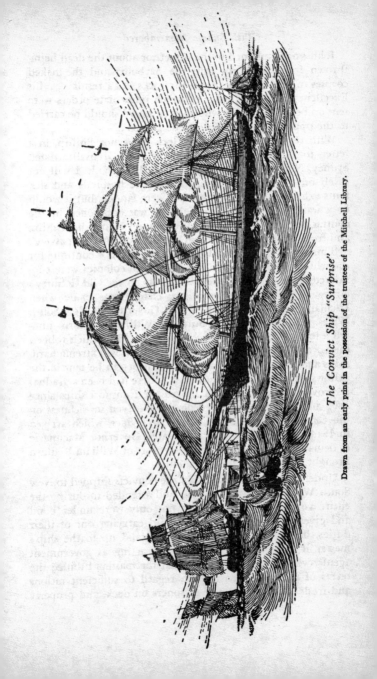

The Convict Ship "Surprise"

Drawn from an early print in the possession of the trustees of the Mitchell Library.

Johnson complained to the Governor about the dead being thrown from the ships into the harbour, and the naked corpses to be seen lying upon the rocks. As a result . . . 'his Excellency, in consequence of which immediate orders were sent on board that those who died on board should be carried to the opposite North Shore to be buried'.

With regard to this Second Fleet, Governor Phillip, in a letter to the Right Honourable W. W. Grenville, dated Sydney, New South Wales, July 13th, 1790, said: 'I will not dwell on the scene of misery which the hospitals and sick tents exhibited when those people were landed, but it would be a want of duty not to say that it was occasioned by the contractors having crowded too many on board those ships, and from their being too much confined during the passage'.

This unmitigated brutality, however, did not continue for the whole period in which the Australian colonies were considered in England to be penal outposts for the Old Country's erring children. A revolutionary change was made when Lachlan Macquarie was appointed Governor of New South Wales. Macquarie and his Surgeon, William Redfern—himself a former convict—evolved a policy in 1814 which robbed the voyage from England to Australia of those extreme hardships and terrors which had made men beg to be sent to the gallows rather than be transported. There had been a gradual improvement in conditions aboard the transport ships since 1802 and a greatly decreased death-roll. Even so, sickness on the *General Hewitt, Surry,* and *Three Bees,* which arrived in 1814, was so widespread as to cause Governor Macquarie to demand a full enquiry, and the report of William Redfern brought about many improvements.

Under this enlightened policy the convicts shipped to New South Wales were watched over and attended to during the entire voyage by surgeons who not only were under bond and given a bonus for the successful carrying out of their duties, but who were better able to stand up to the ship's master if necessary. These surgeons, acting as government agents, were empowered to see that the masters fulfilled the terms of the charter-party with regard to sufficient rations and fresh water, exercise of prisoners on deck, and properly cleaned and ventilated quarters. Moreover, separate ships were provided for female convicts, and later for juveniles. The transported felons on arrival in Sydney were lined up aboard the transports while the Governor himself inspected them and passed judgment on their physical condition. The surgeon who had neglected his charges regretted it when Macquarie had got through with him.

The result of this change in policy and conditions was extraordinary. Judged by the standards of the age, the convict ships plying to Australia became almost pleasure ships; instead of the threat of transportation to Botany Bay being a deterrent to crime, men and women began to commit petty offences in order to have a free ocean voyage with, at the end of it, a chance for making good in a new land. Superintendent Cotton of Newgate Prison has left it on record that his gaol birds used to sing as they left for exile. In 1818, Cotton informed a Police Committee that 'the generality of those who are transported consider it as a party of pleasure—as going out to see the world; they evince no penitence, no contrition, but seem to rejoice in the thing, many of them to court it'. He had, he said, heard prisoners return thanks to the Recorder for their sentences, and seem overjoyed. They shouted and cheered as they were being taken away. Some of them called out to the warders that 'the first fine Sunday we will have a glorious kangaroo hunt at the Bay'.

They knew they would be provided with good clothes and given ample food. They were assured of employment when they were freed. To be a convict in this new strange land was infinitely preferable, from a material viewpoint, to being free in late Georgian England. They were aware, too, that in the new colony taint of conviction brought no shame, for nine-tenths of all the population had been convicted[5]. If fortune were with them, they might perhaps rise to be great merchants like Simeon Lord, with a town house and a country home, fat farms, a seat on the Bench, cards for Government House levees. At worst they would have the food, clothing,

5 By 1840, as new generations were born, convicts and ex-convicts formed only one in ten of Sydney's population.

warmth, and freedom from care which their homeland denied them.

These then were Australia's early citizens. The men and women of the first transports, brutalised by their journey, even if they had not already sunk beyond redemption before leaving England. Others, in many cases, people to whom the status of ex-convict was no cause for shame, but who had deliberately courted the penalty imposed on them. It must be borne in mind that the horrors revealed by eyewitnesses, or substantiated by documentary evidence, were by no means typical of convict conditions. Less than 10 per cent. of the prisoners transported to Australia ever saw the inside of a penal settlement in this country, and many who did do so were there only for brief periods.

CHAPTER 2

Wild Wild Women

THE infant Colony of New South Wales being a dumping ground for female as well as male convicts, the slums and bordellos of England's great cities contributed women to fill the transports bound for Botany Bay. And when, by ill-fortune, an unfortunate woman guilty of a petty mis-demeanour, but still retaining some moral standards, found herself aboard one of the earlier convict ships, her chances of reaching her destination undebauched were exceedingly slim. Prostitutes, procuresses, female sneak-thieves and asso-ciates of criminals emerged from their eight months' trip more degraded even than when they embarked; a woman of virtue who managed to retain it under the conditions ruling in the early convict ships deserved canonisation.

With only one idea in mind: to rid England of as many as possible of its social outcasts, the Home Authorities took no steps to safeguard the moral welfare of the women they were casting out. The result was inevitable: both officers and crews of the transports saw no reason to sentence themselves to months of celibacy, and the female portion of their human cargo was unblushingly shared among them.

There were 191 convict women in the holds of four ships, the *Lady Penrhyn,* the *Friendship,* the *Prince of Wales,* and the *Charlotte,* when in May, 1787, the First Fleet left England for Botany Bay. Some of the women had been sentenced to life imprisonment and others were serving from seven to fourteen years' sentences. Most of these prisoners were what the authorities called 'the very dregs of society', but the contemporary ballad, *Botany Bay,* more crudely described them as 'night-walking strumpets who swarmed in each street, . . . whores, pimps and bastards, a large costly crew'. That many were unrepentant profligates is graphically revealed in the unpublished (and mostly unprintable) Journal of Lieu-

15

tenant Ralph Clark, housed in the archives of the Mitchell Library. Clark, who was aboard the *Friendship*, and had penned his Journal solely for his wife's perusal, said: 'I never could have thought that there were so many abandoned wretches in England; they are ten thousand times worse than the men Convicts . . . In all the course of my days I never heard such expressions come from the mouths of human beings'.

The Journal of Surgeon Arthur Bowes of the *Lady Penrhyn* contains such passages as this: 'I believe, I may venture to say, there was never a more abandoned set of wretches collected in any one place at any one period than are now to be met with in this ship in particular, and I am credibly informed the comparison holds with respect to all the Convicts in the Fleet'. Commenting on the fact that corporal punishment was no deterrent, he adds that neither did he 'conceive it possible to adopt any plan to induce them to behave like rational or even Human Beings'.

Surgeon-General John White, whose *Journal of a Voyage to New South Wales* was published in 1790, in giving evidence of the wanton behaviour of the women afloat, wrote: 'So predominant was the warmth of their constitutions, or the depravity of their hearts, that the hatches over the places where they were confined could not be suffered to lay off, during the night, without a promiscuous intercourse immediately taking place between them and the seamen . . . In some of the ships, the desire of the women to be with the men was so uncontrollable that neither shame nor the fear of punishment could deter them from making their way through the bulkheads to the apartments assigned to the seamen'.

From the Reverend John West[1] we have this eye-witness account of conditions under which some of the convicts came out: 'Both female and male prisoners were commonly forwarded together; the officers and soldiers selected companions for the voyage, and a sentence of transportation included prostitution. It is not incredible that modest women

---

1 Author of *History of Tasmania*. West's great achievement was the origination and leadership of the Australasian Anti-Transportation League.

The Convict Ship "Success"

Drawn from an early print in the possession of the trustees of the Mitchell Library.

rejected life on such terms, and preferred a public execution to the ignominy of a floating brothel. These practices were first tolerated, and afterwards justified as politic'.

Captain Bertram spoke from experience when recording the depravity of these voyages. After stating that the officers had the right of selection of women convicts, he says: 'The unhappy male convicts are denied, save occasionally, these profligate liberties. Sometimes, however, they range into the quarters assigned to the women. The males, accustomed in London to indiscriminate licence, discover the greatest regret at the restraint of their passions, in the grossest oaths and in the coarsest language. The females, who rather resemble the brutes than rational creatures in their excesses, answer their reproaches and rage with equal effrontery and unbounded impudence. It is a scene like pandemonium—a second hell'.

Again, we have a writer referring to Sunday on shipboard: 'A surgeon gave the reading of the Church Service sometimes to a woman, who used to burlesque the whole'. Yet there were officials who defended these conditions. Wrote Surgeon Cunningham: 'Poor Jack is planted in a perfect garden of temptation when among, probably a hundred of these fair seducers'. He then suggested that this promiscuous intercourse on shipboard may help to reform the women by their being 'initiated in the moral principles of personal attachment'!

Surgeon Arthur Bowes mentions the women's 'base ingratitude in plundering the sailors, who at every port spent the whole of their wages in providing wearing apparel and small luxuries for these abandoned women'. By the end of the voyage many of the women were half-naked having gambled away most of their clothing. Masters of transports carrying women convicts always had the difficulty of prostitution. The law did not permit ships' masters to punish their crews for this, and in any case they realised that any such restraint could lead to mutiny. Flagrant prostitution was the inevitable result.

Captain Phillip himself said of the women prisoners aboard the vessels of the First Fleet: 'I am very sorry to say that those we have are most of them very abandoned

18

wretches'. Even before leaving England he foresaw the troubles and problems he would have with them on the long voyage, since he told Lord Sydney: 'I do not know but it may be best if the most abandoned are permitted to receive the visits of the convicts in the limits allotted to them at certain hours and under certain restrictions'.

In later days, to help rectify the numerical disproportion of the sexes in the colony which was responsible for so much vice, some good people in England sent out some free but destitute young women. This was not altogether a success. Twelve of these young ladies, sent out by a religious society, were christened by the sailors 'the twelve apostles'. Apostles they may have been, but not of virtue, since Surgeon Cunningham noted 'a goodly proportion of that chosen band being found in a matronly way by the reverend inspector who visited them on arrival'.

In 1822, John Nicol, a mariner who served on the *Lady Juliana* when that vessel was reserved for women prisoners, published his reminiscences. His journal is illuminating: 'The *Lady Juliana* carried 245 female convicts. Amongst these was Mrs. Barnsley, a noted sharper and shop-lifter who openly boasted that for a century her family had been swindlers and highwaymen. Indeed, her brother, a highwayman, as well-dressed and genteel in his appearance as any gentleman, came to farewell her on board before we sailed from Portsmouth. Other notorious women in our company were Mrs. Davis, swindler and fence, and Mary Williams, receiver of stolen goods, who had spent a long time in Newgate prison'. Then there was Nelly Kerwin, 'a female of daring habits' who had specialised in impersonating the wives of various sailors and drawing their pay envelopes. Her sentence was transportation for the rest of her natural life.

Nicol pens vivid impressions of various other members of the convict cargo (the need for which he explains quite simply—'the colony at that time being in great want of women'), including the 'pretty well-behaved' girl who was rumoured to be the illegitimate daughter of a British Prime Minister. He records the tragedy surrounding the lives of some of the young women convicts. There were, for example,

Sarah Dorset, Mary Rose, and a young Scots girl who moved
him deeply. The latter, obviously cultured, kept to herself
all the time the *Lady Juliana* lay in harbour. Nicol often
saw her crying to herself but he never learned her story. 'The
poor young Scots girl I have never yet got out of my mind',
he wrote years later. 'She died, probably of a broken heart,
before the transport sailed. She was young and beautiful
even in convict dress, but pale as death, and her eyes red from
weeping'.

Most of the women, in Nicol's opinion, were 'harmless,
unfortunate creatures, the victims of the basest seduction'.
Sarah Dorset was a young and pretty girl who left a decent
home, attracted by the pleasures of London. Deserted after
a few weeks of love-making by her 'protector' she had been
forced by want upon the streets, and was taken up as a disorderly person.

'Mary Rose was a timid, modest girl, daughter of a wealthy
farmer, seduced by an officer with whom she eloped to
London. Ordered abroad, her lover left her in the care of his
landlady, an infamous character who rapidly led the girl
down the primrose way'. She was transported for perjury.
'On the voyage out, Mary Rose would not take up with any
man, or join in the ribaldry'. On arrival in New South Wales
she was lodged all the time in the Governor's house until she
was sent back to England by the next ship. (The landlady
had meanwhile confessed to the charge, and so exonerated
Mary.)

John Nicol writes with an engaging frankness of all that
happened on the voyage, including the love life of the crew
and the convict women: 'Once we put to sea every man on
board took a wife from among the convicts, they nothing
loath. I must confess that I was as bad on this point as the
others. The girl with whom I lived was Sarah Whitelam, a
native of Lincoln, a girl of modest and reserved turn, as
kind and true a creature as ever lived.' She was transported
for seven years for stealing a lady's dress. 'I courted her for a
week and upward and would have married her on the spot
if there had been a clergyman on board. I fixed my fancy

20

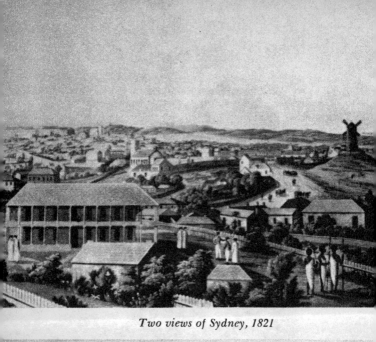

Two views of Sydney, 1821

upon her from the moment I knocked the rivets out of her irons'. She bore Nicol a son on the voyage out.

Some of the women formed a troublesome cargo. A few of the rougher characters got at a cask of port wine in the hold. One of these, Nancy Ferrel, after repeated warnings, had to be made an example of: 'The captain took a flour cask, cut a hole in the top for her head, two in the sides for her arms, and put it on her as a jacket'. For a while Nancy made light of it. She strutted about, smoking a pipe supplied by a companion, and danced a minuet; turning her head from side to side like a turtle, and making the others laugh. Alas, when Nancy found herself unable to sit or lie down, fatigue compelled her to beg to be let out. On promising to behave she was released from the barrel, 'but in a few days she was as bad as ever', says Nicol, adding, 'there was no taming her by gentle means. We were forced to tie her up like a man and give her 12 with the cat-of-nine tails. This alone reduced her to any kind of order'.

Nicol had a soft spot in his heart for the 'noted sharper and shop-lifter', Mrs. Barnsley. 'She was very kind to her fellow convicts; she was a queen among them', he records, and then goes on to say that when the *Lady Juliana* arrived at Teneriffe Mrs. Barnsley bought a case of wine and shared it with her fellow prisoners. He tells a droll story about her spreading the tale among the pious islanders that all of the convicts were being transported for their religious convictions. The women took turns wearing the only crucifix aboard the ship, and so extracted much sympathy and a great many presents from the gullible inhabitants. The devastating Mrs. B. also took over the role of chief midwife for the numerous convicts who had borne children on this epic voyage.

The *Lady Juliana* even had a visit from King Neptune as the vessel crossed the equator, but the ruler of the seven seas added a little spice to the traditional ceremonies by making all the crew confess their amours. 'I was really astounded at the number', Nicol records. A rather naive remark, all things considered. The only incident that slightly marred the jollity of Neptune's visit was when one of the women, alarmed at

21

the sight of him (he was dressed in the skin of a recently-captured porpoise), fainted and had a miscarriage.

Ports of call were highly profitable for the prisoners. At St. Jago they reaped considerable material advantages from co-operation with crews of ships in the harbour, and at Rio de Janeiro, where the ship stayed for several weeks taking in stores, Nicol records that 'the ladies had a constant run of visitors'. Throughout all this, John Nicol was devoted to his Sarah. On arrival in New South Wales he offered to forego his wages if allowed to stay with her in the colony, but the authorities were firm in their refusal. So, pledging her eternal faith, and leaving her his Bible with their names written in it, he sailed away in the *Lady Juliana.* He never again saw Sarah or his young son, John, but continued his voyagings in many parts of the world until he retired from the sea when an old man.

Nicol concludes his autobiography with these words: 'I have been a wanderer and the child of chance all my days. I now only look for the time when I shall enter my last ship and be anchored with a green turf upon my heart; I care not how soon the command be given'.

Taken from the 'Proceedings of the Bench of Magistrates re prostitution on ship *Janus*'[2] are the following disclosures:

'The ship *Janus,* commanded by Captain Thomas J. Mowatt, arrived at Sydney on the 3rd of May, 1820, with 104 Female Convicts from England and Ireland; Mr. Creagh, Royal Navy, having been the Surgeon Superintendent, but who died at Sea when off Van Diemen's Land. Some weeks after these females were landed, and either distributed amongst the respectable Married Settlers, or placed in the Government Factory at Parramatta, it appeared that most of them were in a state of Pregnancy, through having lived in Prostitution with the Captain, Officers and Crew.

'It has transpired that two convict women, Lydia Esden and Mary Long, were sent to Nicholas Bayly, Esquire, of Bayly Park, but they pretended they were unable to work, and tried to return to Sydney, in order, as they said, to get

2 H.R.A., vol. X.

some recompense from the Captain and First Mate, for their Prostitution while on board the *Janus*. Mary Long, who cannot write, said she lived with the Captain during the passage, while Lydia Esden lived with the First Mate John Hedges. Both are pregnant . . .'

'His Excellency the Governor deemed it necessary that such circumstances should be duly investigated by a full Bench of Magistrates, which was accordingly undertaken on the 24th of June, 1820, before Jno. Wylde, Esqr. the Honble the Judge Advocate; Will'm Minchin, Esqr. J.P.; John Thomas Campbell, Esqr., J.P.; Simeon Lord, Esq., J.P.; John Piper, Esqr., J.P.

'The Reverend Philip Connolly and the Revd. Joseph Therry, Roman Catholic Chaplains, with the permission of the Government had come out as passengers in the *Janus*, and gave evidence as follows:—

'*Revd. Philip Connolly*, being duly sworn stated: "I took my passage on board the Ship *Janus*. About three weeks after I had been on board, I had reason to suspect some improper intercourse was going on between the female Convicts and the Sailors . . . the intercourse appeared to me to be general; I have reason to believe there were two or three Women often, indeed Constantly, in the Captain's Cabin—Lydia Esden was one, Mary Long was also one . . . They were in the sleeping Births, both day and night.

"I felt it my Duty to have some conversation with the Captain in the course of a Month after we sailed. I did so frequently nearly the whole Voyage, but there was a time I ceased to do it, Convinced it was useless . . . as to the Sailors, each took their partner from the Prison-room.

"The ship went into Rio, and a letter was sent to the Commodore Bowles, respecting the Mal-practices on board. The Captain and Surgeon in Consequence of this went on Shore, and some bolts and bars were sent on board to keep the Prison secure and to prevent Prostitution. They were shortly removed by the Sailors . . . and I knew of two or three women who visited the Captain after the bolts were removed. Prostitution seemed to prevail more than before . . .

"The Sailors seemed determined to have the women. The

23

Hatches were removed as regularly as they were fastened, and the Captain's remonstrances had no effect, nor could it be expected they would, in consequence of his own example and Conduct, — I mean bad example . . ."

'*Revd. John Joseph Therry,* duly sworn, gave similar evidence to that of the Revd. Connolly; he stated: "I did form an opinion as to what was going on in the Ship—the utmost prevalence of Vice, in respect to illicit intercourse, prevailed. I mean with all the men it was general . . . between them and the female Convicts. I expostulated with the Officers and Captain frequently, but finding my expostulations of no use, I discontinued them."

'*Mary Long,* being duly sworn, stated: "When I have not been confined in the Prison during the night, I have passed my time in the Captain's Cabin. I believe I am at this time in a pregnant Condition. I charge Captain Mowatt with the cause of my being in this Condition. I washed and mended for Captain Mowatt . . ."

'*Lydia Esden,* duly sworn, stated: "I wrote a letter to Mr. Bayly, whose Government Servant I am. I was particularly urgent with him to come down to Sydney to see one of the Officers of the Ship. I complained to him that I was pregnant by the Chief Mate of the Ship, John Hedges. I passed much of my time in his Cabin during the Voyage. The Surgeon knew of my going up and down, and of the other women, too, and did not peremptorily order us to our Prison, but only to be more Circumspect, and not to do it openly, lest the Priests should know of it; for that his living depended on his Character. He said he would have a woman in his Cabin, if it was not for the Priests."

'The Bench of Magistrates, after due consideration, found that Prostitution did prevail to a great degree on board the *Janus* throughout the Voyage from England to this Territory, and that due exertions were not made on the part of the Captain and Officers to repress and prevent the same; and that the charges against Captain Mowatt and his Officers, individually were true and well founded in fact.'

The arrival of the First Fleet women convicts at Botany Bay was the prelude to a spectacle of utter degradation and

licentiousness the like of which has no equal in the foundation of a British colony. Surgeon Bowes has recorded in his
unpublished Journal that 'The men got to them (the women)
very soon after their landing, and the scene of debauchery
and riot that ensued during the night may be better conceived than expressed, particularly when I say that within
one hour of their landing—before they could adjust their
tents in order for sleeping in them—there came on the most
violent storm of lightning and rain I ever saw'. A more lurid
description of the orgies and depravity of the convicts of both
sexes which he witnessed on that same evening is contained
in Lieutenant Ralph Clark's writings to his wife, Betsy, in
England.

So these deplorable excesses continued. Governor Phillip
was unable to cope with the problem and philosophically
hoped such things would soon run their natural course, but
even during the Governorship of Macquarie a contemporary
official described the colony of New South Wales as being
'little better than an extensive brothel'.

CHAPTER 3

The Female Factory

In England, Mrs. Elizabeth Fry and her excellent companions were labouring diligently with their admirable work among the female prisoners of Newgate. When any of these prisoners were shipped to New South Wales the pious band of reformers farewelled them with personal comforts and religious books, together with their prayers and good wishes. What did the prisoners find when they disembarked? No means were available for them to continue their moral regeneration. There must have been many among them who dreamed of starting a new life in a land of peace. Any such vision would have been shattered as they neared the landing place. Reckless, swearing men, and wanton-looking, ragged, foul-mouthed women, were then saluting their approach. The reeking smell from rum shanties met them on their walk to the temporary shelter at the jail, where they were to be lodged for the night. No clergyman was there to receive them.

How the night was passed is told by a Dr. Reed: 'On visiting the gaol in Sydney, the morning after the women prisoners had been landed, I found that many of them spent the night in noise and indecent revelry, occasioned by beer and spirits which had been introduced, and that could not have been done without the knowledge of their keepers'.

The next day the women were conducted to the female factory at Parramatta. They were taken in small boats rowed by convict constables. The fifteen miles' journey often took eight to ten hours, and the helpless women were exposed to brutal treatment and licentiousness on the part of their warders, who made no bones about forcing their attentions on them.

In his report tabled before the British House of Commons, Commissioner J. T. Bigge stated: 'In their passage from Sydney, great irregularities take place; the women

26

frequently arrive at Parramatta in a state of intoxication, after being plundered of such property as they had brought from the ship with them'. Commenting on their arrival at the factory, he reported: 'The insufficient accommodation that is afforded to those females who might be well disposed, presented an early excitement, if not an excuse, for their resort to indiscriminate prostitution; and on the night of their arrival at Parramatta, those who were not deploring their state of abandonment were *traversing the streets.*' Describing the discomforts at the factory, the Commissioner wrote: 'The women have no other beds than what they can make from the wool in its dirty state. They sleep upon this at night in the midst of their spinning wheels'.

A *Sydney Gazette* of 1837 referred to the female factory as 'a hotbed of depravity'. Surgeon Reed, in describing the arrival of women convicts there, says: 'On their arrival the preceding evening, they had not got within the factory before they were surrounded by hordes of idle fellows, convicts, who were provided with bottles of spirits and others with provisions, for the purpose of forming a banquet, according to custom, which they assured themselves of enjoying without interruption, as a prelude to excesses which decency forbids to mention . . .' He goes on to say: 'One of the women, whose disposition had been particularly improved on the voyage, and who retained a strong sense of propriety, exclaimed with tears of anguish: "O God! sir, we are all sent here to be destroyed" '.

So much for Elizabeth Fry's hopes that in their new land her charges would be able to forget the temptations and miseries of their old existence. Commissioner Bigge blamed those in authority, especially the resident magistrate, the Reverend Samuel Marsden, who was the senior chaplain of the colony, for allowing these evils to continue. He demanded why this clergyman-magistrate did nothing to protect these unfortunate women from licentious convicts.

James Bonwick, in his writings of the early days, says: 'Even within the author's experience of the Colony, the female factory, from which women were hired for service in private families, had some forbidding aspects. It was the seat of idleness, the resort of the vicious. The atmosphere was polluted with the fumes of tobacco smoked by the women; and the walls echoed with the shrieks of passion, the peals of foolish laughter, and oaths of common converse. The beginners in the walks of vice associated with the abandoned veterans of crime'.

The first female factory at Parramatta was built over a prison housing male convicts. The filthy floorboards of the women's quarters in this plague spot were warped and open in large cracks through which the women could talk to the men prisoners below. A constable, himself a convict and whose only pay was an extra half-ration, was the night supervisor whose duty it was to keep an eye on the stairway connecting the two floors. But rather than dwell in the squalor of the surroundings allotted to him he shifted his abode to more agreeable quarters nearby, and out of range of his responsibilities.

The new factory was a large three-storied building designed to house 300 women. There were dormitories with twenty double beds in each of them, weaving, spinning and carding rooms, and cells for solitary confinement. It cost about £6,000 to build but so much loam had been mixed in the cement that the building was crumbling before its completion.

It was to the female factory at Parramatta that many of the settlers went to select a wife. What was the procedure? We can do no better than read the evidence of a Mr. Mudie, a settler, who was examined before a committee of the British House of Commons on the system of obtaining a wife from the factory:

'If,' said he, 'a master has a convict that he is anxious to keep, and whom he believes to be well behaved, it is considered a great indulgence if he gives him permission to get a wife from the factory; but the master must enter into an agreement with the Government to feed and support the woman and, in fact, the offspring, to prevent its being a burden on the Government. This being done, the man goes, and he gets an order to the matron of the factory, and, of course, this is for a wife. The women are turned out, and they all stand up as you would place so many soldiers, or so many cattle, in fact, at a fair.

'It is requisite for me to state that the same sort of ceremony, and the same mode, occurs with a free-man; for there are free-men that go to the factory to select a wife. The man goes up and looks at the women; and if he sees a lady that takes his fancy he makes a motion to her, and she steps on one side. Some of them will not, but stand still and have no wish to be married; but this is very rare. Then they have, of course, some conversation together, and if the lady is not agreeable, or if the man does not fancy her from her conversation, she steps back, and the same ceremony goes on with two or three more. I have known of convicts going, and having the pick of one or two hundred without finding one to please them; the lowest fellows you can fancy have said, it wouldn't do; they could not get one to suit. But if he finds one to please him, they get married'.

This arrangement of selecting a wife was a decided improvement on the treatment of convict women in earlier days. The Irish rebel, Joseph Holt, was an eye-witness of the occurrences of which he speaks:—'Governor King's proceeding respecting the poor convict women, on their arrival in the colony was abominable. They were disposed of by Potter, the bellman, as so much live stock. I have seen them afterwards sold—one of them for a gallon of rum, others for five pounds, and so on; and thus they were transferred from one brutal fellow to another, without remedy or appeal'.[1]

Apart from housing convict women, those in service who were found pregnant were sent to the female factory, there to lie in. No attempt was ever made to discover the father. The children thus brought into the world were attended to by thirty convict nurses who resided there and who were engaged solely for that purpose. When the babies reached the age of three, should they survive in such a place and under such conditions, they were transferred to the orphan schools.

Often the convict women got out of their place of detention by arranging with a male convict for a 'marriage'. The

1 'The Memoirs of Joseph Holt' (1838).

gentleman friend would apply to the authorities for permission to take the lady for a wife. As the Government was always anxious to have as many women off its hands as possible, a licence to marry was obtained with little difficulty. Nor were needless and perplexing questions asked or inquiries made as to how many times the lady had already 'married'. At any rate, the prison doors were easily opened under such arrangements.

In the negotiations secretly carried on between the two parties for a matrimonial release, a covenant was usually entered into. The man often made a hard bargain for undergoing the risk and trouble of the woman's release, and insisted on her consent to certain terms of redemption. Surgeon Reed, in 1822, thus referred to these sham marriages: 'Making a contract beforehand that the woman (wife so called) should appropriate a certain quantity of the wages of sin for the support of the man who thus espouses her. In this state the degraded victim of sensuality is often transferred from one master to another, banding about in this shocking and unnatural way until the mere figure is all that remains of the human being'.

Looking back on such pictures, and judging by the standards of today, one can only restrain one's abhorrence by reflecting that there must have been in the colony women of a moral calibre higher than that of the unhappy wretches recorded by observers such as Surgeon Reed, Commissioner Bigge and James Bonwick. But Diogenes setting out with his lantern on a search for one honest man could scarcely have faced a harder task than a nineteenth century philosopher setting out in the very early eighteen hundreds to discover in New South Wales a virtuous woman.

CHAPTER 4

In the Making

HOW did these people live in the new land to which they had been transplanted? As a convict settlement it can hardly be expected that the Sydney of the early nineteenth century should have been a model village. The New South Wales of the early 1800s must not be judged by the standards of the 1960s; it should be remembered that whatever the degradation of society of the Sydney of those days it was very little, if any, worse than many aspects of life in Great Britain and Europe of the same period. The times and the social conditions that were responsible for the drunkenness, brutality and vice of the convict settlement on Sydney Cove also produced the Hounslow Heath atrocities, the English Sabbath cockfights, the fierce drinking and low morality of Scotland, and the ruffianism prevalent in Irish history of the period. It is to the credit of those who administered the colony, both then and later, that, after such an inauspicious beginning, it developed as it did.

Nothing, however, can alter the fact that the mode of life of the great majority of the population of early Sydney was such as would horrify the respectable citizen of today. In 1788, when Phillip established the first settlement, the population consisted of 212 marines, 565 male convicts and 192 women. The proportion of females became even less; at one time there being eight male convicts to every female transported. One writer of that period stated: 'As long as the great disproportion continues to exist between the male and female population in New South Wales, the temptations to illicit intercourse in both, and all the crimes that are committed for the purpose of supporting it, must be expected to prevail'.

In a despatch from Governor Bligh, the Home Authorities were informed that 'in the beginning there were two-thirds of illegitimate children'. The state of the community can be gauged by a proclamation of Governor Macquarie dated February 24th, 1810:

'Whereas His Excellency the Governor has seen, with great regret, the immorality and vice so prevalent among the lower classes of this colony; and whereas he feels himself called upon in particular to reprobate and check, as far as lies in his power, the scandalous and pernicious custom so generally and shamelessly adopted throughout this territory of persons of different sexes cohabiting and living together unsanctioned by the legal ties of matrimony . . .

'His Excellency the Governor, aware of the frequency of such illicit connections, and seeing the shameless and open manner in which they are avowed, to the utter subversion of decency and decorum, is compelled to express in this public manner his high disapprobation of such immorality and his future resolution to repress by every means in his power all such disgraceful connections; and publicly declares that neither favour nor patronage will be extended to those who contract or encourage them'.

The Governor's proclamation failed in its mission. A year later, after a tour in the interior, Macquarie spoke in a general order of 'the total disregard to the common decencies of civilized life'. As the population of the colony increased, so the marriage rate decreased. In 1810 there were 181 marriages; in 1811, 56; in 1812, 43; in 1813, 52; in 1814, 41; in 1815, 62; in 1816, 48; in 1817, 47. An early minister, the Reverend Mr. Cowper, speaking of those times said, 'The Sabbath was unknown', and that 'almost the whole of the Australian population was living in a state of unblushing concubinage'.

Law and order were practically non-existent even in the streets of the townships of that period. Travellers were warned in a proclamation of 1817 not to travel between Sydney and Parramatta except in daytime, because of the number of robberies. A writer of 1821 describes the danger of passing near the locality of the Rocks, where the worst element in Sydney dwelt, as, especially after dark, there was 'the hazard, or rather, certainty, of being stripped and plundered'.

Sydney Cove 1788

Drawn from an early print in the possession of the trustees of the Mitchell Library.

The gaols of the primitive settlements of Sydney and Parramatta were burnt by the convicts, and a number of lives were lost in these outrages. Not that there was any lack of punishment to restrain crime. Hangings were almost daily occurrences, and floggings to the extent of hundreds of strokes were freely administered. The Government acknowledged its own weakness in the various proclamations issued. An order in 1800 proclaims that 'from the late increase of nocturnal robberies there is much reason to suspect that the constables and divisional watchmen are either extremely negligent in the performance of their duty, or that they suffer themselves to be prevailed upon by the housebreakers to be less vigilant than their duty requires, and to connive at their depredations on the honest inhabitants'. Since the constables and divisional watchmen were ex-convicts, the reason for the crime-wave seems obvious.

Strangely enough, in those early days the clergymen of the colony were, in a great number of cases if not in all, also its magistrates. Whether or not this was a necessity arising out of the peculiar circumstances of the day, the fact remains that the combination of two incongruous duties and responsibilities placed the men of God in a very anomalous situation. The Rev. Dr. Lang, referring to this odd position, said: 'In other countries the clergy have often been accused of taking the *fleece*, but New South Wales is the only country I have ever heard of in which the clergy are authorised, under a Royal Commission, to take the *hide* also, or to flay the flock alive'.

Nor was the Rev. Dr. exaggerating when he referred to his fellow clergymen 'flaying the flock alive'. The case is on record of a servant of the Rev. Samuel Marsden, Second Chaplain of New South Wales, committing a small misdemeanour for which his Reverend master flogged him. The servant absconded and went bush, committing another crime before he was recaptured. The magistrate before whom he was then arraigned was the Rev. Samuel Marsden, who promptly sentenced him to death. Sardonically enough, at the gallows it was the Rev. Samuel Marsden who as priest administered spiritual consolation on the scaffold.

That the clergymen of the day, when acting as magistrates, were influenced more by the Old Testament than by the New is shown by the ferocious quality of a judgment taken from the official records of the year 1800. Certain prisoners had been found guilty of attempting to evade their prison labours. Said the Clergymen-Magistrates: 'We do sentence Matthews, as principal, to receive 1,000 lashes; Moore, Galvin and Saunders, 500 lashes; Francis Allen to hard labour, with an iron collar, at Newcastle; William Blake, 200 lashes and three years hard labour'.

No field was considered by these lusty clerics to be outside their scope. One of them, the Rev. Richard Taylor, has left in his reminiscences the following story: 'A poor fellow came to the magisterial clergyman and asked him to speak to his wife, who was often drunk, neglecting his family, and making his life not worth living. Forthwith the clergyman strode angrily down to the man's homestead. "What!" cried he to the woman, "so you won't obey your husband? Well, if words make no impression, blows shall!" Suiting action to words, he then laid his horsewhip over her shoulders most vigorously, whilst the worthless hussy went down on her knees and begged for pardon, promising to behave better for the future. The husband came afterwards to thank his reverence for flogging his wife, the punishment having quite reformed the erring lady'.

The first of the magisterial-clergymen was the mild and kindly Richard Johnson, B.A., who had been appointed by King George III 'Chaplain to the settlement within our Territory of New South Wales' soon after his ordination. William Wilberforce, one of those who recommended him for the post, facetiously dubbed him 'the Bishop of Botany Bay'.

On accepting the appointment the young parson, to familiarise himself with actual convict conditions, enthusiastically decided to pay a courtesy call on some 250 members of his future flock who were imprisoned on the hulk *Leviathan* at Woolwich awaiting transportation to New South Wales. It was his first and last visit. Appalled by the filth and sickening stench of the hopelessly overcrowded dungeon-like quarters he wrote despondently to his friend, Newton, who replied with the advice: 'It will be madness for you to risk your health by going down into the hold of a ship where the air must be always putrid from the breath of a crowd of passengers in chains. If they are sick and want you, let them be brought up on deck'. The chaplain heeded his friend's dubious counsel and, until the departure of the First Fleet, did a pleasant round of the sights of London (he was a Yorkshireman and undoubtedly fascinated by the metropolis), spent a happy holiday at Lymington, and found time to get himself a wife, Mary, who accompanied him to Botany Bay.

The Society for Promoting Christian Knowledge favoured the young parson with Bibles, prayer-books and catechisms, and a formidable library of no less than 4,200 edifying books calculated to console and uplift their fallen readers. Of those books which they presumably expected would be in heaviest demand they obligingly supplied in bulk lots. Thus there were 200 copies of *Exercises Against Lying,* 100 of White's *Dissuasions from Stealing,* 100 copies of *Exhortations to Chastity,* and 50 of Woodward's *Caution to Swearers.*

If the Rev. Richard Johnson refrained from visiting the prison holds on the long voyage to this country he at least saw to it that Divine Service was held every Sunday on two of the vessels of the fleet, and he baptised a number of children. However, when the *Supply* reached Port Jackson and made a landing on Saturday, January 26, 1788,[1] he was unable to hold a religious service the following day because the chaotic unloading of the goods and prisoners was still in progress. The first church service in Australia was held, therefore, the succeeding Sunday, with a congregation of officers, marines and convicts assembled, according to the chaplain's Register 'under some trees'. Lieutenant Ralph Clark (who wrote so bluntly of the behaviour of the profligate convicts) in his Journal said of this memorable service: 'We had a very

---

1 The First Fleet reached Botany Bay on 18th January, 1788, but Phillip at once visualised the area as unsuitable for his project. He explored Port Jackson in a small boat and decided on Sydney Cove as the site for the settlement.

...DNEY GAZETT...

New South ... Wales Adverti...

AUTHORITY.

SUNDAY, MAY 22, 1803.

Numb...

...y ordered, that all Advertisements, Orders, &c. which appear under the Official Signature of the Secretary of this Col... other Officer of Government, properly authorised to publish them in the SYDNEY GAZETTE, and NEW SOUTH W... ...RTISER, are meant, and must be deemed to convey official and sufficient Notifications, in the same Manner as if d... ...larly specified to any One Individual, or Others, to whom such may have a Reference.

By Command of His Excellency the Governor and Commander in Chief

W. N. CHAPMAN, Se...

..., March 5th, 1802.

General Orders.

...W Brown Hayes, a Convict, having ...time past applied to His Excellency ...nor for permission to hold a Free ...edge, previsle thereat and initiate ...hers, which permission, His Ex... ...judged proper to forbid officially ...the Judge Advocate, notwithstand... ...h it appears from the Magistrates ...age of yesterday, that he, Henry ...Hayes, in contempt of that injunc... ...found with several others, assem... ...Free Mason. In consequence of ...his Excellency has Judged it expe... ...order the said Henry Brown Hayes ...abour at the New Settlement to ...r Van Dieman's Land; and it is to ...r understood by all and every His ...r subjects resident or stationed is that ...that any similar meetings without ...ress approbation of the Governor, ...unished to the utmost rigour of the ...as the local circumstances of this Co... ...its Inhabitants may require.

...mand, &c. W. N. CHAPMAN, Sec...
...ent House, May 17, 1803.

...Colonel Paterson having reported ...officially recovered to attend his ...ieutenant Governor and Magistrate ...ts respecting the Police are to be ...the Lieut. Governor as heretofore ...art of Criminal Judicature will atten... ...Monday next, to the trial of such ...s as may be brought before it. ...mand, &c. W. N. CHAPMAN, Sec... ...tent House, May 12, 1803. ...mand of His

...ENCY. W. N. CHAPMAN, Sec...
...ent House, May 18, 1803.

...d of one pound of Sugar per month, ...nessary is directed to issue three ...of Maize, in lieu of three pints of ...ekly, to the male Convicts vic... ...at Parramatta; Women and Children ...tion.

...Officers who are allowed servants ...ment are requested to give in their ...d places where they are victualled, ...ecretary's Office, in order that they ...ive a proportion of Slops on Satur... ...thin Instant. ...mand of His

...ENCY, W. N. CHAPMAN, Sec... ...ent House, May 19, 1803.

SALES BY AUCTION.

ON the PREMISES, on THURSDAY next the 26th Instant, and Following Days, at Ten o'Clock, by Order of the TRUSTEES, and in consequence of the Resolutions of a GENERAL MEETING of the CREDITORS of

WILLIAM COX, Esq

held here on Wednesday last, pursuant to Adravertisement.

The Estate of CANTERBURY, consisting of Nine Hundred Acres, pleasantly situate within Six Miles of Sydney, and from its extent and vicinity to Town, it will become the most desirable and valuable FREE-HOLD in this Colony.

Two FARMS at PROSPECT-HILL, of One hundred Acres.

One Do. adjoining the Town of PARRA-MATTA of Ninety-four, and a Lease for building on, in the Township, of Four Acres and upwards.

About 20 Head of Cows, 2 Horses, a number of Pigs, single-horse Chaise with Harness, &c &c.

ALSO,

The Whole STOCK of SHEEP, consisting of nearly One Thousand Seven Hundred; Part of which are of the Spanish Breed, and reckoned the best in the Colony.

Catalogues of the Lots, and further Particulars may be had, Four Days previous to the Sale, by applying to SIMEON LORD, the Auctioneer, or the Treasurer of the Estate.

ROBERT CAMPBELL.

Sydney, May 21, 1803.

LOST

ON the 28th day of March last, A SILVER WATCH, 2 hands on the Dial Plate, one of which points out the day of the month; Maker's name James Rosey, London, No. 1171. the property of Thomas Legg.

Whoever may have found it, will by delivering it to the Printer of this Paper, receive a Reward of Two Pounds Sterling

Should the above Property be withheld after this Public Notice has been given, every exertion will be made to discover the Parties by whom it may be concealed, and they will be dealt with according to Law.

To be SOLD by AUC...

By S LORD,

AT HIS WAREHOUSE IN SYD...

On MONDAY the 30th Instant, at TEN ... Forenoon.

THE Remainder of the INVEST... Imported per the CATO; Cons...

Capital Looking glasses, richly orna... China plates, dishes, covers, &c. Violins, bowboy, and books of Music Perfumery, lots, and gloves Pallicat handkerchiefs and Norwich Shoes, boots, and worsted hose Pantaloons and breeches Frilled Shirts and ammunition Canes Brass cocks and pocket Knives Saddles and cart harness Shot, Nos 3, 4 and 5 Dip candles, paint and oil Bed Ticking and Feathers Mustard, Arts rent in sacks Thread hosings bindings, pins, ne... Pens ready made, &c &c &c.

SYDNEY.

Yesterday arrived from the Societ... the Nautilus, Mr. E. Simeon Mast... an absence of nearly 17 Months; ... brought a cargo of Pork from Oti... has sustained no damage during her...

Mr Simeon informs us that the ...geret, Capt. Buyers, in consequen... misunderstanding with the nativ... Island of Otimes, was cut from her ...toured on shore, and violently attac... we are happy to add, by the tim... exertions of the Captain and pa... crew, was afterwards got off, and ...gith the loss of only two anchors and...

Yesterday a proportion of Slops ...to prisoners at public labour.

On Friday the infant daughter ... Walburna died at Parramatta, in co... of her months taking fire some day... which accident she was Backlingl... at length expired in considerable...

Governor Lachlan Macquarie
(Original portrait in Court House, Windsor.)

good sermon, the text being taken from the 116th Psalm, and the 12th verse, "What shall I render unto the Lord for all his benefits towards me?" '

Within a few days Johnson was kept busy with his religious duties, attending the sick, marrying convicts (although it appeared that some of the parties already had spouses and children in England), and attending public executions. That he did much good work has long been recognised, but while he was doing it he received little or no encouragement from Governor Phillip and his immediate superiors, and he seems to have been regarded in the light of a nuisance and of little importance in the arduous job of establishing a new colony. Why he found so little favour with the Governor is rather puzzling—even before leaving Portsmouth Phillip complained about the quality of Johnson's sermons.

As neither Phillip nor anyone else had made a move to provide him with a church after five years of waiting for it, Johnson resolved to build one for himself. The result was a quaint structure of wattle-and-daub and thatch from Rush-cutter Bay, which was erected at a total cost of £67. 12. 11½. The poor parson's difficulty was now to get reimbursement for his zealous undertaking, but he found that officialdom paid no heed to his pleas for payment of the account. This is a copy of one of his pleadings addressed to Governor Hunter in December, 1795:

'Sir,

I beg leave to state to you the following circumstances, viz.: That, after having made repeated applications, first to Governor Phillip and afterwards to Major Grose, the late Lieutenant-Governor, for a place of worship to be erected, and there being no prospect of my application being complied with, I was at length (after being in the Colony for about five years and a half) induced and resolved to erect a temporary place for the purpose. That when I had completed this undertaking I laid before the Lieutenant-Governor an estimate of the expenses, requesting that he would transmit the same to the Honorable Mr. Dundas, not doubting but that these expenses would be refunded. But from letters which I have lately received from some respectable friends, some doubts have arisen in my mind whether the application and request which I have made will be complied with. After having declared that my sole intention in undertaking and accomplishing this business was for the good of the service, I submit to you, sir, whether there could be anything unreasonable or improper in my making such request and application.

'Should my conduct in what I have done meet with your approbation, I humbly request, sir, that you make such a representation of the affair to his Majesty's Ministers that those obstacles which have unexpectedly arisen may be removed. I have taken the liberty of inclosing to you, in brief, an estimate of the expenses that I have been at in the above affair'.

Alas, before the Reverend Richard Johnson got paid the £67. 12. 11½ the little church was burnt down, supposedly by convicts who objected to compulsory attendance at the Sunday services. Worn out by hard work, privations, and lack of co-operation from officials, the chaplain left the colony in 1799 and returned to England. He was curate of Ingham, in Norfolk, when he died in 1827. Governor Hunter had paid honour to him when he described him as 'a most dutiful son of the Church of England . . . a very good, pious, inoffensive man', but better still was the tribute paid by a young convict in 1790, when in a letter to his home he wrote: 'On the same account I believe few of the sick would recover if it were not for the kindness of the Rev. Mr. Johnson, whose assistance out of his own stores make him the physician both of soul and body'.

*　　　*　　　*

Here is a letter signed by Joseph Smith from among the 'Voluntary Statements of the People of New South Wales', collected by Caroline Chisholm (1808-77), philanthropist, and possibly 'the greatest of woman pioneers in the history of Australia', as she has been described.

> Macdonald's River, County of Hunter,
> 3rd October, 1845.

'I arrived in the colony fifty-six years since; it was Governor Phillip's time, and I was fourteen years old; there were only eight houses in the colony then. I know that myself and eighteen others laid in a hollow tree for seventeen weeks, and cooked out of a kettle with a wooden bottom: we used to stick it in a hole in the ground, and make a fire around it. I was seven years in bondage, and then started working for a living wherever I could get it.

'There was plenty of hardship then: I have often taken grass, pounded it, and made soup from a native dog. I would eat anything then. For seventeen weeks I had only five ounces of flour a day. We never got a full ration except when the ship was in harbour. The motto was "Kill them, or work them, their provision will be in store." Many a time have I been yoked like a bullock with twenty or thirty others to drag along timber. About eight hundred died in six months at a place called Toogabbie, or Constitution-hill.

'I knew a man so weak, he was thrown into the grave, when he said, "Don't cover me up; I'm not dead; for God's sake don't cover me up!" The overseer answered, "Damn your eyes, you'll die to-night, and we shall have the trouble to come back again!" The man recovered; his name is James Glasshouse, and he is now alive at Richmond.

'They used to have a large hole for the dead; once a day men were sent down to collect the corpses of prisoners, and throw them in without any ceremony or service. The native dogs used to come down at night and fight and howl in packs, gnawing the poor dead bodies.

'The governor would order the lash at the rate of five hundred, six hundred or eight hundred; and if the men could have stood it they would have had more. I knew a man hung there and then for stealing a few biscuits, and another for stealing a duck frock. A man was condemned—no time—take him to the tree, and hang him. The overseers were allowed to flog the men in the fields. Often have men been taken from the gang, had fifty, and sent back to work.

'Any man would have committed murder for a month's provisions: I would have committed three murders for a week's provisions! I was chained seven weeks on my back for being out getting greens, wild herbs. The Rev. Marsden used to come it tightly to force some confession. Men were obliged to tell lies to prevent their bowels from being cut out by the lash. The laws were bad then. If an officer wanted a man's wife, he would send the husband to Norfolk Island.

'Old Jones killed three men in a fortnight at the saw by overwork. We used to be taken in large parties to raise a tree; when the body of the tree was raised, Old Jones would call some men away—then more; the men were bent double—they could not bear it—they fell—the tree on one or two, killed on the spot. "Take him away; put him in the ground!" There was no more about it.

'After seven years I got my liberty, and then started working about for a living where I could get it . . .'

The letter concludes with Joseph Smith's rise to prosperity as a well-to-do farmer in the Hawkesbury district. Caroline Chisholm described Smith in the following terms:

'He was an old man, with a large-featured, handsome, military sort of face, of a red-brown complexion, shaved clean. His dress consisted of a red flannel shirt, with a black bandana, tied sailor-fashion, exposing his strong neck, and a pair of fustian trousers. Out of compliment to the lady he once put on a blue coat with gilt buttons, but, being evidently uncomfortable, consented to take it off again.'

CHAPTER 5

Famine

A MAJOR problem for Governor Phillip was the feeding of his subjects. The Home Government apparently thought it no problem at all, for, after giving the opinion that the settlement would, in a short time, 'be amply supplied with vegetables, and most likely with fish', it laid down the following instructions: 'It is our will and pleasure that you proceed to the cultivation of the land, distributing the convicts for that purpose in such manner and under such inspectors or overseers, and under such regulations as may appear to be necessary and best calculated for securing supplies of grain and ground provisions'.

All this sounded feasible enough on paper, but the Home Government did nothing to help Phillip do its 'will and pleasure'. He was sent to a country of the resources of which neither he nor his government knew anything. Few tools were supplied for the cultivation of the land, and of inspectors or overseers there were none. 'I am without one botanist, or even an intelligent gardener in the colony' Phillip wrote under date September 28, 1788.

The precious cargo of salt pork, flour, rice and peas landed from the store-ships were sufficient only to last for a comparatively brief period. Captain Watkin Tench, writing in 1790, gives a realistic picture of the state of the provisions at that time: 'When the age of the provisions is recollected its inadequacy will more strikingly appear. The pork and rice were brought with us from England: the pork had been salted between three and four years, and every grain of rice was a moving body from inhabitants lodged within it. We soon left off boiling the pork as it had become so old and dry that it shrank one-half in its dimensions when so treated. Our usual method of cooking it was to cut off the daily morsel and toast it on a fork before the fire, catching the drips

41

which fell on a slice of bread, or in a saucer of rice . . . nor was another part of our domestic economy less whimsical. If a lucky man who had knocked down a dinner with his gun, or caught a fish by angling from the rocks, invited a neighbour to dine with him, the invitation always ran "bring your own bread". Even at the Governor's table this custom was strictly observed. Every man when he sat down pulled his bread out of his pocket and laid it by his plate'.

Phillip made every effort to provide a supply of green foodstuffs for his flock. On the voyage out he had procured at Rio de Janeiro and the Cape seeds and plants of many varieties of vegetables and fruit trees. Those that survived the voyage were planted in the garden near his tent, on the present site of the Customs House at Circular Quay. To grow wheat he selected an area next to Sydney Cove, which was given the name of Farm Cove, and is now part of the Botanic Gardens. Writing under date September 28, 1788, Phillip says 'we have about six acres of wheat, eight of barley and six acres of other grain', and in the following month he writes that he had '16 acres under cultivation at a small farm on the public account'.

Lack of agricultural knowledge, however, resulted in insufficient guard against disease, and it was not long before rust attacked the cereal crops at Farm Cove, and the farm had to be abandoned. Many years later when the Sydney Botanic Gardens were laid out plants were placed in the original ploughed furrows, and thus it is that the long oblong beds in the middle gardens came by their shape which has been preserved to this day.

Phillip anticipated the meaning of the impending shortage of food, and apprehended this scarcity as a matter of the utmost seriousness to the settlement. In a letter he wrote to Lord Sydney as early as the 9th of July, 1788, he begged for a regular supply of provisions to be sent out from England 'as the crops for two years to come cannot be depended on for more than what will be necessary for seed'. He also stressed the necessity of sending clothing, especially shoes.

The exhaustion of the supplies brought out in the First Fleet, in addition to rendering the people hungry, had its effect on their clothing. To quote again Tench: 'The distress of the lower classes for clothes was almost equal to their other wants. The stores had been long exhausted and winter was on hand. Nothing more ludicrous can be conceived than the expediency of substituting, shifting, and patching; much ingenuity was devised to eke out the wretchedness and preserve the remains of decency. The superior dexterity of the women was particularly conspicuous. Many a guard have I seen mount in which the number of soldiers without shoes exceeded that which had preserved remnants of leather'.

In spite of the very serious difficulties the settlement was facing, Phillip was optimistic, '. . . I hope a very few years will put this country in a situation to support itself', he wrote in a letter to England. Unfortunately the hoped-for progress was hampered by drought and the lack of speedy relief from England. In consequence, semi-starvation conditions more severe than anything experienced earlier threatened the struggling settlement.

The approaching famine made further reductions in ration supplies necessary, resulting in the already stringent food supplies being cut by one-third. It is to the credit of the governor that in connection with this he proclaimed that 'no reduction of the necessaries of life was to extend to women'. There were occasions when a good haul of fish was obtained, and sometimes a few kangaroos killed, but a plentiful supply of either was not the usual state of affairs. One hunting party that was out for three weeks returned with three kangaroos.

A disastrous blow at this period was the wreck of the *Sirius*, one of the two vessels upon which the settlement depended to procure food from distant lands. At the time of the fatality the *Sirius* was on a voyage to Norfolk Island carrying marines and convicts there to relieve the mainland of some of its population and because of the good reports of the fertility of the island. The *Sirius* was to have gone in quest of food supplies after landing the passengers on Norfolk Island. Though no lives were lost in the wreck, the news of the disaster cast a general gloom over the hungry community.

Phillip immediately convened a meeting of his officers to

discuss the exigencies of the situation. It was then proclaimed that for the future the weekly supply would be reduced to 'no more than two pounds and a half of flour, two pounds of pork, one pint of pease, and one pound of rice to each person'. This allowance applied to every adult and child with the exception of children under the age of eighteen months, who were 'to have only one pound of salt meat'. A curious diet for a child of so tender an age.

All privately owned fishing boats were confiscated for the purpose of establishing a fishing industry, and officers volunteered to take their turns in the boats to see that the fish caught reached their lawful destination and were distributed among the settlers proportionally. The meagre rations had its effect on the fitness of the soldiers and convicts, with the result that both pleaded such loss of strength that they were unable to perform their customary tasks. The governor recognised the justice of the claim and the hours of public work were shortened accordingly.

After the failure of the farming venture at Farm Cove, land in the Parramatta district was put under cultivation, but it was nearly two years after the settlement had been established on Port Jackson that the first harvest reaped in New South Wales was garnered. This was close to the district now called Wentworthville, but at that time part of the country known under its native name of Toongabbie.

The Toongabbie farm covered an area of 1,000 acres under cultivation—800 in maize and the rest in wheat and barley. But it was the most shocking farm that ever existed in this country. George Thompson, who came out in the *Royal Admiral* in May, 1792, and who has left one of the most valuable records extant of the infant colony at that time, wrote this of the Toongabbie farm and its wretched labourers:

'They are allowed no breakfast hour, because they seldom have anything to eat. Their labor is felling trees, digging up the stumps, rooting up the shrubs and grass, turning up the ground with spades or hoes, and carrying the timber to convenient places. From the heat of the sun, the short allowance of provisions and the ill-treatment they receive from a set of merciless wretches (most of their own description) who are the superintendents, their lives are truly miserable.

'At night they are placed in a hut, fourteen, sixteen or eighteen together (with a woman, whose duty it is to keep it clean, and to provide victuals for the men when at work), without the comfort of either beds or blankets, unless they take them from the ship they came out in, or are rich enough to purchase them when they come on shore. They have neither bowl, plate, spoon nor knife, but what they can make of the green wood of the country, only one small iron pot being allowed to dress their poor allowance of meat, rice, etc.; in short, all the necessary conveniences of life they are strangers to, and suffer everything they could dread in their sentence of transportation. Some time ago it was not uncommon for seven or eight to die in one day, and very often while at work, they being kept in the field till the last moment, and frequently while being carried to the hospital. Many a one has died standing at the door of the storehouse, while waiting for his allowance of provisions, merely for want of sustenance and necessary food.'

Joseph Holt[1] in 1800 gives a description of Toongabbie farm almost identical with Thompson's, while a letter written by an ex-convict recalling his bitter experiences of the infamous farm contains these passages:

'We were yoked to draw timber in a gang. We held a stake between us six feet long and six men abreast, and dragged with our hands. Only occasionally were we given scraps of food. 800 convicts died in six months. We cleared the scrub and timber. Each man was expected to clear an acre of ground a week, but the ground was as hard as iron, the timber tough, and the few tools we had were useless. We were dreadfully weak for want of food.

'I have seen 70 men flogged in a day. 25 lashes each was the usual flogging, but I saw Maurice Fitzgerald, an Irish political prisoner, receive 300 lashes. The unfortunate man had his arms extended round a tree, his wrists tied tightly with cords, and his breast pressed close to the tree so that

---

1 Political prisoner, one of the Irish Rebels of 1798. See Chapter 14, 'The Emancipists.'

flinching was out of the question. It was impossible for him to stir. He was flogged by two men—a left-hand man and a right-handed one, so that every one of the 300 blows were given the maximum force. Blood spouted from Fitzgerald's shoulders, and I turned my head away from the sickening sight. Though he was cut to the bone, Fitzgerald never even whimpered'.

Joseph Holt, also an eye-witness to the scourging of Fitz-gerald, has left on record that 'fifteen yards from the sufferer's blood, skin and flesh blew in my face as the executioners shook it from their cats—the day being windy. After feeling the convict's pulse during the punishment, Dr. Mason's (the official medico in attendance) only remark was: "Go on, this man will tire you both before he fails" '.[2]

The shocking death-roll makes it difficult to compute the average number of convicts employed at the farm. However, by 1792, despite outbreaks of fever and chest complaints worsened by exposure and the burden of carrying iron chains, Governor Phillip recorded a maize crop of nearly 5,000 bushels for that year. By then the harsh conditions of labour had sorted the weak from the strong among the convicts, and yielded some remarkably robust characters who were even-tually to win their freedom and become the progenitors of some of the colony's most industrious and worthy families. By 1880, this most terrible of all agricultural projects in Australia was less important and Toongabbie farm was by degrees abandoned. In much later years it was subdivided and sold; part of it now belongs to the Westmead Boys' Home, and part to the Parramatta Mental Asylum.

Governor Phillip returned to England aboard the *Atlantic* on December 11, 1792, to be succeeded by Governor Hunter. The 'pioneer of pioneers' left the settlement with the spectre of famine still haunting the memory, if somewhat less feared. Establishing a new settlement on the shores of an unknown continent 12,000 miles from the mother country was in itself a most arduous undertaking, but Phillip's difficulties and problems were considerably increased by the unpromising

2 *Memoirs* (Holt).

raw material in the shape of colony builders he was given to work with to lay the foundations. Nor was his load lightened by his pessimistic assistant, Lieutenant-Governor Major Ross, who gave him little help and less encouragement. This gloomy Jeremiah spent much of his sojourn in the colony penning mournful predictions to the Home Office that the country was not worth settling and that it was hopeless to continue with the project. 'I will, in confidence, venture to assure you', he wrote in a letter to Under-Secretary Nepean on July 10, 1788, 'that this country will never answer to settle in, for altho' I think corn would grow here, yet I am convinced that if ever it is able to maintain people here it cannot be in less than probably 100 years hence. I therefore think it will be better to feed the convicts on turtle and venison at the London Tavern than be at the expense of sending them here'.

CHAPTER 6

Escape

ALL the circumstances considered—the iron discipline, brutal punishment, and the natural urge in every human being towards liberty—it is small wonder that there were many attempts to escape from New South Wales to other lands. To a great extent, the attempted evasions were due to the very sketchy geographical knowledge of most of the people of the period. Many of the convicts, for instance, were convinced that in the long voyage to Australia they had circumnavigated the world and had come pretty close to returning to their starting point. This theory led to some of the men who had been transported for their part in the Irish Rebellion being so struck with the similarity between the Blue Mountains of New South Wales and the lovely hills of Donegal that they made a dash westwards, firm in the conviction that they were making for their own homes.

Another dream that seduced many to their death was that China was less than 50 miles or so overland from Sydney. There was virtually a stampede to gain this celestial land of promise. Many of the poor unfortunates who made this bid for freedom perished in the bush; numbers of others were recaptured in an exhausted condition.

So seriously did the authorities view the numerous and consistent efforts to escape to other lands, supposedly within easy reach, that it was found necessary to issue on March 23rd, 1803, an official declaration stating: 'The Governor only hopes that the convicts at large will be assured that their ridiculous plans of leaving public labour to go into the mountains of China, Ireland, and elsewhere, can only end in their immediate detection and punishment'.

But the proclamation had little effect; as late as 1814, seven men escaped from a chain gang with the idea of crossing the Blue Mountains and thus reaching the west coast of Australia which they thought was just on the other side. Arriving at the coast it was their intention to build a boat and row across to the island of Timor.

The strangest and most remarkable escape was in 1791, and the venture was prompted, organised and was virtually led by a convict woman, Mary Bryant. On the night of 28th March of that year, William and Mary Bryant, their two children—one a girl of three years, the other a baby boy—and seven men, all convicts, sailed through Sydney Heads in a fishing boat. They steered north along the coast and sailed for 69 days to the top of Cape York and across the Arafura Sea. On 5th June they arrived at Koepang, Timor, having sailed 3,254 miles in ten weeks. Although often in peril from shipwreck, starvation, thirst and hostile natives, the voyage was achieved without loss of life. Handicapped by ignorance of seamanship, yet they navigated their boat, a six-oared ketch, through strange waters to the port they had originally chosen. But freedom was not to be theirs. The Dutch Governor had them returned to England. The ill-treatment to which they were subjected on the voyage to England caused the deaths of Mary's husband and the two children. Convicted again, the survivors were sent to Newgate Prison to complete their sentences.

In the First Fleet itself there was a feeble attempt at escape from one of the transports, the *Scarborough,* and often enough afterwards there were plots and conspiracies and bloodily suppressed outbreaks. One mutiny, however, was completely successful—that which took place on board *The Lady Shore* during her voyage to Sydney in 1797. Oddly, it was not the prisoners who mutinied and took possession of the ship, but the soldiers who were guarding them.

The Lady Shore, heavily laden with stores intended for Sydney Cove, carried 66 female convicts, two male convicts, 70 soldiers (some with their wives and children), and four passengers besides the crew. The soldiers were a mixed bunch, most of them pretty low characters recruited for the New South Wales Corps. Six of them who came aboard in chains had been released from the Savoy military prison on condition that they served in Australia with the N.S.W. Corps for the rest of their lives. The extraordinary method of enlistment for the army in those days resulted in this queer company.

John Black, the 20-year-old purser of *The Lady Shore,* in a farewell letter to his father written just before the ship sailed, commented: '. . . The soldiers are the most disagreeable, mutinous set of villains that ever entered into a ship. Two of the sergeants behaved so ill that Captain Willcocks was obliged to insist upon their commanding officer confining them in irons'.

Of the two male convicts aboard, one had been a notorious London swindler who called himself Major Semple-Lisle and claimed the Earldom of Lisle in Ireland. When the vessel was well down in the South Atlantic the soldiers broke out into open mutiny, ornamented with murder, took possession of all the arms on board, and seized control. The ship's officers were completely taken by surprise, and the captain and mate were shot dead in the first rush aft. The crew looked on while the mutineers forced the officers to surrender amid the wildest confusion of men, women and children. By now, *The Lady Shore,* minus a navigator, had left its course and was plunging into the waves and shipping seas through the portholes.

The ringleaders of the revolt were French military deserters who could not make themselves understood by the English crew, but Major Semple-Lisle, who refused to join the mutineers, spoke fluent French and acted as interpreter. With his help they got the crew working; the carpenter was appointed the ship's navigator and a seaman named Davis was made the boatswain.

All who would not join the mutineers were then forced overside into a longboat. At first it was intended to cast them adrift without food or water, but the pleadings of the purser, John Black, resulted in their obtaining some provisions ere they were left alone in mid-ocean. Twenty-nine people were set adrift in the longboat, comprising the ship's officers—with the exception of the surgeon, who was made to stay aboard against his will—their wives and children, the four passengers, the convict major, the steward and the cabin-boy.

Young John Black proved himself a good navigator and managed to get his boatload of castaways to the mouth of the River Rio Grande. They landed and found themselves three miles distant from a military garrison. It was Portuguese territory, and they were hospitably made welcome by the commandant. Meanwhile the mutineers headed *The Lady Shore* for Montevideo. Unfortunately for them Britain and Spain were now at war and they were promptly thrown into prison and the ship commandeered, to be later recaptured by His Majesty's ship *Tremendous*.

It is interesting to note that John Black came to Sydney in 1801 and decided to settle there. Eventually he became the first manager of the Bank of New South Wales.

There had been a serious mutiny the year before *The Lady Shore* episode. It concerned the transport *Marquis of Cornwallis,* carrying 163 male and 70 female convicts from Cork to Sydney, and in this case, also, certain members of the New South Wales Corps were at the bottom of the trouble. When the transport was off the Cape Verde Islands on September 9, 1795, Captain Michael Hogan received a note from two convicts named Mouton and Royal warning him that a plot to seize the ship had been planned by some of the convicts and soldiers.

The captain had the two informers brought to his cabin on the pretext of a misdemeanour charge and was thus able to hear the full story. The prisoners told him that he himself was to be the first victim and that the ringleaders of the plot were Sergeant Ellis and a group of soldiers. The sergeant had agreed to provide the convicts with knives from which they might forge files to free themselves from their irons. The conspirators corresponded by means of notes, and they planned a dawn outbreak whilst the sanitary buckets were being removed from the prison hold. Some of the women convicts were also in the conspiracy—their part being to put ground glass in the food of the crew.

Captain Hogan alerted his officers and they watched and waited. They soon confirmed the truth of the story, and

Sergeant Ellis was put in irons and flogged so severely that he died a few days later. On learning that they had been betrayed, the convicts attempted an outbreak but it was quickly suppressed and the *Marquis of Cornwallis* reached Sydney Cove safely.

The transport *Chapman* witnessed death and violence in a savage shipboard mutiny that was the outcome of a convict's lurid imagination. Hoping to gain favours, convict Michael Collins told Captain Drake that his fellow prisoners were planning a massed rising. The captain warned his officers, together with the soldiers and crew, but the news unnerved many of them and they magnified the slightest sounds from the convicts' quarters into ominous preparations for an outbreak.

On the night of April 18, 1817, a cook on sentry duty near the prison hold heard a sudden rattling of chains, and shouted an alarm. Soldiers and seamen rushed to arms and fired indiscriminately through the bulkheads. At the time of the alarm most of the convicts were asleep and all without exception were in irons. They cried out for quarter but the firing continued for an hour and a half, with dying and wounded convicts bleeding and suffering in the darkness of the hold. At dawn a strong guard ventured in and counted twelve dead. These were thrown overboard, thirty of the wounded taken to hospital, and the others starved, flogged and double-ironed for the remainder of the voyage.

When the *Chapman* reached Sydney in July, 1817, Governor Macquarie's secretary, Campbell, examined the convicts and was appalled by the reports he heard from them. The Governor ordered an immediate inquiry the result of which he informed the Home Office in London showed 'wanton, indiscriminate and unprovoked cruelty towards the miserably unfortunate men entrusted to their charge'. He placed equal blame on Captain Drake, his officers, Surgeon Dewar (who was in charge of the prisoners' physical welfare) and Lieutenant Busteed, commanding the military escort.

At the inquiry, convict Terry Kiernan told the court that when the shooting began he heard third mate Baxter shout 'Fire away, boys, and kill them all!' Another prisoner, William Leo, said he and three others were chained to the deck in all weathers until they reached Sydney. A rope had been tied round his body and he had been thrown overboard to be allowed to sink eleven times under the water before being dragged back again. Although almost unconscious after the ordeal, soldiers pricked him with bayonets. Later he had been lashed and brine poured on his bleeding wounds. Of 201 convicts aboard the *Chapman* no more than three escaped a flogging during the voyage. After the 'mutiny' all were put on half-rations for the remaining three months of the journey, the officers pocketing the profits — 'If anyone complains about rations I won't flog him, I'll shoot him!' the surgeon told the prisoners.

It was useless the Captain and officers denying the charges, or accusing the convicts of gross exaggeration (the ship's log proved damning evidence of stark brutality), so they blamed each other. Lieutenant Busteed said Captain Drake was drunk 'a good deal of the time on the voyage and could not control his officers. He seemed very far gone in liquor on the night of the firing'. The Captain retaliated by asserting that 'Busteed's troops were in a mutinous and disorderly state', adding, 'and my own crew could not be trusted'. He complained that they had fired without orders, and would not stop when he tried to intervene. Nevertheless, he claimed that undoubtedly the convicts had hatched 'a most horrid conspiracy'.

Members of the inquiry court — Judge-Advocate Wright, Police Magistrate D'Arcy Wentworth and the Governor's secretary, Mr. Campbell—returned a blistering report: 'Apart from the killings, let a humane man figure to himself a fellow-creature, double-chained to a cable and handcuffed for three months—except when he was taken off to be flogged—and existing on half-rations. This was inhuman, barbarous, and cruel beyond all reason—even a mutiny could not justify it'.

On receiving the report, Governor Macquarie determined to have the culprits returned to London to face criminal charges but was bitterly dismayed to find that under the existing laws the ship's officers could not be charged. Captain Drake contemptuously took action to sue Macquarie for unlawfully detaining his vessel during the inquiry. Convicts' lives had no more value in the eyes of the law than those of animals in the early nineteenth century.

*   *   *

The piratical capture of the brig *Cyprus* is a fantastic story of escape which but for the fact of being authenticated history would be dismissed as wildly improbable fiction. The *Cyprus* left Hobart Town on July 28, 1829, for Macquarie Harbour with 31 prisoners, a crew of 12, a medical officer, 5 passengers, including two children, and 13 soldiers. While anchored at Recherche Bay, 50 miles south of Hobart, William Walker, alias William Swallow, led a virtually bloodless coup that even allowing for a deal of good luck was a marvel of planning and timing. A drunken captain, slackness in the military escort, and the call at Recherche Bay all played a part in the outwitting and overpowering of the officers and guard by men desperately determined to avoid imprisonment for years in the dreaded penal settlement of Macquarie Harbour on the bleak west coast of Tasmania.

Walker-Swallow, with 18 other convicts, put the passengers, military guard, crew and the rest of the convicts who were not desirous of joining the mutineers, on the beach with provisions to last them a couple of weeks and then sailed off. Skippered by Walker-Swallow, the only experienced mariner on board, the *Cyprus* headed for New Zealand and after replenishing water supplies sailed for Tahiti. Unable to land there, the vessel continued on to Niue where the escapees stayed for a few months. Some of them decided to remain there but the others set sail for Japan. Finding that Japanese ports were closed to foreign vessels, the *Cyprus* set sail for the China Sea and made port at Canton. There the brig was scuttled. By this time there were only four of the original 19 escapees and they agreed to report themselves as survivors of a wrecked brig—the *Edward*.

Their story was believed and three of them obtained jobs as crew members of a Danish brig bound for New Orleans, while the fourth, Walker-alias-Swallow who now called himself Captain Waldron, signed on for London. Eventually the English authorities learned of the fate of the *Cyprus* and caught up with one of the earlier escapees, Davis, who when questioned inadvertently mentioned the name of 'Captain Waldron'. And so the police were waiting for him on arrival in England. Although he slipped through their hands he was later caught and, with the other three rounded up, together with Davis, brought to trial. With his usual audacity, Walker-Swallow-Waldron made a full 'confession' asserting that he had been forced to go along with the ringleaders because he was the only convict capable of navigating the vessel. His bold unscrupulous lying succeeded in hoodwinking the court and he escaped the gallows. Instead, he was transported again—this time for life.

CHAPTER 7

Care of the Sick

FOR the first few days after the arrival of the First Fleet the time was generally occupied in making preparations for the settlement by clearing the scrub for the erection of dwellings of a temporary nature. Materials for a home for Governor Phillip had been brought from England but the other residences were mostly tents. These were soon pitched, those of the marines being located at the head of the Tank Stream, with the convicts on the west side of it as were also the tents allotted for the sick; the east side was reserved for the Governor.

The First Fleet carried a complete medical staff, from which a principal surgeon, John White, and three assistant surgeons, William Balmain, Thomas Arndell and Dennis Considen, were appointed a medical staff for the colony. A convict, John Irving, was included as junior. Early in February, 1788, work was begun on a hospital building but its accommodation soon became inadequate and after the arrival of the Second Fleet it was found necessary to pitch about 100 tents in the grounds.

The hospital tents were quickly filled; there was an epidemic of scurvy and there were nearly two hundred cases of dysentery which was to prove fatal for many of the sufferers. Gaol fever, scurvy and dysentery were the most prevalent maladies aboard the transports. The hospital quarters were always located in the forepart of the ships—they had to be as far away as possible from the crews' quarters for fear of infection—and were subject to leakages and smells, as well as the maximum motions of the vessels. Ships' masters were expected to provide an accredited surgeon for the voyage, but until the terrible scandal was fully exposed these medical men often worked hand in glove with the master by making little or no attempt to save the lives of the seriously ill. Dead convicts meant less rations used and such surplus foodstuffs could be sold by the master to the hungry settlers on arrival. Convicts on the high seas were at the mercy of the master and surgeon. If these were despicable characters who had agreed to share in fleecing their charges by cheating them of their full rations and letting patients die, there was no redress. Similarly, if there was friction between master and medico it reacted on everybody.

Australia's first general hospital was shipped from England in sections and assembled in Sydney. Twenty years later the structure was in such poor shape that Governor Macquarie realised that he would have to do something about a new building. His great difficulty was lack of finance, but while he was struggling with the problem it was solved for him in quite an ingenious manner. Two men—Garnham Blaxcell and Alexander Riley—approached His Excellency and offered to build the hospital for nothing, providing Macquarie gave them the monopoly for the importation of 45,000 gallons of spirits during the following three years. Blaxcell and Riley knew little or nothing about building or hospitals, but their knowledge of the rum traffic was extensive.

Macquarie was rather dubious about the proposal but his conscience was eased when the Principal Surgeon of the Colony, D'Arcy Wentworth, became a party to the rum contract and so gave an ethical touch to the enterprise. The Governor gave his blessing to the hospital contract and eventually the building was erected in the street named after His Excellency. In addition to the rum monopoly Blaxcell, Riley and D'Arcy Wentworth were given a meat concession worth several thousand pounds, free convict labour, the free use of bullocks for haulage purposes, and six months grace to pay the Government duty of three shillings a gallon on the imported spirits. Naturally, Wentworth took charge of the new hospital.

Surgeon D'Arcy Wentworth, whose son William Charles was to distinguish himself in Australian affairs as explorer and law-maker, came to the colony as assistant-surgeon on the hell-ship *Neptune*. In England he had been involved in most compromising adventures, and between December, 1787, and December, 1789, was tried on two occasions for highway robbery. Both times he was acquitted through the failure of principal witnesses for the prosecution to recognize him in court, and although he was openly referred to in the newspapers as 'the notorious highwayman'. On the *Neptune* he formed an association with a young convict girl, Catherine Crowley, who had been sentenced to transportation for a trivial offence. The girl was sent to Norfolk Island and when Wentworth was appointed surgeon there he lived openly with her. Three children were born of the union. This domestic arrangement was a normal one for Norfolk Island (and indeed for the colony of New South Wales at that time) since there was no permanent chaplain. Even Lieutenant-Governor King involved himself in such a relationship, acknowledging the offspring of it and providing—as did Wentworth—for their education and futures. Wentworth returned to Sydney with Catherine Crowley and their children in the *Reliance* in 1796.

The new rum-built hospital, standing in the first straight street in Australia, was a credit to the enterprising trio. The imposing structure was actually three buildings, the two-storied hospital itself, nearly 288 feet long enclosed by a stone wall in seven acres of ground, and two palatial surgeons' barracks. The latter remain today, one being the State Parliament House, and the other, known as the Old Mint building, is used to house a State Government Department. The hospital has been replaced by the present Sydney Hospital building.

The British Government was not at all happy about the unorthodox manner of the building of the hospital and the Secretary of State, Lord Liverpool, made no bones about his disapproval. He sent the Governor some rather sarcastic letters on the subject, at the same time requesting Macquarie to answer a few awkward questions. One of them enquired 'Was it really a fact that the Principal Surgeon of the Colony was a party to the rum contract?' In his reply the Governor said: '. . . I expected nothing short of the highest commendation, since there was no expense to the British Government, yet a palatial building arose simply by the public drinking 45,000 gallons of spirits'. (It is illuminating to note that from September, 1800, to October, 1802, 69,980 gallons of spirits and 33,246 gallons of wine were landed in Sydney, i.e., an annual consumption of 5 gallons, 3 quarts of spirits, and 2 gallons, 3 quarts of wine for every man, woman, and child in the colony—the average population during that period being 5,807. And this apart from illicit distillation in New South Wales which commenced with agriculture. Many settlers made fortunes from 'bootleg' spirit.)

There is no record of the name of the architect for the three buildings comprising the 'Rum' Hospital, but it has been suggested that Mrs. Macquarie may have designed them since architecture was one of her keen hobbies. However, on completion of the buildings, Governor Macquarie was not altogether satisfied and he called in a survey committee including the noted convict architect Francis Greenway to pass judgment. The committee demanded some major alterations and the enforcement of penalty clauses in the contract for delays and failures, so the extra costs involved for the contractors must have eaten much of their profits. It has been claimed that the trio built the hospital for £50,000 but cleared £150,000 profit for themselves on the deal, despite the fact that they asserted they lost money on the venture. Certainly skippers bringing spirits into the colony were forced to sell it solely to the three contractors who could virtually name their own price. Generally they paid about 10/- a gallon and sold it to the publicans at five times that price, so the profits were enormous.

Conditions at the hospital during Wentworth's administration were revoltingly dreadful. There was no mortuary; the kitchen was used when necessary as a 'dead house', and patients had to cook their own foods in the wards. Rations were issued to every patient individually three times a week, so the wards were virtually a combination of scullery, kitchen and larder. No matter what the complaint or disease, every patient received the same rations of 1-lb. of flour

59

and 1-lb. of meat. There were no vegetables, fruit or milk.

Every evening at sundown the patients—they were mostly convicts—were mustered and locked in their wards until six o'clock the following morning, without any attendants or nurses to look after them. In the beginning there was no segregation of the sexes. No one thought cleanliness necessary for the patients and it was not until thirty-four years after the hospital had been established that a bath-room was installed. It contained two baths for the entire hospital, and then it was thought quite unnecessary.

With the advent of the bathroom came another novelty— an operating theatre. Before that the surgeons did their operations in any part of the building, and there was no such thing as privacy. Visitors to the hospital would crowd around the surgeon while he was operating, often hindering his work. Needless to say, the medicos' methods were very crude. Before an amputation the lines of incision were marked out on the patient's body in ink with a quill pen. Ordinary sponges, never sterilised, were used and after the amputation the severed member was tied up with catgut. Nothing was sterilised; dressings usually comprised a kind of coarse hemp soaked in olive oil. Sometimes the patients recovered, if they were exceptionally lucky; usually septi-caemia or gangrene set in and finished them off. All classes of diseases and complaints were admitted, although little or no effort at classification was made and treatment was practically nil. Cupping or blood-letting was the usual remedy.

James Bowman succeeded D'Arcy Wentworth in adminis-tering the Rum Hospital and he secured some measure of order. Wardsmen were required to sleep on the premises, and Bowman himself made a daily inspection of the patients. Nevertheless, the surgeons were a troublesome enigma. All were employed by the Government and their pay was poor and the perquisites few. True, a shrewd one like Principal Surgeon D'Arcy Wentworth made money in many ways other than medicine—and rum contracts; he held such offices as Commissioner of Roads, Police Magistrate, and treasurer to the Police Fund (the latter was not quite as benevolent as its name suggested, since the Police Fund was really consolidated revenue). It was difficult to get medical men for the colony, and how some of those engaged received their medical training is mystifying. Surgeon Mountgarrett, who had only one arm and a dubious background, engaged in trade contrary to regulations and had been accused of cattle duffing. Of medical officer Henry St. John Younge, Governor Macquarie complained that he 'is by no means a desirable Acquisition in the Line of his Profession. He is exceedingly Ignorant as a medical man, being almost destitute of common Understanding and very low and Vulgar in Manners'. Surgeon Luttrell, who originally came to the colony as a farmer, was described by Macquarie as totally deficient 'in Attention to his Duty in regard to the unfortunate Persons placed under his care . . . he is sordid and unfeeling and will not Afford any medical assistance to any Person who cannot pay him well for it'. Shades of the Hippocratic oath!

When eventually orderlies were attached to the hospital they were chosen at random from among the convicts, those useless for other work generally getting the jobs. The orderlies stole food and belongings from the patients, visitors stole anything they could lay their hands on, and those patients capable of leaving their beds stole from one another. When separate wards for men and women eventuated, a constable was stationed at the entrance to the women's ward to keep the men out. But he could not be there all the time and in any case was open to a bit of bribery to augment his meagre allowance.

Coming to more recent times, it may be added that nurses did not make their appearance in the Sydney Hospital until the late 1860s when Sir Henry Parkes enlisted the aid of Florence Nightingale who sent suggestions and recommendations for the training of nurses. In 1868 Miss Lucy Osburn arrived from England with a staff of five nurses, but they were by no means received with acclaim. The medical profession objected to this new-fangled idea of trained women trying to help patients, and very often the doctors hindered the work of the nurses by keeping them in ignorance of the patients' condition or impending operations. Gradually, however, the existing prejudice against Miss Osburn and her band of workers was worn down, and largely through the work of these devoted women Sydney Hospital really started to get under way. The old Rum Hospital building itself was condemned and the present one opened in 1894.

CHAPTER 8

From the Gallows

ONE of the first permanent government structures erected in Australia was a gallows. An example of the grim injustice and the swiftness of its operation in those days is shown with the case of James Barrett, a youth of seventeen years who stole some food because he was hungry. On February 8, 1788, he was charged, convicted, sentenced and hanged on the gallows within sixty minutes[1].

Curiously enough, one of the first persons recorded as having eulogised the beauty of Sydney Harbour was a condemned man at the foot of the gallows. He did so on Fort Denison, better known as Pinchgut Island. The island has suffered a tremendous change in outline since the First Fleet entered the harbour. It was at that time a conical-shaped rock islet, about eighty feet in height, covered with bushes and stunted trees. Governor Phillip christened it Rock Island, a literal translation of its aboriginal name, 'Mattenwaya'. Soon after the inception of the colony it was recognised that the shark-infested waters would make Rock Island an ideal spot for the safe-guarding of perverse convicts, so accommodation was made there for them. For a short while it was used to house them, and as these unfortunate gentry were fed on a small weekly ration of bread and water they soon coined for it the not inappropriate title of Pinchgut.

In 1796 Francis Morgan was condemned to death for a crime on the North Shore, and the place chosen for his execution was on this island. At the foot of the gallows he was asked, before the hangman placed the rope over his head, if he had anything to say. The only thing worth mentioning, he replied, was the view of the beautiful harbour

---

1 With the limited supplies carried in the First Fleet, food was precious; hence the crime was regarded as a serious one.

from his high elevation. After his execution it was decided to introduce the traditional British custom of gibbeting malefactors in prominent positions. Accordingly the body of Morgan was hung in chains on the top of 'Pinchgut' and dangled there for months.

In 1840, Sir George Gipps, recognising the value of the island as a fortified site and realising that the supply of cheap convict labour must soon cease, commenced its transformation by razing the rocky formation almost to water-level. The project, however, was not sanctioned by the Home Authorities and the work was abandoned in 1842. By then the island had assumed the appearance of a flat area of rubble, a few feet above the tide, and about an acre in extent.

But the position altered in 1854, when Britain and France found themselves at war with Russia. Governor Denison decided that the island should be fortified. In 1857 the present Martello tower and guard-rooms were finished, and the impregnability of the fortress was assured by the mounting of modern artillery capable of hitting a very large object at a very short range, if the target sat very still. The name was changed from Rock Island to Fort Denison in honour of the Governor of the day.

Many people are under the impression that the cells were used for the imprisonment and torture of manacled prisoners. This is not correct. The cells were used for the storage of powder and shot.

The name of Joseph Samuels is immortalized in Australian historical records for earning the title of 'The Man They Could Not Hang'. Sentenced to death for stealing, Samuels and another prisoner—James Hardwick—who was given the death sentence for a similar offence, mounted a cart with ropes around their necks. It was on the morning of Monday, September 20, 1803, and, according to the *Sydney Gazette,* 'the prisoners conducted themselves with a becoming decency' as the hangman fastened to the bough of a tree one end of the rope around the first man to be executed—Hardwick.

The executioner was about to whip the horse when an

officer from a detachment of His Majesty's New South Wales Corps in the foreground of the onlookers dramatically stepped forward carrying a reprieve for Hardwick. (It was customary to withold reprieves to the last minute in order to extract as much suffering as possible from the prisoner.)

Poor Samuels was now left alone on the death cart, and the *Sydney Gazette* records that he 'devoted the last awful moments allowed to him to most earnest and reverent prayer'. His piety was rewarded. When the officer in charge gave the signal and the cart was driven from under Samuels, instead of hanging from the end of the rope he crashed to the ground, unconscious. The rope had snapped in the middle.

Provost-Marshal Smith was a man who supervised an unpleasant duty with a strict regard for law and justice, and also mercy. He, more than anyone else, was shocked at the accident, and hurriedly had the cart backed up again. His assistants picked up the still unconscious Samuels and held him while a new rope was obtained. Again he was hoisted on to the cart and the horse whipped away. But this time the condemned man fell too far and his legs reached the ground, preventing him from being strangled. 'All who beheld the scene were moved by the prisoner's protracted sufferings', said the *Gazette*. 'Nor did some hesitate to declare that the Divine Hand of Providence was at work on behalf of him'.

Samuels 'to every appearance lifeless', was once more lifted on to the death cart and the hangman again carefully examined the rope for any possible flaws, and made certain that its length was correct. For the third time the horse was whipped away, and for the third time Samuels remained alive. The rope snapped near his neck.

The Provost-Marshal was now completely unnerved, and, ordering the dreadful proceedings to stop, he rushed off to Governor King to tell him the lurid story. The Governor immediately granted Samuels a reprieve, an action with which the *Gazette* was in full accord, the newspaper adding piously, 'And may the grateful remembrance of these events direct his future courses'.

Third time was lucky, it could be said, for another man who cheated the executioner in Sydney town. On the morning of April 14, 1801, Private John Boatswain stood to attention as he listened with a heavy heart to the regimental proclamation: 'The regiment to be under arms on Monday next, 19th instant, at half past nine in the morning to attend the execution of John Boatswain, private soldier in the New South Wales Corps, sentenced to die by a general court martial for desertion'.

The sentenced man was led away to the condemned cell to await his end. On the eve of the day which was to be his last the sky became heavy with storm clouds as he ate the traditional meal of extra rations to which the military condemned were entitled. The rain soon came and never eased throughout the night, nor did it seem like abating on the following morning. At 9 a.m. the Commandant looked at the sky and, whether it was because he did not want himself and his officers to be soaked to the skin, or he thought the rain would ruin the spectacle of the military ceremony, or perhaps the rifles would not fire if they got wet, history does not record. He issued another proclamation: 'Raining in torrents. The execution of the prisoner as directed by the orders of the 14th instant, on account of the inclemency of the weather, is deferred until further notice'.

The following day the heavy rain showed no sign of abatement and doubtless John Boatswain who had successfully demanded another 'celebration' meal chuckled to himself as he ate it. The thoroughly annoyed Commandant reluctantly penned a third proclamation: 'Still raining in torrents. Execution further deferred . . .'

Five days passed, but not so the rain, which stayed on in a steady, consistent downpour. And each day John Boatswain was enjoying his privileged 'last' meal. What exactly happened to cause the issue of the fourth and final proclamation is rather mysterious, but it must have caused immense satisfaction to the condemned man when he heard the contents: 'Favourable circumstances having been reported, the Governor of the settlement is pleased to extend a reprieve and to grant a free pardon to the prisoner, John

Boatswain, sentenced to death for the unsoldierly crime of desertion . . .' The following day the sun shone from a clear blue sky.

South Australia's first hanging was the occasion for a picnic holiday. The first sheriff of the colony, Samuel Smart, was appointed before any police force was established, and when he arrested several law-breakers he was shot at by friends of the criminals. The bullet grazed his head and he recognised a youth, Magee, who fired the shot. Magee was condemned to death, and as Adelaide had never had a public holiday or a hanging before, the citizens shut their shops and homes and went out in a body to picnic at the place of execution.

There was no official hangman in the colony in 1829 and no one would accept the job. In ordinary circumstances the sheriff would have officiated, but because he had figured as the victim it was felt not to be in good taste for him to hang his would-be-murderer. A thousand-odd people, including many women and children, assembled around a massive gum tree chosen for the hanging. The hangman took no chances of being recognised. He wore a hood over his head and had padded his clothes heavily. The prayers of the clergyman were drowned by the crowd's whispered speculations about the hangman. The latter's hands, however, and all his movements betrayed his extreme nervousness. So badly did he tie the noose around Magee's neck that the knot slid under the poor wretch's chin, leaving him dangling in mid-air, cursing and shrieking in agony. Panic-stricken at having bungled the job, the hangman took to his heels and fled, while the onlookers yelled in derision.

The mounted troops galloped after the hangman and brought him back to finish his work. Finish it he did, but in a gruesome fashion. Beside himself now with terror, he leaped on the suspended victim and clung to him for thirteen minutes, by the sheriff's watch, before life was pronounced extinct. Then the crowd sat down to eat its lunch and enjoy the picnic.

Public executions were always attractions. Everyone in Hobart town turned out to watch popular bushranger Matthew

Brady mount the scaffold; the men cheered him for his courage and women wept for the man who died more like a martyr than a felon.

CHAPTER 9

Island of No Escape

NORFOLK ISLAND, with its balmy air, its fertile soil, its luxuriant vegetation, its very isolation of beauty truly deserves the title of Paradise of the Pacific. But there was a time when Norfolk Island was a hell on earth. This glorious garden of the ocean with its groves of gigantic pines, so serene and dignified, resounded with the shrieks of prisoners writhing under the lash. No greater contrast could be imagined than the diabolical discipline in a region where nature has spread her gentlest, sweetest charms.

Norfolk Island is 900 miles from Sydney, measures five miles by three miles, and has an area of about 8,500 acres. In the early 1800s it was established as a large penal settlement for the worst of the Port Jackson convicts and those who had been convicted more than once. (A small convict colony had been established there earlier but because of administrative expense and the difficulties of maintaining communications the station was abandoned.) Although nominally reserved for those convicts who, while under sentence of transportation for life committed another offence, the definition was an elastic one and meant in effect the authorities could banish anyone they disliked to the remote Pacific outpost of no escape.

Sir Roger Therry, a former judge and Attorney-General of New South Wales, wrote in his *Reminiscences of Thirty Years Residence in New South Wales and Victoria*, published in 1863, the following description of six convicts from Norfolk Island who were brought to Sydney as witnesses in a trial: 'Their sunken, glazed eyes, deadly-pale faces, hollow, fleshless cheeks and once manly limbs shrivelled and withered up as if by premature old age, created horror among those in the court. There was not one of the six who had not undergone from time to time a thousand lashes each,

69

and more. They looked less like human beings than the shadows of gnomes who had risen from their sepulchural abode. What man ever was, or ever could be, reclaimed under such a system as this?'

Elsewhere, Judge Therry said: 'On one occasion in Sydney I went to see a young bushranger named William Webber who was to be hanged within twenty-four hours. I told him that his voluntary confession had been the means of saving the lives of two other men, and that as a result his death sentence would be commuted to life imprisonment. Webber answered that he would much rather be hanged as he would be sure to be sent to Norfolk Island. "I would prefer death in any form", he said, "than such a state of endurance as Norfolk Island" '.

To escape from this floating hell, convicts deliberately committed crimes though their deliverance would be through the hangman. Death was welcomed as an escape. One convict, without warning, raised his spade and split open the head of the man ahead of him. He admitted that his only motive in the murder was to be hanged—and end the misery of life on Norfolk Island.

For nearly thirty years the island never knew the voice of a minister of religion. It was only on the occasion of a mass execution when thirty-one men were condemned to death because of a convict rebellion that an Anglican clergyman and a Catholic priest were allowed to go there to attend the hangings. The priest, Father Ullathorne, who afterwards became the Archbishop of Birmingham, has left a graphic account of what he witnessed there in his publication *The Horrors of Transportation Briefly Unfolded*. Here are some extracts:

'I was taken to the cells where the condemned men were manacled. The prison was in the form of a square, on one side of which stood a row of low cells, covered with a roof of shingles. The turnkeep unlocked the first door, and said to me: "Stand aside, Sir". Then came forth a yellow exhalation, the produce of the bodies of the men confined therein. The exhalation cleared off, and I entered and found five men chained to a traversing bar. I spoke to them from my heart, and after preparing them and obtaining their names, I announced to them who were reprieved from death, and which of them were to die after five days had passed. (Eighteen of the condemned men had been reprieved, but the officials had not bothered to tell them.) I thus went from cell to cell until I had seen them all. It is a literal fact that each man who heard his reprieve wept bitterly, and that each man who heard his condemnation to death went down on his knees, with dry eyes, and thanked God.

'It may seem strange to the inexperienced that so many men should prefer death to life in that dreadful penal settlement. Let me, then, say that all the criminals who were executed in New South Wales were imbued with a like feeling. I have heard it from several in their last moments, and Father McEncroe, in a letter to me, which I quoted to Sir William Molesworth's Committee on Transportation, affirmed that he had attended seventy-four executions in the course of four years, and that the greater number of criminals had, on their way to the scaffold, thanked God that they were not going to Norfolk Island'.

Came the day of the execution of the thirteen convicts, so envied by the eighteen others who were reprieved. Father Ullathorne described the scene on the scaffold, '. . . When the irons were struck off and the death warrant read, they knelt down to receive it as the will of God. Next, by a spontaneous act, they humbly kissed the feet of him who brought them peace. After the executioner had pinioned their arms, they thanked the gaolers and ascended the ladders with light steps, being almost excitedly cheerful'.

Three Catholics were executed separately from the ten Protestants, and the ghastly affair was spread over two days, 22nd and 23rd September, 1834. The hangings were carried out in the presence of about two thousand convicts on the island herded behind stockades manned by soldiers. The priest, deeply moved by the cruel, inhuman treatment he saw everywhere on the island, records such impressions as this: 'Shackled men are marched out to the fields at daybreak. I noted their shocking appearance, their haggardness of features. They are fettered with heavy chains, harassed with heavy work and fed solely on salt meat and maize bread. Their existence is one of desperation'.

Despite the protests of Judge Therry, Father Ullathorne and other clergy, Norfolk Island's grim record of brutal discipline, savage punishments, frequent injustices and human degradation continued. Custom blinded the governing classes to the evils of the system, but among the courageous few who were prepared to risk unpopularity and ridicule by advocating change was a new commandant, Captain Alexander Maconochie, R.N. A senior naval officer, Scottish-born Maconochie came to Van Diemen's Land in 1837 as secretary to his friend the Lieutenant-Governor, Sir John Franklin. In 1840 he was made superintendent of Norfolk Island. Maconochie was always interested in prison reform. He was himself a prisoner of war in his early days and this may have inspired his life-long interest in penal reforms; but he suffered bitterly for his reforms. The 'mark' system, one of his main innovations, foreshadowed our present system of remission of penalty for good work and behaviour[1].

Under his enlightened administration of the penal settlement on Norfolk Island he achieved extraordinary success in reforming so-called 'intractable' convicts. Yet, when the authorities learned of his astonishing reforms they dismissed him from the post. Misrepresented and derided by contemporaries and later by historians, Maconochie was a man who selflessly dedicated himself to a high ideal—'to make society good by making men better'. One of the few who championed the cause of Maconochie was Father Ullathorne, who said that his name was 'destined to a future celebrity side by side with John Howard'. He also rightly predicted that Maconochie's 'mark' system would eventually be adopted as a universal method in all reform institutions. In one of his many publications, Dr. Ullathorne refers to Captain Maconochie's remarkable success in the case of Charles Anderson[2].

1 Sir John Barry.
2 'On the Management of Criminals' (1866). Also told in *Our Convicts* (Mary Carpenter, 1864).

Charles Anderson was transported to New South Wales when he was eighteen years old. An orphan, his childhood was spent in a workhouse, and when aged nine he was apprenticed in a coal ship, and later joined the Navy. He received a severe head-wound at the battle of Navarino and thereafter when angered or in drink was likely to behave violently and irrationally. As the result of a street brawl he was sentenced to seven years transportation. Uneducated and untutored, and hostile and stubborn of spirit, he proved an incorrigible prisoner. Upon his arrival in Sydney he was sent to Goat Island where the treatment was so severe that, to escape it, he absconded. Apprehended, he was returned to the island, given an additional twelve months to his sentence and compelled to wear irons always. During his imprisonment he received 1,200 lashes for trivial offences such as looking round from his work, or at a boat in the harbour.

After another attempt at escape he was chained to a rock on Goat Island for two years with barely a rag to cover him. He was fastened by his waist to the rock with a chain twenty-six feet long and with trumpet irons on his legs. A hollow, scooped out in the large rock big enough to admit his body, served for his bed, and his only shelter was a wooden lid perforated with holes, which was placed over him and locked in that position at night, being removed in the morning. He was fed by means of a pole with which the vessel containing his food was pushed towards him. None of his fellow prisoners were permitted to approach or speak to him under penalty of a hundred lashes. Regarded as a wild beast, people passing in boats would throw him bits of bread or biscuit. Exposed to all weathers, and without clothing on his back and shoulders, which were covered with sores from repeated floggings, the flies clustered upon his festered flesh, he was denied even water to bathe his wounds.

Later, Anderson was transferred from Goat Island under life sentence to Port Macquarie, where convicts laboured in the lime works. He had to carry lime in baskets from the kilns to barges, and the skin was burned off his back by the lime when it mixed with the sea-water. Anderson

73

escaped again, and when recaptured and given severe lashings was sent to Norfolk Island—the island of *no* escape. Though then only twenty-four, he looked double his age, but fortunately he arrived at Norfolk just in time to come under the merciful administration of Captain Maconochie. The Commandant cleverly put the completely brutalized Anderson in charge of some unruly bullocks on the settlement 'to', using his own words, 'usefully exercise his superfluous energies'. The cure worked like a charm; Anderson showed that he could manage the wild creatures without using the cruelty he himself had suffered, and in doing so found himself.

Anderson's improvement was so great that Maconochie put him in charge of a signal station which was set up on Mount Pitt, the highest point on the island. He performed his new duties with scrupulous care and occupied himself also with a well-tended and fruitful garden. When Sir George Gipps visited the island in 1843 his attention was caught by a prisoner, trimly dressed in sailor's garb, going importantly about his duties. He was astounded when told that it was the man who had been chained to the rock in Sydney Harbour. Even the cynical prison authorities in Sydney who recalled the reformer and forced his dismissal for his leniency to prisoners, grudgingly admitted Maconochie's remarkable results.

A full-length biography had long been needed to reveal the true greatness and social significance of Alexander Maconochie. The need was met in 1958 when the Honourable Mr. Justice John Vincent Barry of the Supreme Court of Victoria published his book *Alexander Maconochie of Norfolk Island*. The work bears the marks of scholarly research, judicial weighing of evidence from numerous sources, and sympathetic understanding. The distinguished author, who has since been knighted, skilfully reveals the inaccuracies and erroneous statements of earlier writers who, referring to Maconochie, asserted that his system was a complete failure on Norfolk Island. Ignorant of Maconochie's importance in the history of penal reform, they yet have thought it necessary to pass judgment on him as a penal reformer. Sir John Barry criticizes, among others, a popular Australian author who in one of his books describes Norfolk Island under Maconochie, to whom he refers derisively as 'Benevolent Mac'. This is completely misleading, says Sir John Barry, and discloses no real comprehension of Maconochie's theories or practices.

Alexander Maconochie made his contribution to an extraordinarily difficult social problem, and society repaid him with derision, hostility, and neglect. The significance of his contribution and his great influence in lessening the sum of avoidable human misery cannot be exaggerated. 'The three universally recognized moral qualities of man are wisdom, compassion and courage' says Sir John Barry, adding, 'Maconochie had these three in generous measure and he brought them fully to the service of mankind'.

Maconochie published several works and pamphlets on prison reform, notably *Crime and Punishment* which deals with the Mark System. He listed the leading defects in the social system of his day that led to crime, such as lack of schools, and especially industrial schools for the children of the poor. He said that long periods of imprisonment were undesirable because they led to deterioration, but release should be earned by self-discipline and industry, and he offered the Mark System as the means by which this could be brought about. Maconochie insisted that recourse to degradation as part of punishment was not only wicked, but foolish, and he was completely opposed to solitary confinement.

The Rev. Dr. Ullathorne was gravely concerned with the problem of homosexuality among the prisoners on Norfolk Island and he repeatedly refers to it. It is to the great credit of Maconochie that during his administration perversion was reduced to a few isolated cases. According to Governor Gipps, after visiting the island and making extensive investigations, unnatural crimes prevailed almost exclusively among the English prisoners, there being very few offenders among the Scots and none among the Irish[3].

---

3 Gipps to Stanley, April 1, 1843. *H.R.A.* Gipps called the problem the 'crime most repugnant to human nature'.

In the 1820s Norfolk Island was usually called Sodom Island, the sexual perversion amongst the convicts being notorious. *The Monitor* newspaper, reporting the execution of a group of Norfolk Island convicts sentenced to death for mutiny in 1827, stated that it was the negligence of their keepers that was the cause of the trouble. The men 'were suffering for endeavouring to escape from the land of Sodom and Gomorrah; a land so defiled, that being *men*, they felt a manly repugnance to enter and sojourn there'.

On religious matters, Maconochie was remarkably tolerant, and he sought to use as a means of reform the re-awakening of good inclinations implanted by early religious training. His treatment of the Jews, of whom there were only about a dozen on the island, was very much to his credit. He obtained from the Chief Rabbi in Sydney the necessary vestments and books, with advice as to what he should do to enable their religious practices to be respected and fostered. He permitted them to use a room as a synagogue, and appointed one of them to act as reader. The experiment was highly successful, and all became reformed characters, helping and counselling one another.

In a pamphlet written towards the end of his life, he describes the circumstances under which he built the churches for the Protestants and Catholics. The construction of the two churches was undertaken without authority, and each accommodated 450 men. The cost, apart from labour and material obtained on the island, was £120 for nails, fastenings and window glass. These were obtained from the stores, and Maconochie was informed by the Works Department in Sydney that he would have to pay this sum from his own pocket. Both the Anglican and Catholic Bishops in Sydney privately told him that if necessary they would raise the amount, but the amount was never claimed; as Maconochie commented, 'the Governor, the late excellent Sir George Gipps, or the Home Authorities, took a wiser view of the irregularity'[4].

After Maconochie's recall, conditions for the prisoners

---

4 *Supplement to a Previous Summary* (1857).

on Norfolk Island reverted to their former horror. Two years after his dismissal an official investigation revealed the incapacity of the new Commandant, the debasement and depravity of large sections of the convicts, and the infliction of severe torture. The solitary confinement cells, from which all light was excluded, were in constant use, but no longer was there only one occupant to a cell, and overcrowding there and throughout the settlement led to gross immorality.

It was at this time in 1846—two years after Maconochie had been removed—that the Catholic Bishop of Hobart, Robert William Willson, visited the island. After accepting the newly-created See of Hobart in Tasmania he did not arrive there from England until two years later, as he believed it best to visit European prisons and acquaint himself before undertaking work that would lie largely among prisoners. The bishop was horrified to see on Norfolk Island some of the tortures inflicted. He found that men were subjected to the 'Spread-eagle', in which their arms and legs were stretched out and they were hung to the wall. He saw the 'tobacco track', which consisted of seizing the convict by the throat and forcibly examining his tongue and mouth for traces of tobacco, which, if alleged to be present, brought severe lashings. Bishop Willson told, too, of seeing tube gags inserted in the victim's mouth and throat, and the torture known as the 'scavenger's daughter' in which men's heads were bent to their knees, and they were trussed and left in that position[5].

From then onwards the English bishop worked unceasingly among the convicts until he finally succeeded in having the infamous Norfolk Island prison abolished forever. The work for which Bishop Willson will always be gratefully remembered centred mainly among the convicts of Port Arthur and Norfolk Island; he brought about many reforms and visited England in 1847 to plead for further improvements relating to convicts and the insane; his crowning success—as the *Australian Encyclopedia* states—was the abolishment of the Norfolk Island penal settlement.

It should be mentioned that Bishop Willson also acknow-

5 *Memoirs of Bishop Willson* (1887).

ledged the worth of Alexander Maconochie. When he was in England, the bishop informed Maconochie that nearly all of the prisoners for whom he had obtained discharges were doing well in Sydney, and most of them advancing fast to prosperity.

CHAPTER 10

Cannibalism Among Runaway Convicts

THERE are a number of documented instances of cannibalism among runaway convicts. *Bell's Weekly Despatch* of January 22, 1832, gives a lengthy account of a confession made by Edward Broughton who with Matthew Maccavoy was executed at Hobart Town. The two men were hanged 'for the wilful Murder of 3 of their Fellow Transports, and eating them as Food'. The confession, signed by Broughton and witnessed by John Bidsee, appears in the journal as follows:

'Broughton said that he was now 28 years of age, and had been sentenced to death for robbing in England, under aggravated circumstances, at the early age of eighteen. He more than once endeavoured to rob his own mother, and his horrible conduct was the means of breaking his father's heart, and hurrying him to his grave.

'He was confined two years in Guildford Gaol, and had altogether spent more years in gaols than at liberty. On his transportation to this Colony, he had scarcely landed in Hobart Town, when he commenced robberies. He was at last apprehended for an outrage he had committed at Sandy Bay, tried and transported to Macquarie Harbour.

'Broughton went on to say that he was one of a party of five convicts, which happened to be at one of the out stations at Macquarie Harbour, in charge of one man, a constable. The convicts consisted of Richard Hutchinson, commonly called "Up-and-down Dick," a tall man, who had, at one time, a large flock of sheep and a herd of cattle at Bark Hut Plains, between the Clyde and Shannon, near the spot where Cluny Park now is, the estate of Captain Clarke; of an old man named Coventry, about sixty years of age; of a

79

boy of a most depraved character, Patrick Fagan, about 18 years old; and the two malefactors, Broughton and Maccavoy, now about to suffer on the gallows.

'Broughton declared the constable had shewed him many personal kindnesses, and refused him nothing in his power; nevertheless, on their departure, he joined with his four companions of robbing him of every article he had, not leaving him even a loaf of bread to subsist on, though he was without a morsel, and 3 days must have elapsed before he could obtain any more from the settlement.

'And Broughton had besides, at various times, tried to be accessory to his death, by letting a tree fall upon him without giving him notice, or by other means, or for no other earthly reason than because he was a constable, and the unwilling or passing instrument of flogging the men, and he therefore hated him.

'One would have thought that these 5 men, thus embarked in a most perilous journey, would have been knit together in one interest for their mutual safety and protection. But the very contrary was the case, as the sequel proved. They viewed each other with the most murderous feeling, jealous of the only axe which they carried amongst them, lest one should drive it into the head of the other, for that was their mode of slaughter upon one another, while the wretched victim was asleep.

'The demon of evil had possession and walked in the midst of them. Every principle, every feeling of humanity was dead amongst them. Broughton called himself a Protestant, and Maccavoy a Roman Catholic, that is they had sprung from parents possessing those persuasions; but as for themselves they had neither of the least spark of religion; they knew no more what it was than the earth on which they trod.

'They walked in each other's company, the one carrying his luckless body to the support of the other whenever it might be convenient for him to sacrifice him for the meal. Fifty times worse than the wretched horde of Abyssinians who are reported to cut the flesh as they travel from the backs of the living beasts.

Port Arthur During Convict Occupation

'As soon as the provisions which they had contrived to carry with them were exhausted, the other four agreed among themselves to kill Hutchinson, and to eat his body for support; and they drew lots among them who should be the one to drive the fatal axe into his head. The lot fell on Broughton, who carried it into execution.

'They cut the body in pieces and carried it with them, with the exception of the hands, head, feet, and intestines. They ate heartily on it, as Broughton expressed it. It lasted them some days, and when it was nearly consumed, a general alarm seized the whole party, lest the one should kill the other. The greatest jealousy prevailed about carrying the axe, and scarcely one amongst them dared to shut his eyes or doze for a moment for fear of being sacrificed unawares'.

Under these dreadful circumstances, Broughton and Fagan made a sort of agreement between them, and while the one slept the other should watch alternately. "We were always alarmed", said Broughton in his confession, and Maccavoy's statement was the same.

'The next that was murdered was Coventry, the old man; he was cutting wood one night, and we agreed in the meantime to kill him. Maccavoy and Fagan wanted to draw lots again who should kill him, but I said no, I had already killed my man, and they ought to do it between them, that they might be in the same trouble as me.

'Fagan struck him the first blow. He saw it coming and called out for mercy; he struck him on the head, just above the eye, but did not kill him; myself and Maccavoy finished him and cut him to pieces. We ate greedily of the flesh, never sparing it, just as if we had expected to meet with a whole bullock the next day.

'I used to carry the axe by day, and lay it under my head at night; forgetting they had knives and razors, I thought I was safe. Before we had eaten all Coventry's flesh, Maccavoy one night started up, looking horribly and bid me come with him to set some snares to try to catch a kangaroo. We left Fagan by the fire, and when we had gone about 100 yards, he asked me to sit down. I had the axe upon my shoulder, and I was afraid he wanted to kill me, for he was stronger than me. So I threw the axe aside, but farther from him than me, for fear he should try and snatch it, and that I might reach it before him if he did.

'But he wanted me to kill Fagan, that he might not be evidence against us. I would not agree to it, saying, "I could trust my life in his hands", and we returned to the fire.

'On our return, Fagan was lying by the fire warming himself, and I threw the axe down. He looked up and said, "Have you set any snares down, Ned?"

' "No," I said, "there are snares enough, if you did not know it".

'I sat beside him, Maccavoy was beyond me; he was on my right and Fagan on my left. I was wishing to tell Fagan what had passed, but could not, as Maccavoy was sitting with the axe close by looking at us. I laid down and was in a doze, when I heard Fagan scream out. I leapt to my feet in a dreadful fright, and saw Fagan lying on his back, with a dreadful cut in his head, and the blood pouring from it. Maccavoy was standing over him with the axe in his hand.

' "You murdering rascal, you dog!" I said, "what have you done?"

' "This will save our life", he said, and struck him another blow on the head with the axe.

'Fagan only groaned after the scream, and Maccavoy then cut his throat through the windpipe. We then stripped off the clothes, and cut the body into pieces and roasted it. We roasted all at once as upon all occasions, as it was lighter to carry and would keep longer, and would not be so easily discovered.

'About four days after that we gave ourselves up at Macguire's Marsh (a hut belonging to Mr. Nicholas, at the junction of the Shannon and the Ouse, or Big River). Two days before, we had heard some dogs that had caught a kangaroo, they were wild dogs, we saw nobody, we got the kangaroo, and threw away the remainder of Fagan's body.

'I wish this to be made public after my death'.

signed, Ed. Broughton.
witness, Jn. Bidsee.'

With Shame Remembered

In July, 1824, eight years previously, Alexander Pearce was executed at Hobart Town for the murder of a fellow convict, Thomas Cox, at King's River. Earlier, Pearce with several other prisoners had escaped from the penal settlement at Macquarie Harbour. Pearce was eventually captured by the military and sent back to prison where he became ill and was put in hospital. Thinking he was dying he told a ghastly story of cannibalism concerning his fellow escapees and himself, but when he recovered he denied it all and said it was merely delirious raving. The authorities, having no evidence of the crimes other than Pearce's own words, took no action.

It was only when some months later Pearce absconded a second time and killed and ate his companion escapee, Thomas Cox, that the truth of his hospital statement was realised. What made the later crime more incredibly vile was the fact that Pearce was not facing starvation but had bread and cheese in his pocket at the time. After eating selected morsels of Cox, Pearce decided to give himself up and returned to the penal settlement. Since there was no legal evidence against his former horrors his execution was carried out for the murder of Cox.

The Hobart Town Gazette in its issues of June 25, July 9 and 23, of 1824, gives the terrible story of Pearce's crimes and execution when 'the large and curious crowd assembled around the scaffold glanced in fearfulness at the being who stood on the gallows before them laden with the weight of human blood and known to have BANQUETTED ON HUMAN FLESH'.

The Rev. Mr. Connolly who attended Cox on the scaffold is quoted in the *Gazette* as follows:

'He would commence by stating that Pearce, standing on the awful entrance into eternity on which he was placed, was desirous to make the most public acknowledgment of his guilt, in order to humble himself, as much as possible, in the sight of God and Man.

'That to prevent any embarrassment which might attend Pearce in personally expressing himself, he had requested

Convict Leg-irons

Fort Denison ('Pinchgut'), Sydney, as it is today

and directed him to say that he committed the murder of
Cox under the following circumstances:—

'Having been arrested here, after his escape from Macquarie Harbour, Pearce was sent back to that Settlement,
where the deceased (Cox) and he worked together in the
same gang. Cox constantly entreated him to run away with
him from the Settlement, which he refused to do for a
length of time. Cox having procured fishhooks, a knife and
some burnt rag for tinder, he at last agreed to go with him,
to which he was powerfully induced by the apprehension of
corporal punishment for the loss of a shirt that had been
stolen from him.

'On the 13th November, they absconded from their duty
into the woods, each of them taking his axe, and the prisoner
being heavily ironed. For several days they wandered on
without provision and reduced by weakness, until on the following Sunday evening the deceased and prisoner arrived
at King's River. A quarrel then arose because Cox could not
swim, and Pearce struck him three times on the head with
his axe. Pearce then freed himself of his irons, and Cox
seeing him about to go off said, in a faint voice, "for mercy's
sake come back, and put me out of my misery!"

'Pearce then struck him a fourth blow, which immediately
caused death; he then cut a piece of flesh off one thigh,
which he roasted and ate, and after putting another piece
in his pocket, he swam across the river, with intent to reach
Port Dalrymple. Soon afterwards, however, he became so
overwhelmed with remorse that he was constrained to re-
cross the river, and, on seeing a schooner under weigh from
the Settlement, he made a signal fire, which on being seen,
induced the pilot boat to put off and take him on board.
He was then conveyed to the harbour, where he publicly
owned the murder, and said, "he was willing to die for it".'

The Rev. Mr. Connolly then addressed the morbid crowd
assembled at the foot of the gallows as follows (quoting again
the *Gazette*):

'He believed it was the recollection of every one present,
that eight men had made their escape, last year, from Macquarie Harbour. All these except Pearce, who was one of the

*St. Matthew's Church, Windsor. Example of Greenway's
architecture*

party, soon perished, or were destroyed by the hands of their companions. To set the public right respecting their fate, Pearce is desirous to state that this party, which consisted of himself, Matthew Travers, Bob Greenhill, Bill Cornelius, Alexander Dalton, John Mathers, and two more named Bodnam and Brown, escaped from Macquarie Harbour in two boats, taking with them what provisions the coal-miners had, which afforded each man almost two ounces of food per day, for a week.

'Afterwards they lived eight or nine days on the tops of tea-tree and peppermint, which they boiled in tin-pots to extract the juice. Having ascended a hill, in sight of Macquarie Harbour, they struck a light and made two fires. Cornelius, Brown and Dalton placed themselves at one fire, the rest of the party at the other. The first three departed privately from the party, on account of Greenhill having already said that lots must be cast for some one to be put to death, to save the whole from perishing.

'Pearce does not know personally what became of Cornelius, Dalton and Brown, but he had heard the two former reached Macquarie Harbour, where they soon died, and that Brown perished on his return to that Settlement.

'After their departure, the party, then consisting of five men, lived two or three days on wild berries, and their kangaroo jackets which they roasted. At length they arrived at Gordon's River, where it was agreed that while Mathers and Pearce collected fire-wood, Greenhill and Travers should kill Bodnam, which they accordingly did. It was insisted upon that everyone should partake of Bodnam's remains, lest in the event of their ultimate success to obtain their liberty any of them might consider himself innocent of his death, and give evidence against the rest.

'After a day or two they swam across the river, except for Travers whom they dragged across by means of a pole, to which he tied himself. Having spent some days in distress and famine, it was proposed to Pearce by Greenhill and Travers that Mathers be killed, to which he agreed. Travers and Pearce held him while Greenhill killed him with an axe. Living on the remains of Mathers, which they were hardly able to taste, they spent three or four days, through weakness, without advancing beyond five or six miles, Travers being scarcely able to move from lameness and swelling in his foot.

'Greenhill and Pearce agreed to kill Travers, which Greenhill did while Pearce was gathering fire-wood. Having lived some time on the remains of Travers, they were for some days without anything to eat—their wants were dreadful—each strove to catch the other off guard, and kill him.

'Pearce succeeded to find Greenhill asleep, took his life and lived on him for four days. He was afterwards three days without sustenance, but fell in at last with the Derwent River and found some small pieces of opossums, etc., at a place where the natives had lately made fires. More desirous to die than live, he called out loudly, as loudly as he could, expecting the natives would hear him, and come and put an end to his existence.

'Having fallen in with some bushrangers, with whom he was taken, Pearce was sent back to Macquarie Harbour, from whence he escaped with Cox, as has been already stated, for whose death he is now about to suffer'.

The *Gazette* adds this finale to its rather ambiguous account of the Rev. Mr. Connolly's address to the crowd at the foot of the scaffold:

'Having stated that the unfortunate Pearce was more willing to die than to live, he concluded this heart-rending and awful narrative by entreating all persons present to offer up their prayers, and beg of the Almighty to have mercy upon the prisoner.

'We trust these awful and ignominious results of disobedience to law and humanity will act as a powerful caution; for blood must expiate blood! and the welfare of society imperatively requires, that all whose crimes are so confirmed and systematic as not to be redeemed by leniety, shall be pursued in vengeance and extirpated with *death!*'

CHAPTER 11

The Pioneer Press

THE background to these incredible events may be glimpsed by examining the early newspapers. Australia's first newspaper, issued from 1803 to 1842, was the *Sydney Gazette and New South Wales Advertiser*. The title of 'The Australian Caxton' has been given to its first editor, George Howe, but, actually, Australia's first printer was a convict named Hughes, although his only productions were handbills. However, George Howe was the Father of the Australian Press, commencing with the first issue of the *Gazette* which he edited and printed.

A convict, also, he was a Creole who had printer's ink in his blood, his father having been Government Printer on the island of St. Christopher in the West Indies. He reached Sydney in 1800 under sentence of seven years transportation, but his offence is not known. It is surmised that he was a political offender, since his father had been involved in political turmoil in the West Indies and the son may have followed in his steps. Soon after his arrival in the colony Howe was appointed Government Printer, and late in 1802 he issued the first book to be printed in Australia—*New South Wales General Standing Orders*. Incidentally, his predecessor, Hughes, besides being a printer, was a bit of an actor and was one of the principal performers at the first theatrical show held in this country in January, 1796[1].

The *Gazette* was the official organ of the Government and had little resemblance to the newspapers of today either in content or appearance. It was of foolscap size, smudgily printed, with the "s's" looking like "f's" in accordance with the typographical practice of the day, and its news was closely supervised by the rulers of the day to conform with

---

1 *The Recruiting Officer*. It was an all-convict cast.

Government opinions. Liberty of the Press did not come to the colony for nearly 20 years, and only then after much persecution. Much of the first issue consisted of official notices, shipping items, and court reports, including an account of some runaway convict labourers (described as "licentious banditti') who had been causing alarm in the Baulkham Hills district. A critic of the *Gazette* later described the journal as a mixture of 'fulsome flattery of Government officials . . . and inane twaddle on other matters'.

Howe received no salary for his services as editor and printer and had to stand all financial responsibility; it was not until eight years later that Governor Macquarie allowed him a salary of £60 a year. Howe gathered the news, set the type, wrote most of the contents under this or that pen-name, and distributed copies personally to his Sydney subscribers who numbered about 300. For the first seven years Howe's trials were legion. His two greatest problems were getting people to pay up and making sure of his supplies of paper and ink. He used to issue pitiful pleas for prompt payment and said he would accept value in kind if the cash was not forthcoming. Farm produce, meat, rum, etc., were all equally acceptable. Because of paper difficulties, from time to time the size, shape and colour of the *Gazette* varied considerably. One issue appeared on brown wrapping paper from the storekeepers; frequently the paper was of three colours. His ink was composed of charcoal, gum, and shark oil. No wonder some of the numbers are today almost unreadable.

And how is this for hereditary influence? Howe's father was a Government Printer; then himself; next his son Robert who succeeded to the position when he died. Another son, George Junior, became the second Government Printer in Van Diemen's Land and founded the *Hobart Town Gazette;* and a grandson was employed in the Queensland Government Printery.

Howe saw better times when he married a rich widow—his second wife (his first had died on the voyage to Australia). He combined store-keeping with journalism, engaged in the sandalwood trade (with Mary Reibey)[2], and was an original subscriber to the Bank of New South Wales.

On George Howe's death a white marble tablet was placed in the original building that housed the *Sydney Gazette*. It bore the inscription:

IN MEMORY
OF
GEORGE HOWE,
A CREOLE, OF ST. KITTS,
BORN 1769 — DIED 1811,
HE INTRODUCED
INTO AUSTRALIA
THE ART OF PRINTING,
INSTITUTED THE
SYDNEY GAZETTE,
AND WAS THE FIRST
GOVERNMENT PRINTER,
BESIDES WHICH
HIS CHARITY
KNEW NO BOUNDS

Sydney Town seldom lacked vivid local items for its newspaper (it appeared as a weekly, twice and thrice weekly, and daily publication during its lifetime) as witness these extracts: 'We observed the stocks full of drunkards yesterday morning, male and female—in fact an overstock'. '. . . Captain Croft of the *Bencoolen*, on arrival in port yesterday, stated that a most awful deficiency had taken place in the ship's bottled ale. Spirits and liquors had disappeared and the cherry brandy had been played the devil with. The crew being always drunk, the Captain gave ten of them into custody'.

Another paragraph tells of a singer 'grossly insulted by a set of noisy know-nothings who had perched themselves in the gallery'. The editor also complains that 'the constables are asleep as usual, and goats in dozens are permitted to roam the streets'. He issues a note of warning to his readers: 'Unless Colonial crayfish are properly bled before boiling the

2 Referred to in *The Emancipists* Chapter 14.

flesh, the person of the eater will be covered with spots the size of a shilling'.

Sydney's first stocks were located in George Street North; later there were others on the corner of King and Elizabeth Streets. Druitt Street also had its stocks and pillories. Drunks were usually the occupants. With their heads, hands, and wrists stuck through the wooden boards and securely fastened, the unfortunates would be left there to be pelted with refuse and rubbish by the onlookers. Here are the words of a *Sydney Gazette,* dated August 17, 1835: 'Stocks with comfortable accommodation for five couples of ladies and gentlemen who cannot pay the usual fines for indulging at the Shrine of Bacchus have been erected at the corner of Bathurst Street. They are accompanied by a whipping post and have a fine appearance. They are quite an addition to the Scots Church which is nearly completed'.

This choice morsel is from a *Sydney Gazette* of 1804, the subject being a notorious old woman who had kept a house for drink and other male needs in the tough Rocks area: 'From twelve to fifteen couples of *spotless* damsels' (the word spotless is underlined) 'robed in white, followed the procession; and after depositing the venerable remains, returned to her late apartments, where *spiritual*' (the word spiritual is underlined) 'consolation was duly administered'.

Occasionally, when reporting the local news, the early newspapers would break into verse. We read in the *Sydney Gazette* of May 29, 1808, this description of a street fight in town between two women, one a little person and the other a veritable amazon:

> *The weaker vessel soon gave way,*
> *And prostrate on the roadway lay.*
> *Her eyes their boasted lustre lose,*
> *And sight itself huge wounds oppose.*
> *From various openings a purple tide*
> *Swells to excess the victor's pride;*
> *Till quite subdued by many a cuff*
> *The small one said she'd had enough.*

Opening the paper must have been a real adventure those

days—one could never know what was likely to be in print about oneself or one's friends. Freedom of the press (after its Government shackles were removed) really meant something; unhindered by influences of advertisers, policies, politics and the struggle for greater circulation. Written in the flamboyant prose of the period those newspapers give a more constructive picture of the era than many history books. There are in them a number of references to the sale of wives for cash or barter. The following is an extract from the *Sydney Gazette* of October 23, 1803, about a husband who bartered his wife for six bushels of wheat and a prize pig. Says the newspaper report: 'The man at Baulkham Hills who lately cried down the credit of his wife did so merely to raise her reputation and enhance her worth, as he was desirous, probably, of making the best of a bad bargain. He has since converted her into an article of traffic, the net produce upon the sale of which amounted to six bushels of wheat and a large black inhabitant of the stye, received from a settler at Hawkesbury'.

Sales of wives, public and private, were by no means unusual. One lady brought for her better half no less than fifty sheep; another was exchanged for five pounds cash and a gallon of rum[3]. Regarding a wench whose husband auctioned her for twenty sheep and a gallon of rum, in 1817, the newspaper referring to the sale reported: 'From the variety of bidders, had there been any more on the market the sale would have been pretty brisk'.

There is an instance in Victoria where a man, after purchasing both a wife and family, took the vendor to law in his endeavour to secure, also, the family feather mattress. A quaintly worded document filed at the Bendigo Court, and still preserved by the descendants of J. A. C. Helm, a solicitor practising in Bendigo in 1859 reads: 'California Gully, Bendigo, August 3, 1859. I hereby agray to sell my wife and famely of churlden for the sum of £1, the land and dwelling house to remain in the poshine of my daughter Jane'.

---

3 James Bonwick (1870).

Apart from the selling of wives, it seems that marriages could be dissolved simply by putting an advertisement to that effect in the newspaper. A formula existed, beginning: 'A mutual separation having this day been entered into between me and my wife, etc., etc'. Here is a tit-bit from an issue of December, 1818: 'NOTICE. Whereas my wife, Jane — —, is again walked away with herself, without any provocation whatever, and, I hear, has taken up with a fellow who looked after cattle in the neighbourhood of Macquarie River. This is to give notice that I will not pay for bite nor sup, nor for any other thing she may contract on my account to man or mortal; and that I am determined to prosecute with the utmost rigor the Law will permit, any person or persons who may harbour, conceal, or maintain the said runaway Jane — —, after the publication of this notice'.

The Derwent Star of Hobart had a spicy style all its own in recording marriages. Apparently the journalists who wrote and edited these forerunners of our modern dailies did so with a lordly disregard not only of other people's feelings but of the consequences (if any but horse-whipping existed) of libel or defamation of character. Witness this item in an issue of 1810: 'Marriage. On Monday, 26th ultimo, R. C. Burrows to Elizabeth Tucker, both late of Norfolk Island. They had cohabited together for fourteen years, verifying the old adage, "Better late than Never".' In fairness to the couple, it should be added that there was no minister of religion or other means of marriage on Norfolk Island at that time.

One of Australia's early newspapers was the *Port Phillip Gazette*. As with other journals of those days, it had immense difficulties to contend with. When a shortage of ink and paper occurred, which was frequently, it was exceedingly difficult to procure more. Like the *Sydney Gazette,* the Melbourne newspaper often used paper of different colours— green, blue, pink and yellow being quite common. Then there were such difficulties as the following notice showed in the *Port Phillip Gazette:* 'To Subscribers. The last week's papers did not leave town till Wednesday owing to the messenger's horse running away, leaving the rider stranded and the papers lost beyond recovery'.

To add to the editor's troubles was the shortage of money. In desperation he put this notice in his newspaper: 'It is no use to honey the matter—payments must be made at least once a quarter, or else I shall run down to heel. Everyone says how well the paper is getting on, when the fact is that I have not enough money to buy myself a shirt or a pair of breeches. My wife is now actively engaged in turning an old pair wrong side out. Come, come, pay up, friends. Keep peace in the family and enable me to wear my breeches out.—The Editor'.

When John Pascoe Fawkner chose the site for the future city of Melbourne he early came to the conclusion that a public-house and a newspaper were two of the most urgent necessities for the development of the settlement as such. The former, of course, came first, and when he got his newspaper going in 1838 Fawkner saw to it that the pub was well boosted in it.

It had taken a long time and a deal of trouble to establish Melbourne. David Collins made a start when he went to Port Phillip in 1803 with about 300 convicts to take charge of the proposed colony, as recommended by Governor King. Unfortunately, Collins made the mistake of settling on the east shore of the bay instead of the west, and within a short time he advised King that the place was unsuitable for a settlement. Apparently Collins made a very cursory examination of the country about Port Phillip and exercised poor judgment in his choice of a site for the settlement. King then authorized Collins to move to Van Diemen's Land, so the convicts together with some free settlers were landed at Sullivan's Cove, where Hobart is now situated.

It was not until thirty-two years later that John Batman of Parramatta came over from Launceston with a party of land seekers in the schooner *Rebecca* and went up the Yarra, landing a little below the present Prince's Bridge. From a tribe of wandering aborigines camped there Batman 'purchased' some 600,000 acres of land for a quantity of blankets and sundry other articles. A few days later he recorded in

Melbourne 1837

his diary the notable entry: 'We went, in the boat, up the large river . . . and . . . six miles up, I was pleased to find the water quite fresh and very deep: this will be the place for the future village'. He marked on his map (seventeen days later) an area on the south bank as 'reserved for a township and other public purposes'. Returning joyfully to Tasmania he informed his partners—14 members of the later-named Port Phillip Association—and within a brief time settlers began to stock the vacant land of Port Phillip. Batman and his associates tried to regularise the land deal with the natives, but were unsuccessful. Governor Bourke proclaimed the purchase void and treated the settlers as intruders and trespassers. Nevertheless, a steady influx of squatters continued and official recognition had to be given to the settlement.

In the meantime another party of prospective land takers, headed by John Pascoe Fawkner, arrived in Port Phillip from Launceston and made their way up the Yarra to the site of the future Melbourne where they promptly squatted, going one better than Batman by simply occupying the land, without attempting to compensate the rightful native owners in any way at all. This duplicated colonisation was the beginning of many quarrels between the rival claimants, but it gradually sorted itself out. Fawkner, who was a townsman (he had been an innkeeper and a lawyer of some sort in Launceston) developed the town of Melbourne, while Batman, who was an agriculturist and grazier, devoted himself and his followers to pastoral enterprise that eventually spread over the country to as far as Geelong.

When George Howe commenced the *Sydney Gazette* in 1803 he had at least a few cases of second-hand type and a primitive printing press, but Fawkner possessed neither and he had to be content with a hand-written newspaper. The copies of each issue were the work of several calligraphers but these men were all masters of the craft and their superb copperplate writing is something to marvel at. Since forgery was at its peak at that period, perhaps the writers had come to this country because of that accomplishment.

Fawkner's newspaper was not merely a single sheet. *The*

Advertiser, Port Phillip, Australia, comprised four pages of foolscap, complete with news, advertisements, Shipping Advice, Wanted, Lost and Found, For Sale, even a 'Poets' Corner'. The manuscript newspaper ran through nine weekly issues, but when the tenth was set up in type it was immediately suppressed for not complying with colonial press regulations. Nevertheless, on February 6, 1839, Fawkner issued the first number of the *Port Phillip Patriot,* which survived until 1843, and on November 22, 1840, he brought out the *Geelong Advertiser,* which still exists.

An examination of a copy of Fawkner's manuscript newspapers reveals, not surprisingly, an advertisement for his public house occupying a conspicuous position. Thus:

> FIRST ESTABLISHED HOTEL
> in Melbourne, Fawkner's Hotel supplies
> to the Traveller and Sojourner all the
> usual requisites of a Boarding House and
> Hotel of the very best quality, being
> mostly laid in from the first Mercantile
> House in Cornwall, V. D. Land, in addition
> to which there will be found mental re-
> creation of a high order. There are provided
> seven English and five Colonial Weekly News-
> papers, seven British Monthly Magazines,
> three Quarterly British Reviews up to July
> and August, 1837.
>
> A very choice selection of Books,
> including Novels, Poetry, Theology, History,
> Philosophy, Chemistry, etc.
>
> N.B.—A late Encyclopaedia. The use
> of any of these books will be free to the
> lodgers at the above Hotel.

Ne'er a word about alcoholic refreshment. Mine host's patrons may have been of a more intellectual type than those of Sydney town.

The *Melbourne Herald* first appeared as the *Port Phillip Herald* in January, 1840. The first issue was distributed free 'to every respectable inhabitant of Melbourne'. Those Melbournians who failed to receive a copy and who might have taken it as a grave reflection on their respectability were calmed by the editor publishing a notice in the next issue to the effect that the runners 'were not fully acquainted with the town, hence the delays and mistakes resulting in some of our respectable citizens failing to receive their copy . . .'

After more than twenty years since its inception, the weekly *Sydney Gazette* saw a rival publication established when W. C. Wentworth and Dr. R. Wardell founded *The Australian*. It appeared first as a weekly and later was issued twice a week, changing ownership several times during its 24 years of life. This uncensored newspaper came into conflict with Darling when it attacked that tyrannical and unpopular Governor[4]. An account of the hanging of eight men in Sydney in 1831 which appeared in *The Australian* illustrates the great gulf that divides the outlook of 1831 from that of today. The article records that the men were hanged for burglary, but they protested their innocence to the last. The editor thought, too, that they were perhaps innocent and mentions something about tainted evidence. However, he sums up things philosophically with these words: 'If in cases like this a few persons must die who are not exactly guilty, the circumstances, however deplored, are in a great degree unavoidable and necessary to maintain discipline in society'.

---

4 On the credit side, important developments took place during Darling's administration. These included Tasmania's separation from New South Wales and the construction of the framework of departmental government round which the Australian civil service system has been built.

CHAPTER 12

Governors Absolute

THE powers possessed by the early New South Wales Governors have been unequalled in the history of the British Dominions. Until 1824 there was no restraining Council influence or legal adviser, and the authority of these Governors was absolute[1]. They could—and they did—condemn, execute or reprieve at will, allot grants of land or refuse them, and there was no appeal. 'The law, Sir? I am the law!' is an oft-quoted remark of Governor Bligh. Still no one would envy these rulers; their worries were legion.

When Phillip left New South Wales the reins of government fell into the hands of Major Grose who became Lieutenant-Governor until the arrival in 1795 of Governor Hunter. But under Grose, and, indeed, for seventeen years after Phillip left, the notorious New South Wales Corps, better known since as the 'Rum Corps', was largely the ruling body of the Colony. Some historians have been unduly condemnatory of the Corps, accepting unreservedly the denunciations of Governors Hunter and Bligh and the attacks of the Rev. Samuel Marsden and the Rev. John Dunmore Lang. It should be borne in mind that these unfavourable views, such as Hunter's statement that the Corps was 'capable of corrupting the heart of the best disposed' were expressed in the heat of dissension. The New South Wales Corps was a body of soldiers recruited in England for special services adaptable to the conditions of New South Wales. They replaced the old naval guard that gave much trouble to Phillip. Quarrels had arisen between the Governor and the marine officers, who objected to performing civilian, and particularly judicial, duties in addition to military ones.

---

1 The Imperial Government omitted to make definite legal provision for the civil government of the colony, consequently many of the orders and regulations of the early Governors were invalid.

The Corps' first years in the colony were relatively tranquil, but gradually some of its members became involved in the rum traffic. The latter was born of the harsh conditions of the early days of the settlements in New South Wales and Van Diemen's Land when intoxicants and other luxuries were difficult to obtain. Settlers used to barter with a member of the military or civil service for a bottle of arrack or rum. So also did convicts; they would band together, ten of them each contributing a portion of their meagre rations in exchange for spirits.

Soon after Phillip's departure the trade was given a sinister turn when Lieut.-Governor Grose, faced with a food shortage, was blackmailed into taking 7500 gallons of spirits from an American trading ship whose captain refused to sell provisions for the colony unless the spirits also were purchased. This and other supplies placed large quantities of liquor (sold by the Government) in the hands of officers, civil and military. Thus it is not surprising that spirits became a currency accepted—and generally demanded—by nearly everyone. Even the Rev. Richard Johnson, the colonial chaplain, paid out as part of the wages of the men who built the first church rum which he valued for the purpose of wages at ten shillings per gallon.

The original members of the Corps were enlisted in the normal manner of those days and contained men who, as agriculturists, pastoralists, explorers and naturalists, contributed greatly to Australia's development in these and other fields. About the beginning of 1800 the quality of the Corps, augmented by drafts from Britain, changed for the worse, since the demands of the Napoleonic war made it more difficult to secure officers and men of the original standard. A number of convicts were enlisted and, although this practice applied to every British regiment and naval ship at that time, undoubtedly had a malign influence on discipline and regimental morale.

The rum traffic was ever expanding. All officers, civil and military, clergy, and other inhabitants, as John Macarthur declared in 1811, 'were under the necessity of paying for the necessaries of life, for every article of consumption, in the

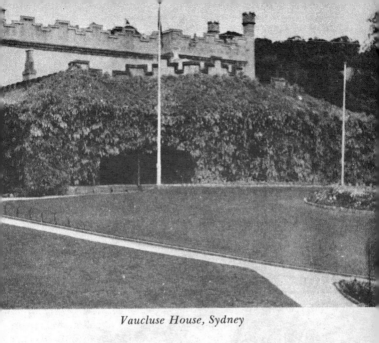

Vaucluse House, Sydney

Ruins of prison buildings on Norfolk Island

John Pascoe Fawkner
(From a copy in the Mitchell Library, Sydney.)

sort of commodity which the people who had to sell were inclined to take; in many cases you could not get labour performed without it'[2]. Officers of the Corps had first access to the cargoes of the supply ships which came to the colony, and this privilege was so misused that it eventually evolved into a system under which all overseas supplies were controlled by, and divided among these officers. Settlers requiring goods were compelled to pay the price the officers demanded, or do without.

Profit for these outrageous racketeers was frequently as high as 500%, and in some instances, 1,000%. Rum which had cost 7/6 to 10/- a gallon was retailed up to £8 a gallon. As soon as it became known that a good trade could be done in spirits at Sydney Cove cargoes were shipped from all parts of the world—chiefly from America. In 1797 Governor Hunter reported that ships had brought to Sydney 'spirits enough to deluge the colony'. He also said that the spirits were sold to settlers 'at an immense profit, to the destruction of all order, to the almost total destruction of every spark of religion, to the encouragement of gambling, the occasion of frequent robberies and several shocking murders'. The widely-held belief that the rum traffic was a monopoly exclusive to the New South Wales Corps is incorrect—the trade was in the hands of civil officers as well as those of the Corps—but undoubtedly the latter was the major shareholder. Many civil officers were replaced by the military, who, not satisfied with being magistrates, took into their hands much control of trade, and became general merchants and importers.

The British Government determined to put down the traffic but neither its urgings nor the efforts of local authorities could extinguish it. Governor Hunter was given positive instructions to stop the trading in spirits, and this he honestly tried to do, but found the task too great. Governor King, his successor, made a bold bid to stop spirits being landed in the colony without his consent, and prevent stills being set up for the manufacture of spirits. In this he was

2 Giving evidence during 'Rum Rebellion' trial.

partly successful, and he had the satisfaction of seeing the colony show signs of prosperity, but, worn out by his constant disputes with many of the leading colonists over the rum traffic, King returned to England in 1806.

The struggle over illicit trading was continued under Governor Bligh. Soon after his arrival an order was issued 'to prohibit the exchange of spirits and other liquors as payment for grain, animal food, wearing apparel, or any other commodity whatsoever to all descriptions of persons in the colony and its dependencies'. Bligh was determined to crush the clique of rum-selling officers in New South Wales, and to purify the official life of the colony. Bligh, the *Bounty* captain who displayed such courage and determination in his great voyage of 3000 miles in an open boat after the mutiny on his ship, soon had many enemies. His governorship was marked by constant wrangling between himself and the wealthier free settlers. Before he had been a week in the colony he quarrelled violently with John Macarthur, one of the founders of Australia's grazing industry, whom he looked upon as the real leader of the opposition to previous governors.

Macarthur, a former lieutenant in the New South Wales Corps, was one of the first military land-holders, having been given a grant of 10,000 acres of land at Camden. From a position of comparative poverty Macarthur had risen, after his arrival in Sydney[3], to one of such affluence that at the accession of Governor Bligh in 1806 he was the richest man in the colony. Bligh asserted that the land held by Macarthur at Camden was obtained by fraud, and that he should not be allowed to keep it. Although Australia owes a great debt to Macarthur for his services—or, more importantly, the services of his sons—in developing the wool industry, his actions were ever dictated by the urge for private gain. Like Bligh, Macarthur was a man of personal courage, with a temper intolerant of opposition, so it was to be expected that when these two domineering persons met violence would ensue. (Macarthur's temper and temperament, in-

---

3 In 1790. It is claimed that he was then £500 in debt.

fluenced by bouts of illness which increased in frequency in later years, ended in madness.)

The trouble came to a head in 1808 in what became known as the Rum Rebellion. The immediate occasion of the insurrection was Bligh's arrest of Macarthur for a breach of the port regulations; the underlying cause was the long-standing grievance of the officers concerning Bligh's determined attempts to crush the rum traffic, and his disposition to interfere with the ordinary trading of merchants and officials. A convict stowaway had escaped on Macarthur's schooner, the *Parramatta,* a fact which rendered the owner of the vessel liable to a penalty of £900.

Bligh at once caused Macarthur to be summoned to answer the charge of allowing a convict to escape, and he also confiscated a still which had been landed in Sydney to Macarthur's order. The court appointed to try Macarthur consisted of the Judge-Advocate, Atkins, and a jury of six officers of the Corps. Macarthur objected to being tried by Atkins, who, he alleged with much reason, was his personal enemy and his debtor. He was supported in his objection by the six military officers. Atkins refused to withdraw from the bench, and the six officers were summoned by Bligh to appear before him to answer for their conduct in taking the side of Macarthur. They declined to appear, as also did Major Johnston, the commandant, who was summoned by Bligh to his presence to discuss the conduct of his subordinate officers.

Major Johnston was now called upon by leading civil and military residents to arrest the Governor. Though such an act was, of course, quite illegal, Johnston marched to Government House, forced an entrance and arrested Bligh, who was formally deposed the next day. Johnston now became Acting Governor, and the New South Wales Corps was virtually the real power in the land for the next two years. Some of the officers who had served under Bligh were dismissed, and new officials took their place. Macarthur was acquitted as a matter of course, and Bligh was put as a prisoner on board a vessel in the harbour.

Johnston carried on the government till Lieutenant-

Colonel Foveaux, his senior officer, superseded him, and later on Colonel Paterson came over from Tasmania and took the place of Foveaux. Paterson liberated Bligh after twelve months' detention on condition of his sailing direct to England. Bligh disregarded his promise and hovered about Tasmania till the arrival of Lachlan Macquarie as Governor of New South Wales.

Governor Macquarie had instructions to reinstate Bligh for 24 hours, and send Johnston to England under arrest to answer for his conduct. Bligh could not be reinstated as he had left Sydney. Johnston was dismissed from his position in the military service, and Macarthur who had sailed for London was not allowed to return to the colony for eight years. Bligh went to England and was made a rear-admiral.

Macquarie's first work was to reinstate all the civil officers who had been dismissed when Bligh was deposed. In obedience to his instructions by the Home Authorities all the military officers save those who had been on outpost at the time of the rebellion (Norfolk Island, Van Diemen's Land and elsewhere) were ordered home. The rank and file were given an option of remaining in the colony through re-enlistment. About half the men of the Corps elected to remain.

Macquarie then turned his attention to the very unsatis-factory state of conditions in the colony. He had written on his arrival in Sydney: 'I found the colony barely emerging from infantile imbecility, and suffering from various priva-tions and disabilities; the country impenetrable beyond forty miles from Sydney; agriculture in a yet languishing state; commerce in its early dawn; revenue unknown; threat-ened with famine; distracted by faction; the public build-ings in a state of dilapidation and mouldering on decay; the few roads and bridges formerly constructed rendered almost impassable; no public credit nor private confidence; the morals of the great mass of the population in the lowest state of debasement, and religious worship almost wholly neglected'. He also said that the colony consisted of 'those who had been transported, and those who ought to have been'.

It was not long before Macquarie set about correcting the immorality, drunkenness and criminality he found in his seat of government, for, as he had indicated, the Sydney of that day was wild and lawless. Respectability was almost non-existent—it was a rarity for couples to bother about going through a marriage ceremony—and the bulk of the population got drunk habitually. Robberies and violent assaults were commonplaces. The new Governor created a civil police force and divided the town into five districts, each with its watch-house and lock-up. The constabulary numbered about 40 members and each was equipped with a Navy cutlass and a watchman's rattle. A few ex-soldiers and sailors were included in the force, but most of them were emancipated prisoners, and even convicts who were still actually serving sentences themselves.

Macquarie's policemen wore blue jackets, flat caps with peaks, and white canvas trousers. They were obliged to call out the time of night during every half-hour of their patrol through their districts, interrogate people found out of doors after the 9 p.m. curfew, see to the good behaviour of licensed victuallers, keep a strict eye upon houses of ill-fame, apprehend drunkards, suspects and sly-grog sellers. On Sundays they were expected to deal sternly with all whom they might find 'breaking or profaning the Sabbath day'. Whether you were bond or free, you had to mind your p's and q's in Sydney town during Macquarie's governorship.

It is interesting to note that in 1837 wheelbarrows were issued for use by the police. Their purpose was to convey drunken persons to the lock-ups. In the case of restive prisoners, their legs could be fastened to the barrow by means of buckles and straps. A *Sydney Gazette* of November, 1837, mentions that the policemen appointed for wheelbarrow duty resembled a muster of coachmen on a street stand. In a later issue, the newspaper has this reference to the subject: 'On Tuesday afternoon a constable in a state of intoxication was observed wheeling a man in a barrow to the watch-house who was also drunk. Instead of taking the man to the nearest watch-house, the intoxicated policeman wheeled him over half Sydney, every now and then capsizing him into the road, to the mirth of the citizens and the gratification of his own drunken propensities'.

In Van Diemen's Land the early Governors had their own troubles. Giving evidence before the English House of Commons on the moral conditions of the island, a speaker described Van Diemen's Land as 'that den of thieves, that cave of robbers, that cage of unclean birds, that isthmus between hell and earth . . .' Sales of wives were common, eligible *de factos* had been auctioned in the open market and, despite the fact that two people had actually married there in 1817, marriage was regarded as an old-fashioned custom that had been relegated to the past. Nevertheless, observance of the Sabbath was strictly commanded by law, and historian Bonwick relates that 'Colonel Collins, first Lieutenant-Governor of Hobart Town, though not susceptible to religious emotion, not devoted to Church celebration, and not conspicuous for the ordinary virtues, was nevertheless sufficiently possessed of the instincts of an officer and a gentleman to observe the proprieties of Sunday service'.

This compulsory Sabbath observance resulted in excellent church congregations, but only numerically speaking. When the Reverend William Bedford pointed out to Governor Arthur that very few of the churchgoers were legally married, and the incongruity of preaching Sunday after Sunday to pews of Hobart's best-known ladies of the town who had no intention of changing their profession, the Governor decided to do something about it. His solution was a simple one that would perhaps not be regarded today as particularly drastic, but it caused turmoil and frenzied panic as no other government order did before or since in Tasmania. Governor Arthur decreed that all government employees had to be married to the ladies they lived with.

To the uproar, the pleas, the threats and appeals, His Excellency turned a deaf ear. Respectability or dismissal was the implacable command. Since most of the ladies living in comfortable concubinage had graduated from the town gaol, few of their gentlemen friends wished actually to marry them. Hence they were cast off to fend for them-

selves whilst their 'protectors' looked around for legal partners of a higher social standing.

Governor Arthur (he was appointed in 1824) also rendered himself unpopular by the adoption of an arbitrary
policy, unsuitable to a community which contained a considerable number of free settlers. About eighteen months
after his arrival in Van Diemen's Land it was proclaimed
an independent colony, and the Imperial Government instituted Executive and Legislative Councils, with advisory
and legislative functions. By dismissing a popular Attorney-
General, and by straining every nerve to destroy the liberty
of the Press, Governor Arthur intensified his unpopularity;
and as his power was almost absolute he was both hated
and feared by a large section of the population. On the
other hand, he strove to the best of his ability to promote
the cause of religion and education, and many churches
and schools were established while he was at the head of
affairs. The public finances were brought into a satisfactory
condition, and after providing for an expenditure of something like fifty thousand pounds per annum, he was en-
abled to carry forward a surplus.

For the better administration of justice, Governor Arthur
divided Van Diemen's Land into police districts, with a
stipendiary magistrate for each; but he caused the laws to
be executed with a Draconian severity which transformed
convicts—many of whom had been transported for minor
offences—into sullen madmen, or ferocious and revengeful
fiends. Men fled from the horrors of the penal settlement
into the solitude of the bush, preferring to face a lingering
death by starvation rather than undergo the tortures of
the oft-repeated lash.

In the year 1825, as many as one hundred escaped convicts with arms in their possession had re-established a
reign of terror in the country districts, such as had prevailed in the time of Lieutenant-Governor Davey. (Davey
has been described as an inefficient and dissipated weakling under whose rule there was a general relaxation from
all the restraints of morality. Nevertheless, by discarding
many 'red-tape' regulations he opened the way to prosperity

for shippers and farmers and his proclamation of martial law throughout Tasmania on 25th April, 1815, checked the bushranging gangs.) Every isolated house was barricaded at night, and behind muskets the muzzles of which glittered from small port-holes stood one or two of the inmates detailed to watch over the safety of the sleeping household.

At length it became a question of whether law or lawlessness should triumph. Arthur placed himself at the head of a strong body of soldiers and civilians and hunted the outlaws down. One hundred and three bushrangers went to the scaffold in the years 1825 and 1826, and once more the plague of brigandage was stamped out. The Crown acknowledged the value of George Arthur's twelve years of service by creating him a baronet on his return to England, and by conferring on him the Governorship of Canada.

The Port Arthur penal settlement in south-eastern Tasmania, the most infamous of the convict stations on the island, was founded in 1830 during the rule of Lieutenant-Governor Arthur. It continued in use until 1877, although a prison for boys at Point Puer, opposite the main settlement was abandoned in 1849. Some eight hundred boys between the ages of nine and fifteen were transported to Port Arthur. One of them, nine-years-old James Lynch, was sentenced to transportation for seven years for the crime of stealing 3 boxes of toys. He probably never knew what it was to own a toy.

As in New South Wales and Tasmania, the other Australian colonies were also trouble spots for their early Governors. Until he was eventually recalled, the Governorship of Hindmarsh, South Australia's first Governor, was marked by long and weary wrangling with the Resident Commissioner, Fisher, and Surveyor-General Colonel Light. The latter had chosen the present site for the infant capital, but the Governor voiced his disapproval in no uncertain terms. There were a number of reasons why the proposed town should have been built nearer the sea, many of them perfectly logical, but Colonel William Light

Port Arthur Suicides' Rock

Drawn from an early print in the possession of the trustees of the Mitchell Library.

persisted in defiance of the Governor until Adelaide was laid along the banks of the River Torrens some six miles from the nearest point on the Gulf of St. Vincent. The wisdom of the move is seen today.

The story of Adelaide's planning has been the subject for innumerable newspaper stories, plays and features. And Colonel Light is regarded as a sort of patron saint by the State. Not that there was much saintliness about the founder of Adelaide. Light was the illegitimate son of an illegitimate father, and his first wife was the illegitimate daughter of an English duke. When Light's second wife eloped with another man by whom she had several illegitimate children, Light brought a mistress with him to South Australia and lived openly with her until his death.

South Australia was planned to be a model colony— one of those places so perfect in theory and such failures in practice. The man who planned it, Edward Gibbon Wakefield, had studied and developed a theory of systematic colonization while serving imprisonment for decoying a schoolgirl heiress, Ellen Turner, whom he married at Gretna Green. This was his second runaway marriage with a wealthy minor. The first was Eliza Pattle, a rich ward in chancery only 16 years old, whom Wakefield ran off with to Scotland and married in 1816. On their return Wakefield's charm brought about forgiveness, and the Lord Chancellor agreed to a settlement on him of about £2000 per annum. Four years later, his wife died leaving him with two children. His second runaway marriage brought down the wrath of the schoolgirl's parents who had Wakefield sentenced to three years imprisonment for abduction and the marriage annulled by Act of Parliament.

Although Wakefield had never been to South Australia, or indeed any part of Australia, he maintained that his theory of colonization was perfect for the proposed new settlement. He proposed, firstly, that Crown lands, when required for agriculture, should be sold at a high price to compel labourers to work for landholders until they had saved enough to buy land. Thus the scarcity of hired labour was to be overcome. The labourers would earn their living

View of North Terrace, Adelaide 1841

(and incidentally their master's) by tilling the soil, but how they would ever acquire sufficient money on their low wages to become landowners themselves was not explained.

Wakefield did not lack support for his scheme; many of the idle rich of old England were intrigued, and the South Australian Association was formed. Things might have worked out, too, but the tillers of the soil refused to remain happy and contented peasants while their masters over-worked them endeavouring to obtain quick results. Land speculation and mismanagement, both in Adelaide and in London, caused chaos. The colonists were often hungry, and it was at this period that South Australians acquired their nickname of 'crow-eaters'. Strangely enough, even to-day, the coat of arms of South Australia features a crow. Governor Gawler was so appalled by the state of affairs that he spent his private fortune in paying the wages of workmen engaged on public works. When he appealed to the British Government for money to help the just-about bankrupt colony, the authorities refused and reminded him that it had been designed to be self-supporting in every way. Eventually Gawler was recalled, and Sir George Grey was appointed in his stead. Fortunately, with the new Governor, the Home authorities sent sufficent funds to enable the worst of the mess to be cleared up, and this, with the jettisoning of the Wakefield theories, set South Australia on the road to prosperity.

Incidentally, during his term of office Governor Gawler nearly lost his life in the South Australian bush. His Excellency, accompanied by an English visitor named Bryan, and Williams, a manservant, had set out on horseback to visit a section of the Murray River. When the trio failed to return search-parties were organised, but it was not until three days later that Governor Gawler and Williams were found in an exhausted state. They told their rescuers that Bryan's horse had become lame and that Bryan had decided to stay with it while the Governor and Williams went on. The two became hopelessly lost and were soon crazed with thirst; they killed one of the horses and drank its blood. The search for the Governor's friend was continued, but it took experienced bushmen a long time before they found him. It was too late—Bryan and his horse had perished.

Victoria's first Governor, Charles Latrobe, had his share of woes. He even had to bring his own house with him from England. When he was commissioned he was advised that there was a serious shortage of dwellings in the colony, so he brought with him on his ship a weatherboard cottage in sections. That same building—Victoria's first Government House—is still standing in Melbourne.

Apart from a dwelling place, Governor Latrobe also brought out with him his Swiss wife. When the boat arrived, a brave showing of flags and bunting greeted them and one or two decorated arches had been erected. Unfortunately, when the vice-regal pair stepped off the boat something went wrong with the gangway plank, and the Governor and his lady stepped nearly knee-deep into mud. Still in their muddy state they were escorted in triumph through the streets of cheering and waving people; history is silent on any comment they may have made.

Here is the concluding statement from the first report of Queensland's first Governor, Sir George Bowen. He wrote it in 1859: 'As to money wherewith to carry on Government, I started with just sevenpence halfpenny in the Treasury. A thief broke into the Treasury a few nights after my arrival and carried off the sevenpence halfpenny mentioned. However, I borrowed money from the banks until our revenue came in'.

CHAPTER 13

Social Panorama

WHAT an astonishing conglomeration peopled the social panorama of Australia's earliest years—patriots and pickpockets, forgers and free-settlers, the highly learned and the illiterate, rum profiteers, civil servants, the fettered and the free. Glimpses of social life in those times can be found in letters of some of the first colonists to their friends and relatives in the 'Old Country' and in the writings of visitors to these shores.

Society at that time was composed of six main levels: (a) The military and officials. (b) Free men of the upper class. (c) Free men of the lower class. (d) Ex-convicts of the better type. (e) Ex-convicts of the lower class. (f) Convicts. An ex-convict whose sentence had been terminated because of good conduct and industrious service was known as an 'emancipist'. An 'expiree' was a convict who had served his term of imprisonment and continued to reside in the colony. The term 'ticket-of-leave' was applied to convicts whose commendable conduct and character had earned them the Governor's permission to work for their own profit. The 'assignment' system was an arrangement under which convicts were sent to work in the service and on the properties of settlers[1].

Governor Macquarie was the champion of the emancipists. He knew that many of them had been transported for petty offences (which nowadays would scarcely be considered as crimes at all) and he encouraged them in every way. As he said: 'When once a man is free his former state should no longer be remembered or allowed to act against him; let him feel himself eligible for any situation which

[1] Under the 'assignment' system the convict, though theoretically not in confinement, was actually so. 'The whole colony was the jail'. (Prof. Scott.)

114

he has by a long term of upright conduct proved himself worthy of filling'. Following up this view, he gave them land to settle on, and assigned convict labourers to them to work it. Besides, his idea was to allow them where they had the ability to act as lawyers and magistrates, and to fill other public offices. This, in the end, brought the Governor into collision with a large number of the free settlers. The first Supreme Court Judge to come to the colony refused to let emancipist lawyers practise before him, and was re-called, while many of the free magistrates refused to sit on the Bench with men who had been convicts. Bitter quarrels were frequent between the emancipists and the 'exclusives' throughout Macquarie's term of office.

The new Governor, Major-General Sir Thomas Brisbane, was without the tact necessary for conducting the affairs of the colony where there were two classes bitterly opposed to each other. On the one side he was beset by a small party of 'exclusives' who claimed to be alone entitled to grants of land, convict labour, and social recognition by the Governor. On the other hand he was annoyed by de-mands for legal rights and social recognition by numbers of wealthy emancipists. Unable to handle these parties suc-cessfully, and not wishing to be mixed up in their disputes, he left much of the control of affairs to his officials and took up his residence at Parramatta. Here he spent a great deal of time at his lifelong study of astronomy. It is said that while in the colony he fixed the positions of over 7,000 stars hitherto scarcely known to astronomers. Brisbane had served in the Peninsular War with the Duke of Wellington, and it is related of him that on sheathing his sword after the battle of Vittoria he exclaimed, looking round from a lofty eminence, 'What a glorious site for an observatory!²'

The civil service was a strange one—a confused muddle of incongruities with officials dabbling in several offices at the one time. Such curious irregularities resulted from the limited number of suitable applicants for the appointments and the inadequate government salaries. Isaac Nicholls, an

2 Brisbane's astronomical achievements brought him greater fame than either his military or vice-regal careers.

ex-convict, became Australia's first postmaster. Before
Nicholls was appointed a chaotic state of affairs existed in
which anyone could collect letters from incoming ships,
and thefts were rampant. Even with Nicholls in charge, the
postal service was a haphazard busines. Letters, according
to Commissioner Bigge, were 'casually delivered to the more
respectable inhabitants of Sydney'; letters addressed to convicts and ticket-of-leave men rarely reached their destination and there was no regular delivery to places outside
the boundaries of Sydney town. Postmaster Nicholls usually entrusted country letters to his acquaintances who
might happen to be passing through the locality of the
addressee. Nicholls received no salary for his job but was
allowed to charge a fee of one shilling each for letters from
overseas and eightpence for local ones. His profits were
estimated to amount to about £100 per annum.

George Cayley, who arrived in Sydney in 1800 as plant
collector for Sir Joseph Banks and who moved about the
settlement very freely, was a keen observer who left on
record his impressions of life in the early colony of New
South Wales. Here are some of his observations:

'The best public building in the colony is a new church
at Parramatta which is not yet finished. Another is also
begun in Sydney, at which place there is a good jail, which
is but lately finished. There are three windmills at Sydney,
two of them built by Government. People are better clothed
now than when I first came here. After making a list of
what one wants, one must apply to the Governor, who
looks over the list. If it meets with his approval he signs it.
Then one must go to the Commissary for him to sign it.
After that one goes to the stores and perhaps may wait a
long time before one gets served. The goods are not exposed for sale but left in a large storehouse with a sentinel
placed at the foot of a step-ladder, where the people sometimes form a waiting crowd, as only one person is permitted
to go up at once.

'There are a few schools, but badly managed. At Sydney
there is an orphan school; none but girls are admitted, yet
children with parents are admitted too'. (The female

116

orphan school referred to by Cayley was flanked on one side by a lumber yard and opposite a military guard-house. Since its object was more in the nature of a protection for the girls' morals than an institute of learning, its location was hardly ideal. Eventually temptation was removed by the transfer of the girls to Parramatta and the installation of less susceptible male orphans in the school.)

'The method of farming is conducted upon a bad principle, and carried on in a slovenly manner. Nothing more is done than break up the ground with a hoe and throw in the wheat, which again is chopped over with a hoe. I have never seen any people weed their wheat, though it is generally overrun with weeds.

'Gardening is in an infant state. It is not uncommon for the colonists to be without vegetables for some months of the year. Potatoes were very bad and stinking on my first coming here, but have improved of late. Watermelons are much thought of . . . Houses are nothing more than simple wretched huts, especially the farmers'. The walls are wattled and plastered with clay, the roof thatched, the floor nothing more than the bare ground. They generally consist of two rooms, and the furniture coincides with them.

'The general mode of living is very mean and wretched. I have known worn-out bullocks killed and issued. Had this meat been exposed for sale in an English market it would have been publicly burnt, but here it was considered prime meat. Though the colony is yet but in infancy, there are a deal of lawsuits and people arrested for debt. A settler, if though he is poor, yet he is out of debt, may consider himself a happy man . . .'

A picturesque description of the lower classes of Sydney in the 1820s is given in a book written by a young Englishman who, in a chapter telling of a visit to a pub in George Street, has this to say: 'In the large tap-room we found a strange assemblage; and stranger still were their dialects and their notions. Most had been convicts, there were a good many Englishmen and Irishmen, an odd Scotchman, and several foreigners, besides some youngish men, natives of the colony. Amongst them was present here and there

117

a woman, apparently the wife of a settler. The few women were all sober and quiet, but many of the men were either quite intoxicated or much elevated by liquor. Their chief conversation consisted of vaunts of the goodness of their bullocks, and productiveness of their farms, or the quantity of work they could perform. Almost everybody was drinking rum in drams; nor were they niggard of it, for we had several invitations from those around us to drink. I could not, however, even at this very early period of my acquaintance with this class of people, help observing one remarkable peculiarity common to them all—there was no offensive intrusiveness about their civility; every man seemed to consider himself just on a level with all the rest, and so quite content to be sociable or not, as the circumstances of the moment indicated as most proper.

'The whole company was divided into minor groups of twos, threes, and fours, and the dudeen (a pipe with stem reduced to three, two, one or half an inch) was in everybody's mouth. I think there was not an individual in the room, but one female, who did not smoke more or less, during the brief time we sat there. Their dresses were of all sorts; the blue jacket and trousers of the English "lagger", the short blue cotton smock frock and trousers, the short woollen frock, fustian jacket, and so forth, beyond my utmost power of recollection. Some wore neckhandkerchiefs, some wore straw hats, some beavers, some caps of untanned kangaroo skin. And not a shin in the room that displayed itself to my eyes had on either stocking or sock . . .'

In his *Reminiscences of Thirty Years Residence in New South Wales and Victoria,* Judge Therry speaks of George Street, Sydney, in 1829 thus: 'George Street—the principal in the town—was brilliant with jewellers' shops, and I soon ascertained that Sydney had been remarkable, even at an earlier period, for the same phenomenon—for it could seem no less to one unacquainted with the reason. This display of splendor was, after all, but a very natural result of the convict element in the town. The receivers of stolen plate and articles of bijouterie in England had chosen Sydney as

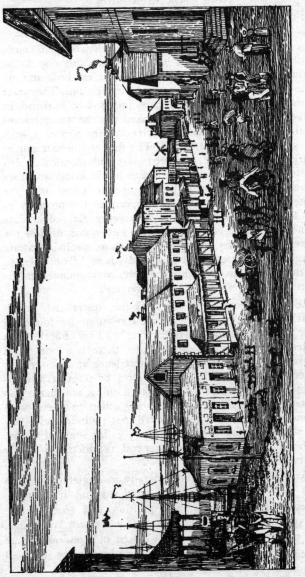

Early View of George Street, Sydney

a safe depot for the disposal of such articles, as agents for such a purpose might at that time easily be found there.

'A lady, the wife of an officer, wore a valuable gold comb, which was snatched out of her hair on coming out of the opera one night in London. The thief escaped, and no trace of the stolen article was found in England. Two years afterwards—about 1825—the lady joined her husband in Sydney. On the first day she walked out she was attracted by the display of brilliant articles in the shop of a well-known jeweller of that period. The first article that caught her eye, prominently displayed, was the identical stolen comb. She communicated the fact to her husband, and they visited the shop. Terms were proposed, either that the name of the consignor of the property or the property itself should be given up. The shopkeeper did not hesitate for a moment. He gave up the comb rather than disclose the name of the party who sent it to him, probably aware that, on the disclosure of how and where he obtained it, all the other articles in his shop similarly obtained might be subjected to a compulsory surrender'.

Robert Dawson, Chief Agent of the Australian Agricultural Company, described social conditions he found in New South Wales in 1831 thus: 'The less I say of Society the better. As in all small communities there is a jostling of interests, and a contention for precedence and power that generate parties which are kept alive by unprincipled individuals who, having sprung from nothing, and having no character to lose, delight in reducing others to a level with themselves. Let it not be suggested that I allude exclusively to those who have been involuntary exiles, some of whom, both in their dealings and general conduct, are highly desirable.

'An opinion prevails too generally in England that men who have been sent to gaol, convicted and transported, generally remain felons in disposition, and are therefore not to be trusted. This I can assert, of my own knowledge, is a mistaken notion . . . I was placed in a position where I had ample opportunity of making observations upon all

classes of them, and of seeing them tried in every variety
of situation and employment . . .

'In 1826 I had from the penal settlement of Port Macquarie an assignment of 50 men . . . Most of these men
were very much disposed to profit by the encouragement
I held out to them . . . Indeed, I experienced more gratitude from several of these very men than has ever fallen
to my lot from any class of people either at home or abroad.

'I always slept when at Port Stephens in the midst of a
large body of convicts, with my doors neither bolted nor
locked, and . . . was never molested, or lost to the value
of sixpence . . . nor was I ever better or more faithfully
served . . . I hope, therefore, that what I have stated will
. . . cause others to think less harshly of this class of banished
human beings, for although some of them may be past
redemption, yet there are many who, though apparently
irreclaimable, require but encouraging opportunities to
revive latent virtue and good feeling'.

*   *   *

A highly profitable business for Sydney traders in the
1830s was the importation of tattooed Maori heads. An
examination of the New South Wales Customs returns on
which duty was payable during those years will show in
the list of items—BAKED HEADS FROM NEW ZEA-
LAND. If you walked down George Street or adjoining
streets in Sydney town you would surely see these gruesome objects for sale in the windows of several shops. Or
you might be accosted by a street peddler—probably a seaman—offering you smuggled heads at a cheaper price than
those sold in the shops.

Prices for Maori heads in the shops generally ranged
from one to two guineas, according to the amount of tat-
tooing on them, but all were well baked and neatly stuffed
with flax. The tattoo designs depicted a man's family background and prowess in battle; thus the higher a Maori was
in the social scale and the more battles he survived, the
more his face was tattooed.

Behind this once popular sale of Maori heads lies one
of the many tragic aspects of the impact of European civi-

lization on a native Pacific people. One of the first Europeans to record a vigorous moral protest against this exploitation of traditional art for commercial gain was the Reverend Samuel Marsden who visited New Zealand as a missionary. 'When I first came across this barbaric business', he wrote, 'I recoiled in horror and disgust. Soon after my arrival in New Zealand a well-meaning native offered to collect a few samples for me. I told him and the other Maoris present that if anyone dared to mention such a vile proposal in my presence again I would see that the offender was immediately charged with murder. The Maoris were astonished at my attitude. They believed that I, like all the other white men who visited them, came only for the purpose of head-hunting'.

Traders visiting New Zealand offered knives, tomahawks, and other such goods the Maoris coveted in exchange for the heads of their enemies. Later, the Maoris were willing to supply heads only for muskets, and eventually when their consciences began to trouble them they refused to part with any more heads.

This change of attitude did not suit the owners of the trading vessels visiting New Zealand. Some of the more infamous of the traders turned head-hunters themselves and massacred tribes of Maoris to obtain their heads. One of these culprits was Captain Stewart of the brig *Elizabeth,* who figured in the massacre of 500 Maoris to clinch a trading deal. In its later stages head sellers sometimes paraded their living victims before a buyer and undertook to decapitate any heads selected, and even have the heads tattooed to order before decapitation.

Major-General H. G. Roberts, the hero of the Maori Wars, became so interested in the heads of his enemies, that he published a book on the subject. He gave detailed recipes used in the baking, cleaning and drying of the heads most efficiently, all with his own illustrations. One chapter explained the meanings of the various tattoo designs.

It was not until after some years of this gruesome trading in baked Maori heads that Governor Darling of New

South Wales decided that it must stop. A proclamation was issued and the new ruling was printed on the front page of the *Sydney Gazette,* also the *Sydney Monitor:*

GOVERNMENT NOTICE

Colonial Secretary's Office,
Sydney, 16th April, 1831.

WHEREAS it has been represented to his Excellency the Governor that the masters and crews of vessels trading between this Colony and New Zealand, are in the practice of purchasing and bringing from thence human heads, which are preserved in a manner peculiar to that country: And whereas there is strong reason to believe, that such disgusting traffic tends greatly to increase the sacrifice of human life among savages whose disregard of it is notorious, his Excellency is desirous of evincing his entire disapprobation of the practice above-mentioned, as well as his determination to check it by all the means in his power, and with this in view, his Excellency has been pleased to order, that the Officers of the Customs do strictly watch and report every instance which they may discover of an attempt to import into the Colony any dried or preserved human heads in future, with the names of all parties concerned in every such attempt.

His Excellency trusts that to put a total stop to this traffic, it is necessary for him only thus to point out the almost certain and dreadful consequences which may be expected to ensue from a continuance of it, and the scandal and prejudice which it cannot fail to raise against the name and character of British Traders, in a country with which it is now become highly important for the merchants and traders of this Colony, at least, to cultivate feelings of natural goodwill; but if his Excellency should be disappointed in this reasonable expectation, he will feel it an imperative duty to take strong measures for totally suppressing the inhuman and very mischievous traffic in question.

His Excellency further trusts that all persons who have in their possession human heads, recently brought from New Zealand, and particularly by the schooner *Prince of*

Denmark, will immediately deliver them for the purpose of being restored to the relatives of the deceased parties to whom the heads belonged; this being the only possible reparation that can be rendered, and application having been specially made to his Excellency to the purpose.

By His Excellency's Command,

ALEXANDER M'LEAY

If tattooed Maori heads no longer grace the mantelpieces and whatnots of homes there are many still to be seen in the museums of Europe. Incidentally, in the year 1896 a group of Maori visitors in the Canterbury Museum in Christchurch, New Zealand, saw the head of one of their family displayed in a glass case. They laid a complaint before the Dominion Governor and as a result the museum curator, Sir Julius Von Haast, was told to put the offending exhibit out of sight or take the consequences.

* * *

Surgeon Peter Cunningham, R.N., who made four voyages to New South Wales as surgeon-superintendent of convict transports, was a highly observant visitor to these shores. In 1827 he published *Two Years in New South Wales,* one of the most valuable of all the records of this particular period kept by individual observers that Australian archives contain. Especially interesting are his impressions and comments on the colonial youth of his day—the Currency Lads and Lasses:

'Our colonial-born brethren', he says, 'are best known here by the name of "Currency" in contradistinction to "Sterling", or those born in the Mother Country. The name was originally given by a facetious paymaster of the 73rd Regiment quartered here—the pound currency being at that time inferior to the pound sterling. Our currency lads and lasses are a fine interesting race, and do honor to the country whence they originated. The name is sufficient passport to esteem with all the well-informed and right-feeling portion of our population; but it is most laughable to see the capers which some of our drunken old sterling madonnas will occasionally cut over their currency adversaries in a quarrel. It is then "You saucy baggage, how dare you set up your currency crest at me! I am sterling, and that I'll let you know!"

'To all acquainted with the open manly simplicity of character displayed by this part of our population, its members are the theme of universal praise; and, indeed, what more can be said in their favor than that they are little tainted with the vices so prominent amongst their parents? Drunkenness is almost unknown with them, and honesty proverbial; the few of them that have been convicted having acted under the bad auspices of their parents or relatives . . .

'The men of low rank are fonder of binding themselves to trades or going to sea than passing into the employ of the settlers as regular farm servants. This, no doubt, arises partly from their unwillingness to mix with the convicts so universally employed on farms, partly from a sense of pride; for, owing to convicts being hitherto almost the sole agricultural labourers, they naturally look upon that vocation as degrading, in the same manner as white men in slave colonies regard work of any kind, seeing that none but slaves do work . . .

'The young girls are of a mild-tempered, modest disposition, possessing much simplicity of character; and, like all children of Nature, credulous and easily led into error. The lower classes are anxious to get into respectable service from a laudable wish to be independent and escape from the tutelage of their often profligate parents; and, like the "braw" Scotch lasses, love to display their pretty curly locks, tucked up with tortoiseshell combs, and slip-shod or barefooted trip it merrily along . . . They do not commonly appear to class chastity as the very first of virtues, which circumstance arises partly from their never being tutored by their parents so to consider it, but more especially from never perceiving its violation to retard marriage. They are all fond of frolicking in the water, and those living near the sea can usually swim and dive like water-hens'.

In July, 1839, the Australian statesman, Sir Henry Parkes, came to Australia with his wife as assisted immigrants. Parkes was then aged 24 years and full of optimism, but he was soon disillusioned as witness this letter he addressed to his family in Birmingham a few months later. Nevertheless, his subsequent career should be a source of inspiration to immigrants of today.

Sydney, New South Wales,
1st May, 1840.

My dear Friends,

This is a duty I ought to have performed months ago and you will think harshly of me for this neglect. I have no excuse to plead save that I was unwilling to sadden your hearts with a tale of misery. I waited from day to day, and from month to month, hoping to be able to give a cheering account of this country, but it is a sad one I write at last. I have been disappointed in all my expectations of Australia, except as to its wickedness, for it is far more wicked than I had conceived it possible for any place to be, or than it is possible for me to describe to you in England.

We came to anchor in Sydney Harbour on the morning of the 25th July, 1839, my dear wife having been safely delivered of a little girl on the 23rd., when we were a few hours sailing clear of Bass's Straits. Our little blue-eyed ocean-child gets on very well and is now of course more than nine months old. I thank God for this blessing.

"He moves in a mysterious way,
    His wonders to perform".

or this sweet one of ours could never have out-lived the many ills which every day of its short life hath brought. I had but two or three shillings when we got to Sydney, and the first news that came on board was that a four pound loaf of bread was selling at half-a-crown! and every thing was proportionably dear.

There was no place for the emigrants to go till such time as they could engage with masters, or otherwise provide for themselves. When they left the ship they had to do as best they could. Poor Clarinda, in her weak state, had no one to do the least thing for her—not even dress her baby or make her bed, and in a few days she was obliged to go ashore with her new-born infant in her arms and to walk a mile across the town of Sydney to the miserable place I had been able to provide her as a home, which was a little low, dirty, unfurnished room without a fireplace, at 5/- per week rent. When she sat down overwhelmed with fatigue, on a box which I had brought from the ship, within those wretched walls, I had but 3d. in the world, and no employment.

For more than two weeks I kept beating about Sydney for work, during which time I sold one thing and another from our little stock for support. At length, being completely starved out, I engaged as a common labourer with Sir John Jamison, Knt., to go about 36 miles up the country. Sir John agreed to give me £25 for the year, with a ration and a half of food. This amounted to weekly:

10½ lbs. Beef—sometimes unfit to eat.
10½ lbs. Rice—of the worst imaginable quality.
 6¾ lbs. Flour—half made up of ground rice.
 2   lbs. Sugar—good-tasted brown.
 ¼ lb. Tea—inferior.
 ¼ lb. Soap—not enough to wash our hands.
 2   figs Tobacco—useless to me.

This was what we had to live upon and not a leaf of vegetable or a drop of milk beyond this. For the first four months we had no bed other than a sheet of bark off a Box-tree, and an old door laid on two cross pieces of wood, covered with a few articles of clothing. The hut appointed for us to live in was a very poor one. The morning sunshine, the noon-tide shower, and the white moon-light of midnight gushed in upon us alike. You will perhaps think had you been us you would have had a few vegetables at any rate, for you would have made a bit of garden and cultivated them for yourselves, but you would have done no such thing. The slave-masters of New South Wales require their servants to work for them from sunrise to sunset, and will not allow them to have gardens lest they should steal a half hour's time to work them.

I should mention that our boxes coming up from Sydney on Sir John's dray were broken open and almost every thing worth carrying away was stolen. I made this at first a very grave complaint, but only got laughed at and told that it was nothing.

During the time I was at Sir John's, I was employed mostly in a vineyard consisting of sixteen acres of land. I was there during the vintage season, and left just as we had done wine making in the middle of last February, having been in his service six months. The estate of Sir John is named "Regentville", and is situated about three miles from the small town of Penrith on the Nepean River, and about the same distance from the first range of Blue Mountains.

I have been in Sydney now better than two months, part of which time I have worked in a large Ironmongery Store in George Street, which was founded by Macdonald, who now resides, I believe, at Birmingham. I am at the present time at work for Messrs. Russell Bros., Engineers and Brass Founders, Queen's Place, George Street. I get 5/- per day finishing brass work. Good brass founders get 7/6 and 8/- per day.

I think I could get plenty of light turning to do and a good price for it if I had a lathe, which I will try to get before long. I am very unsettled, at present, on account of my health. This brass business does not suit me at all. I have not been able to do any work for the past week. I think I shall be obliged to go into the country again.

As soon as I get settled I will write and arrange with you how you may forward me a few things which I should like to get from England, as soon as I can remit the money. In the mean time be pleased to write immediately and let us know how all our dear friends have fared since we left home—I hope well. Address: Mr. Henry Parkes, Ivory Turner, at the General Post Office, Sydney. You must pay the land postage or the letters will not be sent with the mails on board ship. Send me some Newspapers, write on the wrappers of them "Newspapers Only". Send me all the news you can.

I have seen but one person since I have been in the Colony of whom I had any knowledge of in England. That was Sampson Moore who was transported about two years ago from Mosely Street, Birmingham. I met him in Sydney. He was then staying in the hands of the Government at the New Prison at Woolloomooloo. For the encouragement of any at home who think of emigrating, I ought to add that I have not seen one single individual who came out with me in the *Strathfieldsaye,* but most heartily wishes himself back at home. Mr. Isaac Aaron, who lived in Deritend is practising in this Colony as a Surgeon at Raymond Terrace on the River Hunter.

With my heart's prayer for you all,
I remain,
H. PARKES.

A P.S. follows giving wages in Sydney for good workmen, house rentals, further greetings and messages including 'Tell John Barney I would advise him by no means to come to this Colony'. The letter was addressed to his sister Sarah to whom he again wrote a few months later but in a more optimistic tone, having secured a position in the Customs House.

The Rocks, a small district of high land lying west of Sydney Cove and at present in the process of being developed into one of the city's most impressive areas, was settled very early in the history of Sydney. Because of its central situation it soon became the haunt of men of the sea and those who battened on them. Grog shops and shanties, licensed and unlicensed, abounded among the primitive dwellings lining the lanes and byways. Alexander Harris (*Settlers and Convicts,* 1847) described The Rocks as being 'St. Giles and Wapping in one' where in Cockroach Lane, Frog Hollow and elsewhere in the area congregated all the worst characters of the colony.

An appallingly vivid picture of the district was penned in a report which appeared in *The Sydney Morning Herald* of October 7, 1858. Written by a correspondent, the article was the first of a series entitled 'The Social Cesspools of Sydney'. The writer (he was William Stanley Jevons, who was to become a famous economist at Manchester University) referred to 'several so-called streets' of The Rocks 'with their small and comparatively ancient stone cottages, so unevenly and irregularly built that the doorstep of one residence sometimes approximates to the eaves of another. Where the erections are of wood, their dilapidated, filthy appearance is all the more striking. The interiors of these abodes usually consist of two dirty, bare rusty-coloured chambers, of small size and yet too large for the scanty articles which constitute the furniture'.

The correspondent said that the streets were 'the habitual resorts of vicious and filthy humanity, from which the malaria of crime and disease necessarily arises and taints the social atmosphere', adding, 'Of the inhabitants I will not say much; in some cases misfortune may have led, and may keep them here; but in others, the unhappy, debauched, wicked face, the slovenly, dirtily clothed persons, tell too plain a tale. A young intoxicated woman with a black eye and bruised forehead, and a shrivelled old dame with a face of yellow-brown colour sitting in a poverty-stricken room—they were striking pictures of the first and last stages of vice'.

In further articles on 'The Social Cesspools of Sydney' the writer describes the 'flowing stream of filth' with the system of open drains running through the streets, dammed by the walls of houses, and often spilling into their backyards. 'Nowhere is there a more complete abandonment of all the requirements of health and decency' he sums up.

Shocking as we may view such conditions, it is well to remember that many parts of the London of the 1850s were equally as bad. As for drainage—well, by a coincidence the day following the printing of the article on that subject, *The Sydney Morning Herald* published a dispatch, datelined London, Friday, July 2, 1858, 'From our City Correspondent.' Among the reports is the following: 'The entire sewage of London having been thrust into the Thames, the river has this year been a mass of putrid corruption and the stench has been frightful, producing fever and cholera in several instances. The Law Courts and Parliament have at times been almost deserted by reason of the smell'.

Perhaps the best known part of The Rocks was Essex

Street. Here was located 'Gallows Hill' where gathered large crowds to watch hangings in the old jail near George Street. As the years passed, The Rocks district quietened down and parts of it became highly respectable. Notable people born there included two Prime Ministers (Sir Edmund Barton and Sir George Reid) and the distinguished orator and statesman William Bede Dalley. The artist Conrad Martens was another famous resident, and both Joseph Conrad and Jack London took up temporary abode there when they visited Sydney. Here at the 'Ship and Mermaid' and other hostelries Conrad and London heard many a salty yarn, some of which they used in their famous stories.

A notorious gang known as 'The Rocks Push' operated in Sydney up to the 1890s, but at the turn of the century much of The Rocks was resumed by the Government and its warren of slum houses was demolished. Further resumption and demolitions occurred with the building of the Sydney Harbour Bridge, and the dwindling district and its all but vanished atmosphere became merely a decorous residential one. The tremendous transformation that will be taking place with the giant development scheme could scarcely have been foreseen by the early critics when they expressed themselves of the state of affairs at The Rocks.

* * *

Gambling is an inherent part of the Australian make-up. No matter how you look at it, Two-up is an Australian tradition and all States, with the exception of South Australia, conduct lotteries under government management or control. Here in Australia government-controlled lotteries flourish to an extent greater than in any other country, in proportion to population, the revenues from ticket sales amounting to more than twenty million pounds a year. Religious, moral and economic arguments against government-sponsored lotteries are frequently expressed by church leaders and others, but without discernible effect on public or parliamentary opinion in the five States in which the lotteries flourish.

Two-up, a game born of the monotony and boredom of colonizing—an escape from the tiresome job of digging postholes or mine shafts—is undoubtedly an offshoot of the old English game of pitch and toss, which came to Australia with the First Fleet. This simple form of amusement failed to satisfy the gambling instinct of the first new Australians; hours of play resulted in very little money changing hands. So they boldly tossed two coins at once and bet to their limit on whether they would fall heads or tails. Over the next one hundred years the game developed into one unique to this country with complicated rules and a strange jargon that is as Australian as a didjeridoo and as sudden in its outcome as the crack of a drover's whip.

An economic disaster caused Australia's first lottery. The colony of New South Wales was hit by a great drought from 1838 that continued into the next decade and began to undermine the financial structure. Shop business dwindled, warehouses were unable to unload their stocks, and soon fortunes were being swept away as Banks and companies crashed.

The Bank of Australia was among those that went insolvent and the liquidators in Sydney announced that they would raffle its assets—lands and businesses held as securities on dishonoured mortgages to the value of more than five million pounds. So was held the first public lottery in Australia, and it was a sensational event. Sydney went lottery crazy, and during the four days of the drawing in January, 1849, crowds packing the City Theatre in Market Street were at fever pitch. Shops and streets were all but deserted, but the lottery ticket sellers did a great business. Although lottery tickets were £4 each—a large sum in those days—there was scarcely a person who did not have at least a share, no matter how small, in a ticket.

Now that Sydney had succumbed to the lottery craze the Bank of Australia advertised that it would hold a further lottery to dispose of some remaining assets. Leading citizens began to wonder if private lotteries would solve their own financial difficulties. Always one to make the most of an opportunity, the astute lawyer and politician William Charles Wentworth decided to inaugurate a lottery for his own benefit. He realised that this would be a golden chance to dispose of some of the vast properties he held which because of the economic crash had dropped alarmingly in value on the current market.

Accordingly, it was announced by 'a group of public-spirited citizens' that they had 'persuaded' Mr. Wentworth to dispose of his properties—'a large mass, such as it is believed no other single individual in the Colony is possessed of'—so that he might be able to devote his full time to the affairs of his country. (Much of Wentworth's properties had been acquired in lieu of payment from clients affected by the great depression.) It was planned to sell 12,000 tickets at £5 each with a prize for every ticket.

The 'prize for every ticket' was a sure-fire attraction and the general public was enthusiastic. Some of the more sober-minded citizens had misgivings and one newspaper ridiculed Wentworth's scheme, beginning with 'When a Patriot consents to be trotted out like a horse for so amazing a price, we think ourselves entitled to walk round him at our leisure. And we shall do so . . .' Among its many criticisms the newspaper editorial asserted that the price of a ticket could purchase more land than most were likely to win in the lottery.

Despite adverse criticism applications for tickets poured in for the two lotteries being advertised side by side— William Charles Wentworth's and the Bank of Australia's. Then the Government began to have doubts about the outcome of such lotteries and so the Attorney-General called on Mr. Wentworth and threatened to prosecute him; at the same time the liquidators of the Bank of Australia were also warned to discontinue their intentions of holding another lottery. Both lotteries were thereupon abandoned. Thirty-two years later when George Adams established his sweepstake at Sydney, it was a technical evasion of the law against lotteries, the prize-awards being decided not entirely by the blind luck of the draw, but by a contingent sporting event.

In 1893 the Bank of Van Diemen's Land Ltd., Hobart, went into liquidation. Remembering how the Bank of Australia in Sydney had successfully disposed of most of its assets when in a similar plight, the Tasmanian bank decided to do likewise. The bank directors put the assets into a lottery—300,000 tickets at £1 each—the first prize being the bank building itself and the land on which it was built at Miller's Corner, Hobart. Second prize was an hotel, and all the other prizes consisted of bank properties in various places. Tickets were fully taken up.

Today, the policy adopted by Tasmanian Lotteries is to offer bigger prizes than lotteries on the mainland. In 1955 a sweep was organized on the Melbourne Cup, offering as first prize Hadley's Orient Hotel at Hobart, which was officially valued by the Tasmanian State Treasury at £200,000. The gigantic scale of this lottery made it probably the biggest in the world.

CHAPTER 14

The Emancipists

A GOODLY-SIZED volume of *Who's Who* could have been compiled from names in the ranks of the emancipated, so prominent were many of them in the affairs of the infant colony of New South Wales. Worthy men and women were intermingled with a few rascals and opportunists—in short, mixed types found in every community both then and now. A number of former participants in the Irish Rebellion of 1798 were to be found in emancipist society. They included the Irish Protestant clergyman Henry Fulton, Joseph Holt, Michael Dwyer (a leader in the guerilla warfare), and three Catholic priests: James Harold, James Dixon and Peter O'Neil.

Because his confession to having been implicated in the rebellion was obtained 'under pressure', Henry Fulton was privileged to transport himself for life[1]. He sailed for Australia in the *Minerva* on August 24, 1799, but was granted a conditional pardon the year after his arrival. Henry Fulton worked for seven years as a chaplain on Norfolk Island before he was fully pardoned, when he resumed his duties in New South Wales. Later he became a member of the civil court, and Governor Macquarie made him a magistrate. Governors Bligh and Macquarie favourably regarded the Reverend Henry Fulton, and he loyally supported Bligh on the deposition of that Governor. He was a chaplain in the Penrith district at the time of his death in 1840.

Joseph Holt, a land-holder of Wexford who had led a detachment of yeomanry during the Irish Rebellion, was banished, and sailed to this country in the same ship as the Rev. Henry Fulton in 1799. The following year he became manager of William Cox's farm in Sydney, but was arrested soon afterwards on suspicion of being implicated in a conspiracy

1 Bishop of Derry to Archbishop of Canterbury.

of Irish prisoners. Holt was released but wrongly imprisoned again in 1804 and exiled to Norfolk Island for alleged complicity in what became known as the Castle Hill Rising, a mutiny of some of the Irish convicts. Given a conditional pardon, he was entrusted with important work in Hobart and Sydney, and when he was granted a full pardon in 1811 he returned to Ireland the following year. Joseph Holt died in poverty in Dublin in 1826 regretting he had ever left New South Wales. His *Memoirs* were published twelve years after his death.

In 1821 the emancipists claimed that their adult population numbered 7,506 and their aggregate wealth £1,123,600 sterling, as against £597,464 sterling of the free settlers. Considering that the colony was but thirty-three years old, the ex-convicts had certainly accumulated riches to a degree impossible in the Old Country. Truly the penal settlement had been established in a land of limitless opportunity.

Here are a few of the many emancipists who have gained a permanent niche in Australia's history:

SIMEON LORD

Simeon Lord was one of the most powerful and richest of the colonists, a magistrate, the owner of immense land holdings around Sydney as well as large properties in country areas and Tasmania. His palatial town house, a three-storey mansion in Macquarie Place, was built of sandstone with fittings of polished cedar, and was probably the finest in the colony. Only seventeen years after his arrival in Sydney Town as a convict Simeon Lord had amassed his fortune through astute and shrewd (if sometimes a little shady) business deals and trading. One of his biggest commercial successes was the establishment of a woollen mill at Botany where he manufactured cloth and blankets; he owned another mill at Orange, and he produced various articles not hitherto manufactured in the colony. His greatest enemy was the wealthy John Macarthur, leader of the aristocratic squatters, and the two men hated and fought each other for thirty years. The only truce in their life-long feud was when they combined to oust Governor Bligh in the Rum Rebellion.

Lord was nineteen when he arrived in this country, having been convicted at Manchester, on 22nd April, 1790, for stealing '100 yards of muslin valued at sixpence and 100 yards of calico valued at fourpence'—values which were 'controlled' in order to bring them below the dangerous level of one shilling. This sum at the time could carry the penalty of hanging. For a brief period Lord was assigned to an officer of the New South Wales Corps before he was transferred to an ex-convict woman named Bligh who had established a prosperous bakery in The Rocks area of Sydney. Lord was a general handyman and bread carter for Mrs. Bligh 'and was something more beside' (whatever that may imply), according to one historian. At any rate it was Mrs. Bligh who financed the first of his many successful ventures when he set himself up as an auctioneer. By 1806 he had become rich through trade in sealskins, sheepskins, timber, coal, wheat and the products of the South Sea Islands, and was registered as a shipowner.

Governor Macquarie accepted Lord as one of his 'most meritorious men'. He entered into contracts with him for the supply of grain from abroad, appointed him to the magistracy, and admitted him to the society of Government House. Lord had by now become one of the three leading merchants of Sydney. It is said that on one occasion in court when Lord in his role of magistrate abused a woman who was facing a charge, she answered him: 'You are a great man now, Mr. Lord, but remember you came to the colony in the same situation as I did'.

Lord's elevation to the Bench of the Supreme Court, as well as the countenance given him by Macquarie, was regarded with disfavour in England and was debated in Parliament. Henry Bennet, M.P., complained of Lord that 'as soon as he came down from the seat of justice he got into a cart and sold blankets; one of the most indecent acts that could possibly be exhibited'. Bigge, the inquiry commissioner[2], had little or no admiration for Lord and brought

---

2 J. T. Bigge came to the colony to inquire into Macquarie's administration.

pressure to bear on Macquarie to obtain Lord's resignation from the Commission of the Peace.

More than a dozen streets in Sydney are named after Simeon Lord, whose descendants are legion. He married a convict girl and by her had six sons and two daughters; there were about 40 grandchildren at the time of his death in 1840. Men who are leading figures in financial institutions and Australia's pastoral industry are among the direct descendants.

SIR HENRY BROWN HAYES

The ranks of the emancipists included at least one member of the order of knighthood—Sir Henry Brown Hayes—the original occupant of the estate which he called Vaucluse and which is now incorporated in the Sydney suburb of that name. Though he was a convict, Sir Henry insisted on living as a gentleman. Naturally, it was bound to cause trouble with some of his fellow free citizens, but Sir Henry was an Irishman, and the Irish are never afraid of opposition. His story is an intriguing one.

A former military captain and sheriff, Sir Henry Brown Hayes was a widower and a well known man-about-town living in Cork; a dashing figure who sported the very latest Savile Row clothes and the finest of accessories. He was thirty-five years old, and had received a knighthood seven years earlier when there came to Cork on a visit the attractive Mary Pike, heiress to a fortune left by her father, a famous banker.

Whether it was her face or her fortune that attracted Sir Henry is not clear, but certainly it was Miss Pike who sent the Irish knight to Botany Bay on a sentence of life imprisonment. He did his utmost to persuade the young lady to marry him but she was firm in her refusal. Having failed to win her by fair means he plotted what the prosecuting counsel was later to describe as 'a foul deed'. Hayes forcibly abducted her to his country manor, *Vernon Mount*, where with a man garbed as a clergyman and some of his friends as witnesses he tried to induce Mary Pike to go through a 'wedding' ceremony. Again he failed; the unyielding Mary flung the ring at her would-be husband and refused to sign any paper. Sir Henry, realising that Miss Pike was a lady who knew her own mind and nothing would make her change, wisely released his prisoner who lost no time in returning to her friends and issuing a warrant for his arrest.

So it was that in August, 1801, Sir Henry Brown Hayes was brought to trial; the judges sentenced him to death but later commuted the sentence to transportation for life to Botany Bay. As it happened, his transportation was a pleasure cruise compared with the rigours suffered by ordinary prisoners. His first move on learning what ship was to carry him to his exile was to pay the captain £500, a handsome gift which not surprisingly earned him extraordinary privileges on the voyage. Free officials travelling on the same ship—the convict transport *Atlas*—were incensed to find Hayes monopolizing most of the limited space and available comforts. Thomas Jamison, on his way to take up the surgeon-generalship of the colony, was so furious that he left the vessel at Rio de Janeiro and took passage in the *Hercules*. The latter reached Sydney ten days ahead of the *Atlas*, and scarcely had his ship docked when Jamison instituted an action against Sir Henry for 'threatening and improper conduct'.

When Hayes reached Sydney he was immediately sentenced by the magistrates to six months' imprisonment as the result of the surgeon-general's charge, but apart from serving that term he was not kept in confinement for long. Though a convict according to the strict letter of the law, the fact of him being a man of rank and open purse, and one who had done nothing more than attempt to trick an heiress into marriage caused him to be allowed to live as a captured officer on parole. Nevertheless, his activities in the affairs of the colony involved him so much that the authorities were forced to restrain him. He applied to hold a meeting to form a Masonic lodge, and although his application was refused he held the meeting just the same. Reference to this episode is contained on the front page of the *Sydney Gazette* of May 22, 1803. Under the heading GENERAL ORDERS, it reads:

'Henry Brown Hayes, a convict, having some time past applied to His Excellency the Governor for permission to hold a Free Mason's Lodge, preside thereat and initiate new members, which permission His Excellency judged proper to forbid officially through the Judge Advocate, notwithstanding which it appears from the Magistrate's proceedings of yesterday, that he, Henry Brown Hayes, in contempt of that injunction, was found with several others assembled as Free Masons. In consequence of which, His Excellency has judged it expedient to order the said Henry Brown Hayes to hard labour at the New Settlement to be formed at Van Diemen's Land; and it is to be clearly understood by all and every His Majesty's subjects resident or stationed in this Colony, that any similar meetings without the express approbation of the Governor, will be punished to the utmost rigour of the law, and as the local circumstances of this Colony and its inhabitants may require.

> '*By Command, &c., W. N. Chapman, Sec.*
> *Government House, May 17, 1803.*'

It may be added that Sir Henry was never sent to Van Diemen's Land. The charge that he was concerned in the convict insurrection of March, 1804, at Castle Hill earned him a month's imprisonment on Norfolk Island, and he was confined in the Newcastle coalmines for several months because of open sympathy with the deposed Governor Bligh. When Bligh was vindicated he saw to it that Sir Henry received a full pardon. A resident of Sydney Town in his time has left on record this impression of him:

'Sir Henry Brown Hayes is a witty gentleman, though rather impetuous, and fond of entertaining. He has established himself comfortably in a district near Sydney which he has called Vaucluse. He named it thus because it reminded him of the beautiful valley in France of that name, which he had often visited. He is apparently resigned to a life in exile, but he is continually obsessed by a sense of injustice. This obsession tends to crop up in his conversation at all times and causes embarrassment to his guests who do not like to be reminded that Sir Henry is, after all, a convict. On one festive occasion at his home he suddenly squashed a fly and exclaimed: "That's how I'd like to crush John Philpot Curran!" Some of the women guests blushed at this reference to the eminent Crown Prosecutor who was the means of Sir Henry being convicted'.

After receiving his pardon in 1812, Hayes returned to Ireland. Before leaving he leased his home, Vaucluse House, to an old friend, Samuel Breakwell, who sold it to Captain John Piper. It was bought later by William Charles Wentworth who enlarged it and by his deeds filled its rooms with history. Hayes's connection with Vaucluse House is best remembered by his attempt to banish snakes from the precincts of the home by surrounding it with turf brought from Ireland, and therefore endowed by St. Patrick with anti-snake properties. When the turf arrived he waited for the next St. Patrick's Day and, on that auspicious occasion, had a trench six feet wide and two feet deep dug right round the house. A gang of convicts, Irish to a man, shovelled the blessed soil into it. The bill of lading for the imported soil was in existence late in the last century, and when excavations were necessary in recent years in the grounds of Vaucluse House, workmen unearthed part of the trench of Irish sods.

When Sir Henry Brown Hayes died at the age of seventy, a Cork newspaper concluded the obituary notice as follows: 'The gracious and gentlemanly manner he possessed made him endeared to every person who had the honour of his acquaintance'. Miss Pike, no doubt, excepted.

FRANCIS HOWARD GREENWAY

Francis Howard Greenway, Australia's first architect, came to this country in 1814 to expiate the crime of forging an endorsement on a building contract. Trained as a painter and architect, he had practised in Bath, and his arrival solved a problem for Governor Macquarie whose pleas for the services of an architect had been ignored by the Home authorities. Government building contractors of early Colonial Sydney were making easy fortunes, with no architect to supervise their work. There were no proper plans other than rough sketches drawn by government officials, and no estimates, and so the contractors combined to use poor materials and to tender scandalously high prices.

Greenway reached Sydney in the convict transport *General Hewitt,* and was at once employed by Macquarie in reporting on government buildings then nearing completion. Greenway was aghast at the state of affairs he found in connection with some of them. He told Macquarie that 'most of the public buildings, from bad construction, bad materials, ignorance and wilfulness of the workmen have very early fallen into decay and ruin'. He reported, too, on Sydney in general that 'the town will not be safe from fire until proper regulations are made . . . with designs of regular streets . . . and suffering no capricious variation'. He insisted on proper building laws and wanted all refuse of the townspeople to be drained into a common sewer.

In March, 1816, Macquarie appointed Greenway Civil Architect at a salary of three shillings a day, and while in receipt of this princely remuneration he planned some architectural gems, a few of which grace New South Wales today. They comprise St. James' Church at Sydney, the Convict Barracks (now used as a court-house), the Government House stable walls (which enclose the N.S.W. Conservatorium of Music), St. Luke's Church and the former hospital at Liverpool and the church of St. Matthew at Windsor. In most cases these buildings have been altered and added to by less skilled hands, but they still retain their beauty of architecture. A noted architect said of Greenway's work that 'with the barest means and economy in execution he produced architecture that has never been excelled in any land, giving the simplest structures a monumental scale, beautiful proportions and delightfully textured walls'.

Greenway begged the Governor to allow him to replan the whole of Sydney as a handsome model city with 'as grand a square as any in Europe'. The British Government, horrified at such extravagant ideas for what was to them but a penal outpost, promptly ruled out the architect's grandiose scheme. The building contractors were not the only ones hostile to supervision by Greenway; many of the free settlers resented the appointment of a convict to the important—if ill-paid—post of Colonial Architect. Moreover, Governor Macquarie was often a trial to the troubled architect. The Governor fancied himself as quite an authority on architecture and frequently altered Greenway's plans, so much so that Greenway had to protest to His Excellency. On one occasion he wrote to the Governor that it was distressing for him as a professional man to have to conform to his sketches of a building that 'has no claim to classical proportion or character'.

But Greenway had to face his greatest set-back and eventual decline with the advent of Commissioner J. T. Bigge who came to the colony to inquire into the administration of Macquarie. As with other emancipists, Bigge treated Greenway with scant respect. He forced him to alter plans, abandon others, and held that his style of work was 'too grand for an infant colony'. As the result of many disagreements with his superiors Greenway was dismissed, and the old contract system of building was re-introduced.

Although Greenway had been given a full pardon, there was no scope privately for an architect, and he suffered neglect and poverty. He tried unsuccessfully to obtain payments from the Government for architect's fees concerning various buildings, but his claims were rejected on the grounds that such work had been done while he was still a convict. His death in 1837 passed almost unnoticed; the exact date and cause of his death and the place of his burial are unknown. Greenway's wife had died five years earlier, and there were several children. One of Greenway's sons was afterwards well known as a clergyman in New South Wales.

MOLLY MORGAN

Much of the site of the city of Maitland, New South Wales, was at one time known as Molly Morgan's Plains. The fabulous Molly Morgan was a ratcatcher's daughter, twice convicted in England and sentenced to transportation to Australia, who died a wealthy woman with the local title of Queen of the Hunter Valley.

Born in Shropshire, Molly Jones was a pert, rosy-cheeked country lass when she married William Morgan, a wheelwright and carpenter, to whom she bore two children. She already was the mother of a child whose father, a well-to-do farmer, refused to marry her. To provide a little extra for the struggling family Molly succumbed to the temptation of stealing a few shillings' worth of hempen yarn, but her pilfering was detected and she was brought to trial and sentenced to transportation for five years.

Although she sailed for Botany Bay aboard the hell-ship *Neptune,* one of the vessels of the second fleet, Molly Morgan's good looks and easy virtue gained her many privileges and she endured little of the sufferings of other convicts. The officers found her attractive enough to provide her with extra rations and accommodation separate from the others. Even on arrival in New South Wales, the merry-eyed Molly saw her prison guards vying for her favours. It was not long before she was transferred to Parramatta and practically a free agent.

Three years after her arrival in the colony her husband, William Morgan, came with a new batch of prisoners transported also for stealing. Because of his good behaviour William was allowed to live with Molly, but he soon raised objections to his wife's flirtations with soldier friends. This was a handicap to the saucy wench and she decided to escape from the environment. Offering herself as mistress to Captain Locke of the whaler *Resolution* on condition that he take her back to England, the proposition was accepted. Locke found her so pleasing on the voyage that when his vessel arrived in England he offered her a permanent home on the *Resolution* as his companion. She declined and, after collecting her children from relatives who were looking after them, moved to Plymouth where she worked as a seamstress.

A prosperous brassfounder, Thomas Mares, proposed marriage to Molly, and although she had a husband working out his sentence in far-off Australia, she accepted. The 'marriage' was happy enough in its early stages, but following a quarrel Molly set fire to Mares' home and it was burned to the ground. Infuriated, Mares called in the police but the firebug had escaped to London. There she was caught and at the Croydon Quarter Sessions on October 10, 1803, was sentenced for the second time to transportation.

Fortunately for this lucky prisoner she still had good looks and a much admired figure so it is not surprising that in a short time she was the holder of a ticket-of-leave. She was fortunate, too, inasmuch that her rightful husband, William Morgan, on his release bothered her not at all but quietly disappeared from the scene. Molly, with the help of a 'protector', a member of the Parramatta garrison, acquired a few acres of land and some horses and cattle.

Prosperity came quickly. Her herds increased so rapidly that when puzzled officials investigated they found that many of the beasts were ones reported as stolen. Her freedom lost, the incorrigible Molly was sent to the Coal River convict camp. Once again her charms came to her rescue and, although now in her forties, she dazzled the military men in this womanless penal outpost, who treated her more like a guest than a prisoner. Another ticket-of-leave was soon forthcoming.

Molly was more than ever determined to amass riches, and do so quickly, but in a more or less legitimate enterprise. She decided, too, to remain in the Hunter River district where she had many men friends and admirers. Cedar-getters and settlers were moving into the fertile valley and Molly Morgan opened a rough grog shanty for the thirsty newcomers as well as the troops and coal miners in the newly discovered coalfields. The slab and bark shanty was well patronised, and about 1818 Molly opened an inn at Wallis Plains on the present site of Maitland. Her hostelry—the Angel Inn—stood opposite where is now the post-office and proved a magnet for the increasing population of the prosperous district. The buxom but still fascinating proprietress was the toast of the town. She amassed riches enough to be considered one of the wealthiest in the colony, and the district in which she lived, Wallis Plains, was much better known as Molly Morgan's Plains. Here she bought up large blocks of river frontage land and all the area that now comprises the main business centre of West Maitland.

Governor Brisbane so admired her success that he gave her the use of convict gangs to clear her land. Despite the fact that she was still legally married, she went through another 'marriage' ceremony with Thomas Hunt, a handsome young garrison soldier. Yet even in her sixties she remained sprightly and shapely and always a shrewd and clever businesswoman. Her business acumen did not harden a 'heart of gold' and she was renowned and respected for great kindness and humanity. On one occasion she made a wild nonstop ride to Sydney in a last minute attempt to plead with the Governor to spare the lives of some convicts sentenced to be executed for stealing fruit from an orchard. Her intercession saved them from the gallows. Little wonder that Molly Morgan was revered as the 'Queen of the Hunter Valley'. Before her death in 1833 she had subdivided her land and sold it in small blocks for business premises and residential sites, and had retired to her 200-acre farm at Anvil Creek, near Greta.

SOLOMON WISEMAN

The man who gave his name to Wiseman's Ferry, New South Wales, must have possessed some remarkable qualities. Solomon Wiseman came to the colony in 1806 after his conviction for stealing '704 pounds weight of Brazil wood' on the Thames, where he was employed as a lighterman. For that offence he was sentenced to death, later commuted to transportation.

After earning a ticket-of-leave, Wiseman settled on the Hawkesbury at this spot, long before the road was made. Four years later he obtained a licence for an inn, and when in 1826 work was begun on the new road from Sydney to the Hunter River he established a ferry where the road crossed the Hawkesbury on his property. For many years the ferry was used for transporting across the river large numbers of stock bound for the Sydney market.

The Rev. T. Atkins, who ministered to churches on the Hawkesbury, wrote of Wiseman in 1859 as a man of considerable natural ability but 'deeply read in the corruption of human nature'. Be that as it may, Wiseman was known locally as 'The King of the Hawkesbury'. There is a cave on the northern side of the river bearing the name of the

Judgment Cave, where—in keeping with his name—Solomon Wiseman is supposed to have sat and delivered judgment. There are about twenty houses today in the village of Wiseman's Ferry—or Wiseman's, as it is called locally. The homestead of the King of the Hawkesbury is now an hotel. The original portion of this fine old building has walls about three feet thick. He built his house—as most pioneers did—with a view to its lasting. It is two-storeyed with magnificent circular steps leading up to the verandah.

But he was an extraordinary person. To quote Judge Therry's reminiscences: 'He was quite a character—a person of great natural shrewdness and of considerable prosperity. He was very hospitable, walking round with a telescope under his arm so that he could see his visitors coming from afar. At the time I visited Solomon Wiseman (it was about 1830) he was surrounded by all the substantial comforts that a farmer with a like income enjoys in England. His household consisted of his wife, an amiable Englishwoman, and four sons, remarkably fine youths varying from thirteen to eighteen years of age. Being inquisitive as to how these youths were brought up, and how he provided for their education, I found his notions on the subject of education curious and original. He said education was a point on which he was not particular; and asked me what was the good of it? adding the observation that the acquisition of wealth was the main lesson of life. I told him that, amongst other things, "Education aided in the acquirement of property". "Oh", he said, "my views are quite different. I have four sons, and I say to Richard, 'There's a herd of cattle for you', and to Tom, 'There's a flock of sheep—look after them'. So, in five years' time they become rich, each the owner of large herds of cattle and flocks of sheep. Now that's what I call education, for by it they acquire means to live". It was idle to reason with mine host on the advantage of the observance of duties, and the restraints that education was designed to confer. He looked only to the one point of material gain, and discarded every other consideration. In literary attainments of any kind Solomon

147

was sadly deficient, and took unmerciful liberties with the English language and English history . . .'

DR. WILLIAM REDFERN

An emancipist who played a full part in the life of the Sydney community was Dr. William Redfern. The crime for which he was transported to these shores had been a sympathetic attitude to participants in the *Nore* mutiny when he was a surgeon's mate, and still in his 'teens, aboard the *Standard*. He was accused of having encouraged the crew of his ship to take part in the mutiny by urging them to be 'more among themselves'. Court-martialled, he was sentenced to death but, because of his youth, the sentence was commuted to life imprisonment. Redfern's implication in the mutiny was out of humanitarian motives; he wanted to see improvements of the very bad conditions of the navy of those days.

Right from the day of his arrival in the colony he was employed as a prison doctor, so great was the shortage of medical men. In 1802, just one year after his landing, he was granted conditional emancipation, and the following year received a free pardon. In 1808, Lieut-Governor Colonel Foveaux appointed him assistant-surgeon on the colonial medical staff. Since he was unable to produce evidence of his medical qualifications, he submitted himself to a professional examination before a special tribunal comprising the principal surgeon of the colony, and the surgeon and assistant surgeon of the New South Wales Corps. Redfern passed the examination and was given a certificate—the first medical diploma in Australia.

Dr. Redfern's medical skill made him the most popular doctor in the colony; he became physician to both Governor Bligh and Governor Macquarie, and his services were sought by people in all classes of society from leading families down to the paupers he attended without fee. Redfern established an extensive private practice, and when Governor Macquarie built the new Sydney Hospital (the southern wing of which still exists as the Housing Commission building) he was placed in charge.

Hand-written page of 'The Melbourne Advertiser'

Lost.

the 17 Decr inst between
[...]borne and the End of
[...] Salt water River A Lady
[...]dome gold Ear Drop
[...]ver will bring the lost
[...]ring to the office of this
[...] shall be handsomely rewarded Decr 27th 1837.

Wanted,

good serviceable Cartman
in [...] Apply at this
Office Decr 27 [...]

For Sale.

[...] for Breeding or for the
[...]chers. 20 Choice Pigs
[...]ly At Faulkners Hotel.

On Sale.

[...] Head of Prime Cattle
[...] are adopted for Breed
[...] [chain?] Stock, a part are
[...] for the Supply dairy
used by the Butcher. For
[...]ence enquire of S R Fawkner

Also

[...] to 30 good useful horses
[...]ater part of these useful
[...] are quiet Saddle Horses
[...] will carry a Lady, enquire
[...] the office of this paper

Notice

[...] 100 to 2000 ft of good timber
[...] first 24000 at 29 [...] 1000
[...]ndow Sills of Sydney
[...]ne and large size [...]

2000 5 ft paling for Sale at
12/ per Hundred, they are of
V.D Land manufacture have
are ready for delivery, orders
on V.D Land will be taken
in payment of the above
Timber and Stone by.
Jno P. Fawkner

Port Phillip Packet

This fine fast Sailing cutter
will be Kept as a Regular
Trader between this Port
and Launceston, carries
from 30 to 40 Bales of Wool
and is confidently expected
to arrive at this Port on
the 10th inst. for particulars
Enquire of Capt Ackers
January the 1st 1838

Wanted by the Commercial
World at Williams Town
and Melbourne, About 40
Beacons good Sea Tree Stakes
would answer to mark the
Channel from the outer An-
chorage to this Town, who
ever will perform this
Service Shall be entitled to
the Public Thanks

A quantity of [...] saw sup-
er New Zealand Pine in
Log, and Flooring Boards
Apply to Mr Horatio Cooper
or Mr Hugh Mc Lean
Williams River.

Batman.

John Batman
(From an old print.)

Redfern had a rather brusque manner and, refusing to toady to anyone, made enemies with those who thought he should be a little humble and ever conscious of his former 'felony'. He had a bitter opponent in Commissioner Bigge, who asserted that Redfern had been transported for 'the most foul and unnatural conspiracy that ever disgraced the page of English history' and that he displayed 'an irritability, or rather a violence of temper, both towards his inferiors and superiors'.

Redfern expected in 1818 to succeed D'Arcy Wentworth as principal surgeon, and Macquarie recommended his appointment to the London authorities, describing him as 'a man of very eminent talents and an excellent scholar and possessing universal knowledge'. Nevertheless, Redfern was passed over and the appointment was given to James Bowman. Registering 'severe mortifying disappointment that my most sanguine hopes and best prospects in life are thus utterly blasted', Redfern resigned his commission as assistant surgeon. This was a victory for Commissioner Bigge, who made no efforts to hide his personal enmity towards Redfern. When Macquarie made Redfern a magistrate for the colony Bigge vigorously opposed the appointment, and the Governor was ordered to remove him from office. Macquarie's policy of rehabilitating emancipists had no greater opponent than the Commissioner.

Wishing to obtain relief from their disabilities as citizens, New South Wales emancipists sent Redfern and Edward Eagar to England in 1821 to present a petition to the king. The delegation was successful, and the position of the emancipists was improved by a new parliamentary act in 1823. While in England, Redfern's health broke down and when he returned to Australia he relinquished his medical practice and devoted the rest of his life to agricultural development. He was granted 2620 acres of land near Minto and he acquired large areas in Bathurst, Cowra and the Port Phillip district. Redfern's town estate covered much of the ground of the suburb that now bears his name. One of the first directors of the Bank of New South Wales, Redfern was actively associated with benevolent and phi-

lanthropic societies and took a keen part in welfare work
for the aborigines. He died in Edinburgh in 1833, during
a second visit to Britain.

MARGARET CATCHPOLE

There is some doubt as to the exact year that Margaret
Catchpole came to Australia. Henry Fulton, a former rector
of Windsor and Richmond, says that she was aboard the
transport *Nile,* which arrived in December, 1801, and *The
Australian Encyclopaedia* has accepted that date.

Margaret Catchpole was born in Framlingham near Ipswich, Suffolk, in 1762. She gained local fame in her native
English village when, as a young girl, she rode bareback
one stormy night to fetch a doctor some miles distant for
the wife of one of the villagers. On another occasion she
jumped fully dressed into a river to save the life of a
drowning child. There are variations of her romantic association with some of the men who followed, along the picturesque coastline, the illegal but popular practice of smuggling. One of these men was a sailor-smuggler named Will
Laud.

At the age of thirty-five Margaret Catchpole took a horse
from the stables of her employer, where she worked as a
domestic, and, dressed in male attire, rode to London, a
distance of seventy miles, in approximately eight hours—
no mean achievement. Why she did this is not clear; her
action may have been caused by a desire to meet Laud. On
her arrival she tried to sell the horse, but was arrested and
sentenced to death; soon afterwards the sentence was commuted to imprisonment for seven years.

She had served about two years in a jail at Ipswich when,
by an odd coincidence, Will Laud was imprisoned in the
same jail for having smuggled goods in his possession.
Margaret promptly arranged for his release by payment of
his fine, and he in turn arranged for her to escape, which
she did by effecting a remarkable climb (with the aid of
a clothes-line) over a wall 22 feet high. Her lover kept her
in hiding, but the soldiers found her whereabouts and
came to arrest her. Will Laud, in attempting to shield her,

was killed, and once more she was sentenced to death; again the sentence was commuted, this time to transportation to New South Wales for life.

And so we find Margaret Catchpole in Australia. Because of the shortage of domestics she was not sent to the Female Factory at Parramatta but was assigned as cook and laundress to the Commissary Palmer and his family living at Woolloomooloo. Strangely enough she never married—and this in a community where women were at a premium. Credence is thus given to the story that she had sworn to remain faithful to the memory of her lover, Will Laud. Certain it seems that one aspirant for her hand was the brilliant young botanist, George Cayley, sent to Australia as a plant-collector by Sir Joseph Banks.

'I wonder', the descendant of an early settler remarked in a reminiscent mood, 'if any of the present generation of Australians know how the very early settlers of Sydney interpreted the musical notes of the butcher-bird? My grandfather used to tell many tales about Margaret Catchpole. One was that so many men asked her to marry them that even the butcher-birds began to mock them. If you listen to one of these birds, especially in the early morning in autumn—it is then that the butcher-bird sings his sweetest songs—it requires no stretch of imagination to hear him say: "Pretty Margie Catchpole, won't you marry me?" My children are so sure that this is what the butcher-birds say that they always call them "Pretty Margie Catchpoles".'

In her middle-age she worked as a nurse and midwife in the Hawkesbury district; some of Australia's most noted pioneers were assisted into this world by the very capable hands of this worthy woman. When the terrible floods of 1806 devastated the Hawkesbury flats she was a gallant figure in heroic rescue work. She made her home at Richmond Hill (near the junction of the Grose and Hawkesbury rivers), and it was there that she sustained a fatal illness through going in bad weather to the help of a neighbour in distress. Her death occurred on 13th May, 1819, five years after she had received her pardon.

The Mitchell Library, Sydney, possesses a number of

letters Margaret Catchpole sent to relatives and friends in
England. Like most people in her circumstances at the
time, she had received no education other than the little
she had acquired herself. In a letter she wrote in 1803 she
was apparently referring to George Cayley when she stated
'i have at this time a man that keeps me compeney and
would marrey me if i lik, but i am not for marring, he is
a gardner, he com out as a Botnes . . .'. She mentions in a
letter to her uncle and aunt her work as a midwife and names
several of the families she attended, adding, 'It is a wonderful Countrey for to have children in, very old women have
them that never had non Before'.

'i am well Beloved amonkst my Betters', she says in
another letter, and refers to being of 'a good spirit'. In a
letter dated 8th October, 1806, Margaret mentions that
she walked 50 miles (she was then aged 44) to collect a
parcel sent to her from England. Further evidence of her
hardiness is shown when a year later she wrote proudly
that she was 'not at a lors in no part of the world' and
added that she was then 'as suppel as ever'.

Today you can see the little slab cottage on a hill at
Richmond where Margaret Catchpole spent the last years
of her life, but though she lies buried somewhere in the
cemetery of St. Peter's Church, Richmond, her grave is unknown.

ANDREW THOMPSON

'It is the interposition of Providence to save the Colony
from utter ruin, for never was there a more artful or greater
knave'. So said Captain John Macarthur, thankfully, on
hearing of the death of Andrew Thompson on October 22,
1810. Yet Governor Macquarie mourned the passing of
his 'good and most lamented, departed friend' and had a
long eulogistic epitaph engraved on Thompson's tombstone in the cemetery adjoining St. Matthew's Church,
Windsor. Moreover, the Governor named Thompson
Square, Windsor, in his honour. Enemies of the deceased
asserted that Macquarie's 'most sincere and affectionate
esteem' for Andrew Thompson was allied to the fact that
the late emancipist had left one-fourth of his reputed

£25,000 estate (a goodly sum in those days) to His Excellency.

Knave or not, Andrew Thompson deserves due recognition for his multitudinous pioneering undertakings. Macquarie described him as the founder of Green Hills, now Windsor, and was pleased to invite him to Government House—the man who had been successively and successfully convict, constable, convict-superintendent, farmer, shipbuilder, bridge-builder, brewer, publican, illicit distiller, flood hero, inventor, smuggler and chief magistrate. Macarthur's hatred of Thompson stemmed from the latter's gate-crashing of the rum traffic, which clashed with his own interests and those of the rum monopolists of the New South Wales Corps. Nor did the illicit distilling which Thompson is believed to have operated endear him to other rum racketeers.

Thompson was sentenced to transportation in 1792 at the age of seventeen. Although *The Australian Encyclopaedia* states that his conviction was for house-breaking and burglary, some historians claim that he was sentenced for setting fire to a haystack. At any rate he quickly won the favours of his overseers and was made a constable at Toongabbie. Within five years he acquired land in the Hawkesbury River district and received a full pardon. The enterprising emancipist built a bridge at Green Hills and was permitted to charge a toll on it. It was also at Green Hills where he established a brewery (later to become the Windsor hospital) and opened a public house. Earlier he had been made superintendent of convict gangs in the Hawkesbury district, and in that capacity had earned a reputation of being a stern taskmaster and disciplinarian. It is said that he quelled an incipient uprising of one of the gangs by knocking out the ringleaders with his bare fists.

As a shipowner, Thompson traded with his vessels as far as New Zealand. In 1809 he received as a grant an island in Pitt Water[3] which he named Scotland Island, so honouring his Scottish parentage, and there he engaged in ship-

3 Now known as Pittwater.

building and erected large salt works for extracting salt from sea-water. At the launching of one of his ships, the *Geordy*, the *Sydney Gazette* described the vessel as 'one of the finest ever built in the colony'. It seems, however, that his most profitable venture on Scotland Island was an illicit distillery—certainly he was fined £100 in 1807 for illicit distilling, although the fine was later remitted.

During disastrous floods on the Hawkesbury in 1806 and 1809 Andrew Thompson was responsible for rescuing more than one hundred people, and, in so doing, seriously undermined his health. Although highly regarded by the three Governors of his time—King, Bligh and Macquarie—and although the possessor of riches, broad acres, a town house in the present Macquarie Street, and now a self-educated man of wide knowledge, he was spurned by the die-hards. Fellow guests at Governor Macquarie's dinner parties, including the Rev. Samuel Marsden, resented the ex-convict's presence and snubbed him openly. The Rev. Samuel Marsden was such an incorrigible 'exclusionist' and possessed such a peculiar Christian outlook that he refused to act as roads commissioner with Thompson, saying that it ill became his cloth to consort with a former convict. When Macquarie appointed Thompson Chief Magistrate for the Hawkesbury, other magistrates refused to sit on the Bench with him. Their 'indignity' was of short duration, for Thompson died shortly after the appointment.

In a *Sydney Gazette* of December, 1804, there appears a notice requesting the return of various volumes including books of poems by Burns and Milton which had been 'borrowed from the house of Mr. Andrew Thompson at the Green Hills, Hawkesbury', and 'from forgetfulnes' had not been returned. It was earnestly requested that residents who had any of the books in their possession should kindly 'return the interlopers' to their owner. This tactful advertisement is the first public reference to the existence of a private library in the colony.

MARY REIBEY

The name of Australia's first businesswoman is commemorated in a thoroughfare in Sydney called Reibey Lane, which runs between Pitt Street and Macquarie Place. A pitiful convict girl at thirteen, Mary Reibey (her maiden name was Haydock) became the richest lady in the land. She was transported to New South Wales in 1790 for stealing a ride on the village squire's most treasured cob; her 'crime' was probably the result of a youthful prank and a love of horses together with an absence of parental control. Her parents were dead and she lived with a grandmother.

Aboard the convict ship *Royal Admiral* the young girl was battened down with screaming, cursing, convict women, the scrapings of London's gutters and brothels crowded together for the very long voyage to Sydney Cove. Mary's youthful eyes witnessed degrading sights no child of thirteen should have seen when the sailors came down into the hold to take their pick of the women. A compassionate ship's officer removed the terrified girl from the iniquity of the hold and assigned her to help a wardress with her work.

In Sydney Mary worked as a nurse-maid in the household of Major Francis Grose where she was highly regarded, but no one imagined that she would become the most important colonial woman of her day. In 1794, when she was seventeen, Mary married Thomas Reibey, who had been an officer in the *Britannia*[4]. After her marriage she lived on a farm in the Hawkesbury district owned by her husband, and there her first child, a son, was born. Although happy enough, Thomas Reibey was a sailor at heart, and restless ashore, and Mary wondered if there was a way to hold him to her yet enabling him to have the seafaring life he loved without sailing around the world.

The young wife was gifted with remarkable business ability and she saw a solution for her problem. She sensed that there was a fortune to be made in coastal shipping trade, especially with the sealing industry in Bass Strait. Heeding Mary's advice, Thomas engaged in local shipping and within nine years was the owner of three schooners.

---

4 Several publications state that he was an officer on the transport that brought Mary Reibey to Australia—the *Royal Admiral*.

He next entered into partnership with Edward Wills and purchased another schooner for trading. Mary was happy, too, with his appointment as a pilot in Port Jackson, and under her guidance he acquired warehouses and property in The Rocks area and at Macquarie Place. Although she was now the mother of three sons and four daughters, Mary Reibey became increasingly business-minded. She not only controlled the selling of merchandise that was brought to Sydney as a result of her husband's trading ships, but she also supervised a wine and spirit business for him.

At first Sydney society cruelly snubbed Mrs. Reibey, dismissing her as a 'government girl', not allowing her children to mix with their own, and never including her in their social functions. Soon, they realised that she and her husband were a power to be reckoned with and respected. The Reibeys' ever-expanding prosperity and importance could no longer be ignored and they were honoured with invitations to Government House by succeeding Governors. Society ladies now humbled themselves and fawned for invitations to the Reibeys' dances and soirees.

Mary's happiness suffered a grievous blow when her husband died at the age of forty-two. She then took over the entire management of the merchandising and the supervision of farms on the Hawkesbury. Governor Macquarie presented her with a grant of 200 acres at Airds, which she called Toad Hill Farm. In 1812 she opened a new warehouse in George Street, Sydney, and extended her shipping activities with the purchase of two more vessels, the *John Palmer* and the brig *Governor Macquarie*. Commercial groups and government officials sought her astute advice and guidance, and it was on her premises that the Bank of New South Wales was founded in 1817.

By now Mary was a forthright personality who demanded respect and got it. She had lost her faith in human nature so young that she was quite equal to the pitfalls of business life in Sydney of those days. One story told about her illustrates this admirably: that she refused to pay a bill for repairs to her watch until she had counted the jewels to make sure the watchmaker had not robbed her. Her cariage was well known to the Hyde Park gatekeepers and here were stories of the way she used to defy the park egulations and gallop her horses while the attendants pretended not to see her. She was proud of her carriage, for which she had imported white Arab horses.

She set up her eldest son, Thomas, who had been trading in Tasmania for several years, on a property near Hadspen in northern Tasmania. 'Entally House', the home itself on the property, furnished in period style and complete with lodge, was acquired in 1950 by the Tasmanian Government as a splendid example of colonial architecture. Mary Reibey also established another son, James, on a property near Hobart. In 1820 she took two of her daughters—Celia and Penelope Ann—to England to further their education and to attend to some of her overseas business interests. She visited her Lancashire village, where her wealth and fine bearing created a deal of excitement. Relatives who had spurned her now received her with affection and vied for her favours. Mary had no desire to stay in the country that had sent her away as a convict and at the end of the last term of her daughters' finishing school she and the girls sailed for home—a trip made in conditions of luxury.

After her return from England Mary Reibey paid a visit to 'Entally' to be present at the christening of her first grandson, also called Thomas. She arrived in Launceston in her own ship, berthed at Reibey's wharf (owned by her son), and drove to 'Entally House' in her London carriage drawn by handsomely mounted and groomed horses. The country around her son's property was virgin bushland, but leading to the fine freestone home with its square towers slotted with musket holes as a protection against bushrangers was a drive of noble English trees. Fine stables, barns, kennels and servants' quarters could be seen, and in the background were flocks of sheep and dairy herds.

As Mary stepped from her carriage her daughter-in-law, Richardia, with the baby Thomas in her arms, greeted her. It is recorded that at the christening next day by the Rev. John Youl, Mary, holding her first grandchild in her arms prior to the ceremony, said to the assembled company: 'No one must point a finger of scorn at him. He will be a leader among men. He will have the best teachers and go to Oxford or Cambridge and embrace the wonderful traditions of England'.

Mary Reibey's business affairs continued to prosper, and she made more investments in town property in Sydney. On 2nd June, 1828, the following paragraph appeared in the *Sydney Gazette:* 'Mrs. Reibey, with a perseverence and spirit of enterprize that truly astonishes us, after having erected many elegant and substantial buildings in Macquarie Place . . . and in the centre of George Street, has now turned her attention towards the improvement of Castlereagh Street, where a noble pile of buildings will soon ornament that hitherto neglected part of the capital'.

She was tireless in everything she undertook. She interested herself in charitable organizations and in church work, and also in literature, education, politics, and questions of town planning. Her last years she spent at her home in Newtown, Sydney, where she died on 30th May, 1855, at the age of seventy-eight. She was survived by three daughters and numerous grandchildren.

The young Thomas fulfilled the prophetic utterance of his doting grandmother. He was ordained a minister of the Church of England in 1843—the first clergyman to be ordained in Tasmania—and later was appointed Archdeacon of Launceston. About 1870, as a result of a disagreement with Bishop C. H. Bromby, he resigned his religious office, entered Parliament and eventually became Premier of Tasmania. Being possessed of considerable means he accepted no salary during his thirty years of clerical life, and indeed he donated the land and built his first church and rectory out of his own pocket. It was as late as 1912 that this worthy grandson of a worthy and remarkable woman pioneer died at the age of ninety-one.

CHAPTER 15

The French-Canadian 'Patriotes'

IN 1946 the writer was in the little township of Dapto, in the Illawarra district of New South Wales, and had the pleasure of meeting Mr. James Marceau, who was then in his 89th year. James Marceau was the son of Joseph Marceau, one of the French-Canadian patriots exiled to Australia for participating in the Papineau Rebellion.

Maps of the Sydney area show three little bays in the municipality of Concord commemorating the French-Canadians' exile here—France Bay, Canada Bay and Exile Bay—yet the complete history of these political prisoners in Australia has never been written. Many people are familiar with the story of the Irish convicts; familiar, also, is the history of the 'Scottish Martyrs' who, for sedition, were transported to these shores in 1794. Hunter's Hill, near Sydney, was named by one of them—Thomas Muir—after his father's estate near Glasgow. Little known, however, is the story of the Canadian 'Patriotes' who came to this country in 1840—most of them under sentence of transportation for life.

The Sydney *Shipping News* of February, 1840, contains a paragraph stating that Her Majesty's Storeship *Buffalo* arrived from Quebec, via Hobart Town, with 58 rebel Canadian convicts, having landed 83 other Canadian rebels in Van Diemen's Land. The Sydney batch of convicts were all French-Canadians, and their ranks included two surgeons, two lawyers, merchants, clerks, tradesmen and farmers. Those convicts who were landed at Hobart were all British-Canadians. But both parties were political prisoners who had not taken kindly to British rule in their homeland.

The Canadian Constitution Act passed by the British House of Commons in 1791 conferred the franchise right

159

and a parliament to be elected by the people of both Upper and Lower Canada. The latter was occupied by the French-Canadians while Upper Canada was the home of the British-Canadians. Many of the French-Canadians were anti-British in outlook and the extremist element began forming a movement to oppose actively any form of British rule. Their ultimate aim was the creation of an independent republic with their leader Louis Joseph Papineau—Speaker of the Assembly of Lower Canada for more than twenty years—as the first President.

Many British-Canadians of Upper Canada also wanted an independent nation of their own. They, however, were more forthright than their French neighbours in their denunciation of the Mother country's rule. Led by William Lyon Mackenzie, they protested against the abuse of power by a high-handed autocracy representing the British Government.

Benjamin Wait, one of the leaders of the dissatisfied British-Canadians, afterwards wrote these words: 'Canada complained of the absence of all security for life and property—of taxation without representation—of the destruction of the liberty of the press—of packed juries—of a judiciary entirely dependent upon the Crown—of education for the rich and none for the poor . . .' When he published his book *Letters from Van Diemen's Land*, he began with the quotation from Bacon, 'It is better to fail in striking for so noble a thing as Liberty than not to strike at all; for reform never dies'.

In 1837 small rebellions occurred in both Upper and Lower Canada. The French uprising took place at La Brule, but was suppressed by British troops. A rebellion by the British-Canadians was also suppressed, and in both cases many prisoners were taken and some of the leaders hanged. Desultory skirmishing continued in the woods and forests culminating the following year—1838—in uprisings again in Upper and Lower Canada. The rebels again failed—the British-Canadians being defeated at the battle of Prescott and the French-Canadians at Point Peel Island. Again, many prisoners were taken and some of the more promi-

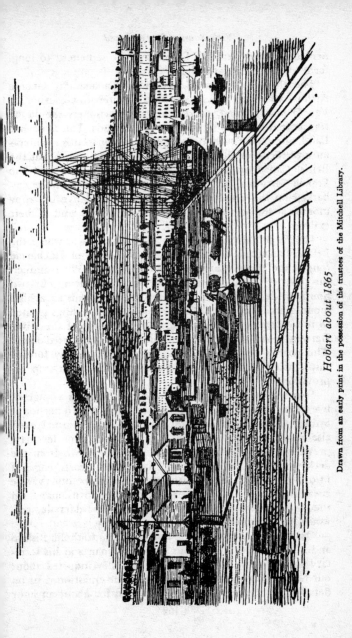

Hobart about 1865

nent of them executed. The others were sentenced to long-term and life imprisonment.

The then Lieutenant-Governor of Canada, Sir George Arthur, who had previously been Lieutenant-Governor of Van Diemen's Land, decreed that the prisoners should be transported to penal settlements in Bermuda, Van Diemen's Land, and New South Wales. Of those sent to this country—most of them for life-imprisonment—it was decided that the British-Canadians were to be landed at Hobart, and the French-Canadians at Sydney. And so the rebels were embarked on the vessel *Buffalo*, there to spend five unhappy months at sea before sighting the shores of the land of their exile.

The *Buffalo* dropped anchor at Hobart Town, where the British-Canadians disembarked. In the diary of Ducharme (one of the French-Canadians) is this extract: 'We examined the town (Hobart) as well as we were able during our two hours on deck. To us it appeared somewhat rustic; a high mountain cuts off all the back country. Its buildings seemed to us fair enough, and the land on both sides of the River Derwent good and level. We noticed well-cultivated fields. The port is very spacious and is visited by many foreign ships, chiefly American and French whalers who stop for provisions'.

Two weeks later Ducharme records: 'After a voyage of five months we entered Port Jackson and came to anchor at Sydney Cove. When we came on deck for our usual exercise we gazed with horror on this land that some few days previously we so ardently desired. Looking down from the deck we saw miserable wretches harnessed to carts, engaged in dragging blocks of stone to public buildings; others were breaking stones; the sight of this brought to us many sad thoughts, for we believed that within a few days we, too, would be employed in exactly the same way.

'On the 27th we received a visit from the Catholic Bishop and a priest. The Bishop was an Englishman and his secretary an Irishman: both spoke French. They inquired about our health, listened to our narratives, and questioned us on details of the voyage, etc. We conversed for about an hour and a half. They told us they would see that no obstacle would be placed in the way of our carrying out our religious duties, and they terminated their kindly visit with general prayers.

'On the 28th the Bishop came back again to see us with his secretary and another priest. We were agreeably surprised at their interest in our misfortunes, and to see that they did not worry about the difficulty and danger of climbing up and down the ladders on the ship's side, and of seeking us out on the lower deck, a dark and uncomfortable place, so as to extend to us their sympathy. At ten o'clock, in the depths of the hold, on an altar built of boxes, Monsignor Polding—for such was the Bishop's name—said Mass. We had decorated the altar with a number of religious images in our possession, and these in addition to those brought by the priests made the altar quite seemly. Doubtless God found it so, for it was a work of the most ardent devotion'.

On leaving the ship the prisoners were sent to a penal settlement called Longbottom, near Cabarita, now part of the municipality of Concord. They were housed in the old barracks or stockade that Governor Phillip had originally established at a point half-way to Parramatta as a resting place for convicts who had to trudge in their heavy nailed boots, and often in irons, along the road to Parramatta.

When the Canadian prisoners arrived at the barracks they were assembled in the yard and addressed by a sergeant in command of the platoon of soldiers there. He pointed to the boundaries they must never cross unless on their way to their daily labour and accompanied by the guards. The penalty for breaking bounds was fifty strokes of the lash. They were warned, too, that punishment by the lash would be inflicted on anyone guilty of insubordination to the guards or to other superiors, or to the breaking of any of the many regulations. One of the latter was absolute silence among the prisoners while in their quarters. Speech was forbidden even during the evenings when they returned from their hard work, and throughout the night.

Each day they were sent out in gangs in the custody of

soldiers and were obliged to work very hard for long hours on roads and buildings. Among the various public works on which they laboured was the building of the Victoria Barracks at Paddington. The stone used in its construction was quarried on the spot, and all of this was done by the French-Canadians. Until recent years a stone cottage was standing in Erskineville Road, Macdonaldtown, which was the work of some of these same prisoners. It had been built for Mr. Joseph Sly and was later purchased by Mr. A. T. Holroyd who was at one time Master in Equity. According to a newspaper of those times, the first wood blocks ever used for the paving of Sydney streets were made and laid by these exiles. They were employed all round the districts of Burwood and Enfield and helped largely in the laying-out and upkeep of many of the properties there.

The rations allowed to the prisoners were little better than those allotted to them on the voyage out. They were given only two meals a day—in the early morning and at mid-day. For the morning meal it was coarse porridge, and at mid-day some meat and poor quality bread. No vegetables were supplied, and never were they given supper or any meal in the evening. Thus, after having laboured the whole day, with only the mid-day break for a poor meal, they returned in the evening worn out with fatigue and hungry, to be locked up for the night without a meal until the following morning. It was during this time that two of the prisoners died. Both were natives of Montreal, married, and each the father of six children.

How were the British-Canadian prisoners faring in Tasmania? Here are some extracts from a booklet entitled *Narrative and Recollections of Van Diemen's Land*. It was written by one of these prisoners—Stephen Wright:

'The overseers whom the superintendent placed in charge of us were men of the worst type—felons and convicts condemned for the most awful crimes that shuddering humanity records. We were harnessed two and two; four men being placed before each cart. We were then marched to work a distance of two miles to the stone quarry where we filled our carts. We were obliged to draw them laden with

Melbourne's first Government House.

Government House, Adelaide, 1837

from fifteen to eighteen hundredweight, and drag them over broken ground a distance of one mile. Rain or shine, wet and dry, over rocks and mud, we never did less than thirteen journeys a day.

'. . . After the first month of toil many of us frequently collapsed in performing the tasks imposed upon us. Night after night have we been dragged to the huts in a state of utter prostration and insensibility. And if we complained that we were not equal to the strain of the labour we were taken before a magistrate (no defence being permitted) and sentenced to seven days solitary confinement for the first offence, twenty-one days for a second offence. The only food allowed during this period was a quarter of a pound of bread per day. This living grave known as solitary confinement was a vault without light and without any room for standing erect. It was two feet wide and six feet long, ventilated with a few tiny crevices in the stone. The filth of these dens of infamy surpasses all description. The blood almost stops circulation while undergoing this inhuman torture. And this we received for the most trivial indiscretion.

'The first time I was incarcerated it was for the following misdemeanour: On returning from work in the midst of a tempest of rain and piercing wind, and being wet to the skin, and seeing a good cheerful fire burning in the kitchen, I committed the awful outrage of warming my shivering limbs. That taste of comfort cost me seven days solitary confinement in the vault with a scrap of bread and some filthy water my only allowance each day.

'. . . After being at this camp for some months we were removed to another one in the interior to prevent any attempted escape. Our men were in a deplorable condition and like so many swine would eat peelings and rubbish thrown from the door of the chief felon who presided over us. At our new camp we were engaged in building the road between Launceston and Hobart Town. The law prevented any person giving us food or tobacco. And if either was found on us the donor was fined and we were subject to twenty-one days solitary confinement'.

View of Perth, 1856

Stephen Wright's *Narrative* is not merely a recital of the prisoners' sufferings. He could appreciate the beauty of nature even in the midst of so many privations, as witness this extract: 'The scenery of the island would require the pen of a poet or the brush of a painter to do anything like justice to it. The trees were covered with a foliage of unusual beauty, and hundreds of feathered warblers from the wild-wood soothed us at our labours; while the mountains rose in forms of grandeur whose tops were lost amid the clouds of heaven. Nature seemed to console us, and I felt for the first time in my life that

> *Man's inhumanity to man*
> *Makes countless thousands mourn.*

Meanwhile in Sydney, as a result of the unceasing intercessions of the clergy, conditions were improved for the prisoners there. They moved to a new home, a sort of barracks they erected for themselves on the Parramatta Road nearly opposite to where is now the entrance to the Burwood Park. Within a year after their arrival they were granted tickets-of-leave. Immediately the released men showed their gratitude by applying themselves to charitable and cultural works to help the community in general. They opened night schools for the illiterate in outlying districts of Sydney. The medical men gave their services free to the poor. The merchants and clerks took clerical jobs in offices and warehouses where their business knowledge was a great asset to their employers.

But five and a half more years were to pass before the exiles were free to return to their homeland. At last came the day when the British Government granted free pardon to every one who had participated in the Papineau rebellion. Sir George Gipps, the Governor of New South Wales, then sent for those under his charge and received them with kindness and courtesy. He informed them that they were free to return to Canada, and that money had been subscribed to pay for the passages of those who desired to do so. All but one wished to return to their homeland.

The Canadians' departure from these shores was a big loss to the community, and it is not surprising that they were sadly missed by the many friends they had made in all walks of life. The man who decided to remain in New South Wales was a bachelor named Joseph Marceau. He became a farmer and settled in Dapto, where he married Mary Barrett. They had nine children, descendants of whom are still in the Dapto district, and these constitute the sole remaining link with the French-Canadian Patriots of the Papineau Rebellion.

It may be added that Papineau was pardoned—the authorities admitting their error in making him an outlaw. A warrant for high treason had been issued against him, and for six years the sum of one thousand pounds had been offered for his apprehension. Though that amount in those days was a fortune, no one betrayed him, despite the fact that he moved about freely. After his pardon he re-entered Parliament, made a visit to France, and died in Montreal at the age of eighty-five.

'Whatever opinion may be held of those who took part in the Rebellion of 1837-38, whether justified or not, there can be no question that we are now enjoying the advantages gained by that struggle'. So commented a member of the Canadian Historical Society in recent years. 'There can be no question', he added, 'either as to the cruel treatment meted out especially in Lower Canada, where houses were burnt and savagery reigned, or to those who were executed, particularly those banished—political prisoners who were treated as felons and herded with the vilest of convicts. We remember that it is difficult sometimes to say what constitutes treason. When successful the leader is a hero, a patriot; when unsuccessful, a rebel and a traitor'.

CHAPTER 16

Black and White

It has been said that Australia was conquered without a single shot being fired. Unfortunately for the original inhabitants of this land, the statement is untrue. From the time of Captain Cook's landing party firing warning shots at the two naked natives who boldly advanced with spears and waddies to defend their rights, until a century later, there were constant clashes between the aborigines and the white newcomers. Most of the early conflicts were matters of reprisal, on one side or the other, between those defending their sacred grounds or their womenfolk and the newcomers objecting to their stock being speared or stolen. The attitude in most cases was that if a black killed a white it was murder, but when whites killed blacks it was 'teaching them a lesson'.

Governor Phillip estimated that at the date of his arrival there were about 1500 natives living in the vicinity of Botany Bay, Broken Bay and Port Jackson. He had strictly prohibited every person in the settlement from molesting the natives or depriving them of their weapons and belongings, but his orders were often ignored even by his own officers. Many of the convicts, too, openly stole native implements or forced their attentions on the young women of the tribes. So began the conflict between the white man and the aborigine. It is not a story to be proud of, this ousting of the aborigine from his hunting grounds, the destruction of a primitive and ingenuous race by degenerate white settlers and their convict servants. A whole way of life was to be trampled underfoot, a whole culture mocked and derided because it belonged to another age, and a whole people required to fit into a mould devised by a foreign and determined invader.

From the day of his first landing in Botany Bay until the

time he left Australia to return to England, Phillip evinced
the keenest interest in the aborigines' mode of living and
psychology. He was disappointed to find that the natives
had no wish to reciprocate interest in the newcomers and
he was at a loss to understand that quality of reserve which
is a common characteristic of the Australian aborigine.
Phillip complained that they deliberately avoided coming
into contact with the white people and questioned whether
this avoidance was due to 'dislike or contempt'.

The Governor was convinced that natural curiosity would
lure the natives to inspect the settlers' preparation of land
for cultivation, the erection of buildings, and the white
man's animals, but the aborigines remained aloof and completely indifferent to the invaders' presence. Despairing
of establishing amicable relations with them by ordinary
means, Phillip decided on the extraordinary plan of seizing
a couple of the men by force and after introducing them
to the ways of civilisation to release them so that they could
tell their people that the white man wanted to be friends
with them.

The scheme was not altogether a success. Two terror-
stricken natives were captured at Manly Cove after a desperate struggle, but one of them effected his escape. The
other was taken to Sydney where he was bathed, shaved,
given a hair cut and clothes, while every effort was made
to reconcile him to his captivity. The native's terror gave
way to astonishment as his captors endeavoured to entertain
him. He soon showed his intelligence by quickly learning
to pronounce the names of things which were taught him,
and he dined, European fashion, at a table next to the
Governor's.

Captain Tench records that 'he ate heartily of fish and
ducks, which he first cooled. Bread and salt meat he smelled
at but did not taste. All our liquors he treated in the same
manner and could drink nothing but water. On being
shown that he was not to wipe his hands on the chair which
he sat upon, he used a towel which was given to him, with
great cleanliness and decency'. Unfortunately, just when this
apt pupil was making such good progress with the English

language, and looked like becoming an emissary between the newcomers and his own people, he contracted a white man's disease, smallpox, and died.

Determined to continue his experiment, Governor Phillip ordered the capture of two more male natives. Lieutenant Bradley of the *Sirius* was dispatched on this 'friendly' mission and succeeded in overpowering two young warriors who bore the names of Bennelong and Colbee. The latter escaped from his captors within a week, despite the fact that he was wearing leg-irons. On the other hand, Bennelong (most historians spell the name thus, but Collins refers to this native as 'Bennillong', whereas Tench prefers 'Baneelon') settled down in his captivity and thoroughly enjoyed his new environment; so much so that when the Governor returned to England he took the native with him. Phillip also took another aboriginal with him, Yemmerrawannie, but this native died in England. Bennelong was introduced to King George III and was lionised by London high society.

Describing this remarkable personality, Tench says he was 'of good stature and stoutly made, with a bold, intrepid countenance . . . his powers of mind were certainly far above mediocre. He acquired knowledge both of our manners and language faster than his predecessor had done. He willingly communicated information; sang, danced and capered; told us all the customs of his country, and all the details of his family economy. Love and war seemed to be his favourite pursuits, in both of which he had suffered severely'.

Bennelong returned from his visit to England attired in London's latest fashion, but his pride in his sartorial elegance was considerably jolted when he beheld his sister hurrying to the boat to greet him wearing only a welcoming smile. In Sydney Bennelong comported himself (according to David Collins) as 'quite the man of consequence' but his latter days were unhappy when he found that he was not wholly acceptable in the white man's world and it was not easy to settle back in his former life among his own people. He was ultimately killed (January, 1813) in a

tribal fight[1]. He is commemorated today in the naming of
Bennelong Point on the eastern part of Sydney Cove—site of
the Opera House building—where he once lived, and his
name is given to a Commonwealth electorate. There are
certain aspects in Bennelong's story that seem to find sympathetic echo in the case of the noted full-blooded aboriginal
artist, the late Albert Namatjira, torn between his tribal laws
in Central Australia and the existing laws of the white man.

Australian history is blemished with treacherous slayings
and maltreatment of its original inhabitants and the counter
attacks by the avenging natives. The 1830s were a bad
period; greatly concerned about the clashes with the aborigines, the Secretary of State in London 'in the most earnest
manner' reminded colonists of the 'solemn nature of the
obligation by which we are bound as men and as Chris-
tians towards that Race . . .' The massacre at Myall Creek
in 1839 is one such instance.

Camped near the Dangars' Myall Creek pastoral holding
in northern New South Wales, near the present town of
Inverell, at that time was a tribe of aborigines who, so it
was said, had been helping themselves to some of the stock
on occasions when they were short of provisions. Twelve
of the station-hands, mostly assigned servants, ruthlessly
herded all the natives—28 in number, of both sexes and all
ages—into a hut, roped together, and there slaughtered them
without mercy. Incensed at the outrage, Governor Sir George
Gipps had eleven suspects arrested and brought to Sydney
to stand their trial for murder. All of them were acquitted,
but seven of them were re-tried before Sir William Burton.
This time all seven were found guilty and, despite many
public protests, were hanged in December, 1838.

The *Sydney Herald*, which sided with the landholders,
protested about white men being hanged for the deaths of
natives, but the *Sydney Monitor* saw the justice of it and
was bitter that only seven of the eleven paid the penalty.
The editorial leader in the *Monitor* of 19th November,
1838, had this to say:

---

1 The *Australian Encyclopaedia*. Some historians claim that he was killed
in a Sydney street brawl.

'The trial of eleven men for the slaughter of a company of Aborigines of both sexes and all ages, from sucking infants to hoary hairs, took place on the 15th inst., when they were *acquitted*.

'From the violent articles published by the Colonial Press during the last months against the black natives, we had been impressed with the belief, that not only had these slaughtered aborigines committed some wanton murders on our stockholders residing in their neighbourhood, but that their slaughter had been perpetrated in retaliation for such murders.

'But in all the evidence given on the trial, our readers will perceive, that the eight-and-twenty persons put to the sword by the eleven stock-keepers are not accused of committing any personal violence whatever, at any time, either on these eleven men, or on their neighbours. The only thing laid to their charge, by the murderers, is, that they had committed a "depredation" on some sheep *once;* and had once "rushed" the cattle in charge of *one* of the prisoners. The nature and extent of the "depredation" on the sheep is not explained. With respect to "rushing" of cattle, our readers lately arrived in the Colony will please to understand, that cattle when much left to themselves, "rush", that is, make off at full gallop to a great distance, and into the glens and passes difficult of access to their keepers, on falling in with either blacks or whites. There is however an exception to this rule as regards such cattle as are inspected once a fortnight or so, by their stock-keepers. On seeing their own keeper they will not "rush" unless his visits have been very few and far between. But if cattle see the *Blacks,* they are apt to rush on all occasions, even cattle that are reckoned to be pretty tame. If therefore the "rushing" of the cattle be in future to be considered as an apology for putting the Blacks to the sword, the whole race must soon be exterminated, inasmuch as they get their living not by staying at home, but by hunting in their native wilds.

'But the company or tribe of Blacks put to the sword by these eleven men, had not only been innocent of all personal violence, but they had become domesticated *among these very men*. One of them (Kilmaister) has been the chief cause of their taking up their residence near his hut, and he himself seems to have formed a friendship for them; for, in the evening on his return from his journeys after his cattle, he was in the habit of playing and dancing with their children. One of the witnesses indeed states that this man always denied being of the party. But the man made no attempt on his trial to prove an *alibi;* and other witnesses swore to him being of the party.

'The Blacks, it appears, were residing near the hut of Kilmaister, in peace and confidence as usual, when a party of men, mounted, and armed with swords and pistols, galloped up to the place. From the manner of the party, the Blacks, who are by no means so deficient in intellect as they are represented in books, perceived danger and ran for safety into the hut. They were taken out, and tied one by one to a long rope, used to catch cattle by the horns. Perceiving their fate, they began to weep and moan. The women, though tied, contrived to carry their infants in a net slung from their shoulders. Being all secured, men and boys, women and girls, and sucklings, one of the horsemen led the way, with the end of the rope attached to himself or horse. The other ten horsemen divided into two parties of five each, five placing themselves on one side of the rope, one behind the other, and five on the other side. The funeral procession then commenced its march, amid the tears and lamentations of the victims. It must bave been a heart-rending sight to see the aged Black, named "Daddy," led to the slaughter, a man of giant-like stature, and probably brave as he was magnificent in his form; the tears rolling down his aged cheeks at the sight of his wife, children, and relatives. The children perhaps scarcely knew their sufferings until the sharp steel had passed through their bodies, and put a speedy end to their troubles.

'Arrived at the place chosen for the catastrophe, the slaughter began. All, however, we can glean from the evidence is, that two shots were fired. The sword it should seem did the rest without noise, except the cries of the victims. Decapitation appears to have been considered the readiest way of despatching them, from the great number of skulls afterwards found.

'After the slaughter, a fire composed of dead trunks of trees, and many yards in extent, was kindled, and the headless bodies and skulls were placed on the pile . . .

'It is not improper that these eleven men should have counsel hired for them. *Three* counsel however was rather a luxurious number. But while three gentlemen, (the *masters* of these men for instance,) might have hired one counsel each *privately,* it is not to the credit of New South Wales that a *general subscription* should have been raised among the magistrates and graziers of Hunter's River, to an amount much larger than even three counsels could demand.

'What was there in this murder of eight-and-twenty poor helpless betrayed men, women and children, that should induce the magistrates and gentlemen of Hunter's River to hire Counsels for the murderers? Do they hire Counsel for other men when tried for murder? . . .

'The verdict of acquittal was *highly popular!* It was with exertion that the Chief Justice could prevent the audience *from cheering*—such was their delight! The aristocracy of the Colony, for once, joined heart and hand with the prison population in expressions of joy at the acquittal of these men.

'We tremble to remain in a country where such feelings and principles prevail . . . For the verdict of Thursday shews, that only let a man or a family be sufficiently *unpopular* with the aristocracy and the prison population of the Colony *conjoined* (in this case), and their murder will pass unheeded. Money, lucre, profit—*these* are thy Gods, O Australia . . . In consequence of these eleven men being visited in prison, and otherwise "comforted and abetted" by the Magistrates and Gentlemen of Hunter's River, not one of them turned King's evidence!'

There was a widespread belief at the time of the trial that the men concerned in the massacre were acting on the orders of others. As already stated, after the acquittal seven of the eleven men were re-tried before another Judge, found guilty and, despite many public protests, were hanged.

It may be mentioned that at an earlier date when Lieutenant Nathaniel Lowe of the 40th Foot Regiment was charged with the murder of an aborigine he was acquitted without even being called to the witness-box. In defending Lowe, his lawyer, Dr. Robert Wardell, asserted that the trial was illegal, pointing out that aborigines were not allies, subjects or enemies of the King of England because they did not have the status of human beings. Killing such creatures, therefore, could scarcely be described as murder. Furthermore, he quoted a distinguished German 'authority' to show that all aborigines were cannibals and that a Christian had every moral right to exterminate such sinners.

Governor Macquarie endeavoured to change the aboriginal way of life to conform to that of white civilization, but his attempts though well meant were pathetically naive. Perhaps he could be described as the originator of the present National Aborigines' Day when he set aside the 28th day of each December for a festival at Parramatta known as the Native Meeting. The *Sydney Gazette* of January 4, 1817, contains a flowery account of the odd proceedings:

'On Saturday last the 28th ult, the town of Parramatta exhibited a novel and very interesting spectacle, by the assembling of the native tribes there, pursuant of the Governor's gracious invitation. At ten in the morning, the market place was thrown open and some gentlemen, who were appointed on the occasion, took the management of the ceremonies. The natives having seated themselves on the ground in a large circle, the chiefs were placed on chairs a little advanced in front, and to the right of their respective tribes. In the centre of the circle thus formed, were placed large tables groaning under the weight of roast beef, potatoes, bread, etc., and a large cask of grog lent its exhilarating aid to promote the general festivity and good humour which so conspicuously shone through the sable visages of this delighted congress.

'The Governor, attended by all the members of the Native Institution, and by several of the magistrates and gentlemen in the neighbourhood, proceeded at half past ten to the meeting, and having entered the circle, passed round the whole of them, inquiring after and making himself acquainted with the several tribes, their respective leaders and residences. His Excellency then assembled the chiefs by themselves and confirmed them in the ranks of chieftains to which their own tribes had exalted them, and conferred upon them badges of distinction; whereon were engraved their names as chiefs, and those of their tribe. He afterwards conferred badges of merit on some individuals in acknowledgment of their steady and loyal conduct in the assistance they rendered the military party, when lately sent out in pursuit of the refractory natives to the west and south of the Nepean River.

'By the time the ceremony was over Mrs. Macquarie arrived and the children belonging to, and under the care of, the Native Institution, fifteen in number, preceded by their teacher, entered the circle, and walked round it; the children appearing very clean, well clothed and happy. The chiefs were then again called together to observe the examination of the children as to their progress in learning and the civilized habits of life. Several of the little ones read; and it was grateful to the bosom of sensibility to trace the degrees of pleasure which the chiefs manifested on this occasion. Some clapped the children on the head; and one in particular, turning round to the Governor with extraordinary emotion, exclaimed, "Governor, that will make a good settler—that's my Picaninny" (meaning his child). And some of the females were observed to shed tears of sympathetic affection at seeing the infant and helpless offspring of their deceased friends, so happily sheltered and protected by British benevolence. The examination being finished, the children returned to the Institution, under the guidance of their venerable tutor; whose assiduity and attention to them merit every commendation.

'The feasting then commenced, and the Governor retired amid the long reiterated acclamations and shouts of his sable and grateful congress'.

Among the native chiefs who were 'honoured' with

'badges of distinction' by early Governors was Bungaree, who died in 1830. Writing to the *Australian Home Companion* in 1859 a contributor recalled this intriguing personality:

'King Bungaree and myself were contemporaries; but there was a vast difference in our ages. When I first knew him he was an old man over sixty, and I was a boy of twelve. Round his neck was suspended, by a brass chain, a brass plate. On this plate, which was shaped like a half moon, were engraven in large letters the words BUNGAREE, KING OF THE BLACKS. On the plate was also engraven the arms of the colony of New South Wales—an emu and a kangaroo.

'His Majesty changed his manners every five years; or rather they were changed with every administration. Bungaree, like many of the aborigines of New South Wales, was an amazing mimic. The action, voice, bearing, attitudes, the walk of any man he could personate with astonishing minuteness. It mattered not whether it was the attorney-general stating a case to the jury, the chief-justice sentencing a criminal to be hanged, a colonel drilling a regiment in the barrack square, a Jew bargaining for old clothes, a drunken sailor resisting the efforts of the police to quiet him—King Bungaree could, in mere dumb show, act the scene to give you a perfect idea of it.

'Now as the Governor for the time being was the first and most important person in the colony, it was from that functionary that King Bungaree took his cue. And, after having seen the Governor a few times and talked to him, Bungaree would adopt his Excellency's manner of speech and bearing to the full extent of his wonderful power.

'When first I knew Bungaree, the Governor of New South Wales was General Darling. Bungaree then walked the streets with his arms folded across his breast, his body erect, his pace slow and measured, with something of a military swagger in it, and the only salute he vouchsafed was a dignified but very slight inclination of his head . . . But when Darling left and Bourke became his successor how very different was the demeanour and the deportment

of King Bungaree! He walked briskly up George Street
with his left hand on his hip and his right arm moving to
and fro, took off his cocked hat periodically in recognition
of salutes (most of them imaginary), and when he neared
the guard-house at the bottom of Church hill he would
raise his right hand in the air and shake it, as a signal to the
sentry *not* to turn out the guard to present arms to him'.

In 1841 Commissioner McDonald was sent to investigate
the robbery of a shepherd's hut at Ramornie, in northern
New South Wales. It was alleged that aborigines had stolen
supplies of flour and sugar. McDonald organised a large
party of border police and station-hands to punish the natives, who were found camped on the banks of the Orara
River. The camp was surrounded and, at a given signal,
it was rushed. Men, women and children were shot down
indiscriminately. It was afterwards discovered that the robbery had not been done by the natives but by a dishonest
hut-keeper.

True, there have been instances of atrocities by the natives,
the worst in Australian history being the massacre of
19 whites—men, women and children—who were taken by
surprise and murdered on 17th October, 1861, at Cullin-
la-ringo station, near Springsure, Queensland. Nevertheless they were minor in numbers compared with the considerable slaughter by the whites. Whenever the natives
were guilty of killings there was invariably a terrible revenge by the settlers. Tribes were almost exterminated in
some areas; in 1865 the Halifax Bay tribe in North Queensland was estimated to number about 500 individuals and
by 1880 it was reduced to 22.

The Perth Gazette and Western Australian Times of 19th
and 26th May, 1865, featured the daily journal of a ferocious, punitive, three-months' expedition against a tribe of
aborigines. This was written by its commander, 'Maitland
Brown, Esq'. The reason for the expedition was the disappearance of three explorers who had left Roebuck Bay in
search of new pastoral land. They had taken with them
four horses and food to last fourteen days, and when they
had been missing for two months it was presumed that they

had been killed by the natives. Maitland Brown headed a search party of eight men including two troopers. Here are some extracts from his published despatches revealing the ruthlessness and mentality of Brown, apart from the unbelievable attitude of readers of the newspaper who expressed no abhorrence of the ferocious measures he took.

The party arrived at Cape Villaret where it was intended to follow the tracks of the missing explorers southward along the coast. Here the troopers rode out and captured five natives of the Roebuck Bay tribe and brought them in for questioning. They made 'vague statements' but confirmed the story that the three white men were dead. 'Two of the captives showed a restlessness and awful dread of their position which goes in my mind to prove that they had assisted in the murder'. (Already, Maitland Brown is judging his captives by mere guesswork.)

Later, while riding near Roebuck sheep-station, a tribe of about forty natives were seen in a thicket of acacia. 'We gave chase at once. I overtook one of them, caught him, and put my gun-strap around his neck, like a noose. Mounting again, I dragged him for some distance towards the edge of the thicket, but he resisted with all his might, as though his death-warrant was sealed. Then my bridle broke, and I had to let him drop, so exhausted from fear and screaming that he stayed alongside my horse, panting for breath, and clutching at the stirrups for support. As I had already choked and frightened him quite enough to compensate for the loss of one nail, I let him go with a laugh'.

On March 27th, the party started overland from Roebuck Bay towards Cape La Touche Treville, and we find the heroic commander writing thus: 'If the natives resist us, I am determined to teach them a lesson. If from any circumstances I imagine them guilty, and can capture them without resistance, I shall put them on board ship, to be dealt with by a magistrate. But I trust that there will be no necessity for capture, and that the guilty natives will either attack us, or resist us in such a manner as will justify us in exterminating them'.

From Roebuck Bay the civilization-spreaders travelled

18 miles on the first day without encountering the enemy, but on the second day they captured three wild natives. Mr. Brown proceeded to 'interrogate' them: 'After pinioning the arms of the three behind their backs, and putting a strap around the neck of each to lead them by, I had them kept apart in order to question them separately'. One of them voiced his protestations so 'I was obliged to convert Mr. Burgess's pocket-handkerchief into a gag for him. This gave him the first taste either he, or his fathers before him, had ever had of a good English bandanna. Despite his strenuous efforts to scream, this proved an effectual nonconductor of sound'.

No information was obtained from the trio so Maitland Brown Esq. and his armed horsemen set out and succeeded in ambushing a tribe of about twenty natives: 'We surrounded and drove them closer together. In a few minutes they threw down their spears, also their kylies and dowaks. Mr. Burgess and myself galloped after a host of lads who, with one man, were scampering over the sandhills. After collecting them together, we brought them to the group in the middle of the plain . . . A majestic-looking fellow (his name was Karimba) appeared over the hill. He stood for a moment, then, instead of running away, walked across the plain towards us. As he came up, we took his spear from him, and put him among the rest.

'As they all had the look of murderers about them, I decided to secure them at once with leather thongs to a long tether-rope. They had not calculated on this, and a murmur of bitter regret at having thrown down their arms, ran through the whole. Karimba resisted, so I split his cheek open with my fist, after which he allowed himself to be tied. We then strung them all to the rope and led them to our camp'. On the journey Karimba collapsed. 'I reproached myself for having tied the rope too tightly around his neck. With a butcher's knife I began to cut the rope. Karimba, feeling the cold steel on his throat, opened one eye. Seeing this, instead of cutting the rope I cut a stick, and switched his carcase with it until life returned'.

Interrogation elicited no useful information from the

captured natives so next day ten were selected for their
'guilty looks' and sent on board the schooner which was
following the coastline to keep in touch with the land expedition. Eventually two other natives were captured, and
these led the commander and his horsemen to the place
where the three missing explorers had been killed in retaliation—according to the natives—for slaughtering some
aborigines. Immediately the two guides were chained together, but, asserted Brown, they attempted to escape so he
had them both shot dead in his presence.

Retribution did not end there. On the return journey
the punitive expedition saw a tribe of about seventy natives—men, women and children—who greeted them 'with
a war-cry. The fighting men, about 25 in number, danced
forward trebly armed, quivering their spears and flourishing their kylies and dowaks' relates Maitland Brown. 'I
galloped through them, and, in passing, shot the man who
had taken the lead in directing the manoeuvres. The report
of my rifle had no effect on them, but, seeing their com-
rade rolling in the dust, with blood gushing freely from
a mortal wound, astonished though it did not daunt them
. . . I fired the remaining barrel of my rifle at three in a
line, and drew my revolver. Williams dashed in and did
good execution. Messrs. Burgess and Francisco also joined,
and the fight went on to the sound of incessant reports of
our arms, the whiz of the kylies and dowaks, the wobbling
of their clumsy spears and the rustling to and fro of the
natives and our horses. In ten minutes all was over. Six
natives remained upon the plain dead or dying, and about
twelve others stand little chance of recovery. The rest retired to the mangroves. The only damage done to our side
was a wound inflicted by a dowak on Williams' mare's
head'.

Magnanimously, the commander pays tribute to the enemy
as a fighter: 'The natives stood their ground with the savage, though not cool pluck of an Englishman. Not one of
the wounded uttered a sound of either fear or pain. Even
after they found they had no chance with us, they dis-

dained to throw down their arms, and resisted savagely to the last'.

The men of the Iron Age had triumphed over the men of the Stone Age. And with the ending of the Battle of Roebuck Bay the noble Maitland Brown Esq. returned in all his glory to receive acclaim and write of his exploits in demonstrating civilization to the heathen savages.

Tasmania's aborigines were never numerous. They were a homogeneous race, quite different in appearance from the mainland natives, having woolly hair, flat noses, wide nostrils, full lips and ears with large lobes. Their faces were very expressive, registering every change of feeling. This primitive but intelligent race did not long survive the impact of white civilization. The skeleton in the Hobart Museum of Truganini, the last of the Tasmanian aborigines, is a sad reminder of the extermination within little more than two generations of a whole community of native people who had lived in Tasmania for thousands of years. A stone implement found near Gladstone was estimated by Professor Edgeworth David to be about 30,000 years old. The British arrived in the island in 1803—in 1876 the Tasmanians no longer existed[1]. It is not a pleasant thought.

The first white settlement was made at Risdon Cove on the River Derwent in September, 1803. Few aborigines were seen, for at that time of the year they were at their hunting-grounds in the central highlands. In May the following year, however, a large party of men, women and children, driving a herd of kangaroos before them, as was their practice in hunting, made an appearance. Without provocation the officer in charge, Lieutenant Moore, gave the order to fire, killing a number of aborigines and wounding others. That was the beginning of what came to be termed 'The Black War'.

According to all reliable authorities the Tasmanian natives were harmless and peaceful people, not likely to have caused trouble had they received decent treatment. Fight-

---

1 At the time of Truganini's death another Tasmanian native was still alive on King Island—a lubra who had been kidnapped and carried there by sealers.

ing weapons were unknown to them. They had no boomerangs, wommeras, spears or canoes, and they had only the crudest of stone implements. Their weapons for obtaining game were merely waddies and pointed sticks, and despite Tasmania's cold climate both sexes usually went naked.

It was but a short time before the aborigines found themselves displaced from their favourite hunting-grounds and their food supply seriously depleted. Most of the kangaroo-hunters and stockmen were convicts, who regarded the natives as sub-human and treated them accordingly. The sealers of Bass Strait, no whit behind the hunters and stockmen, seized aboriginal women whenever the opportunity offered and used them with the utmost brutality. The records of the Aborgines Committee of 1830 are full of accounts of atrocities perpetrated by white men. 'Black women were lured away, babes were murdered and maidens violated . . .'

Lieutenant-Governor Collins did his best to repress 'the murders and abominable cruelties practised upon the natives by the white people'; but the means at his command were inadequate for the purpose. His successors issued proclamation after proclamation condemnatory of the atrocities but they were impotent to restrain the savage propensities of country settlers, liberated convicts, sealers and runaway sailors who were beyond the reach of the law and deaf to the voice of humanity. These shrank from no crime and recoiled from no cruelty. 'The wounded were brained; the infant cast to the flames; the bayonet was driven into the flesh; the social fire round which the natives gathered to slumber became before morning their funeral pyre'[1]. If the women were spared, it was only to become the slaves and concubines of their ferocious captors. Goaded to desperation the aborigines sought revenge but, of course, their waddies and sticks were no match for the muskets and organized might of their opponents. With their age-old fear of the darkness, the natives spent their nights around their

---

1 Hon. Andrew Garran (*Australasia Illustrated*).

watch-fires, and thus exposed themselves to be surprised and butchered as they slept.

In 1830, Governor Arthur attempted by a great drive to have all the natives of the eastern part of the island confined to the south-eastern corner for their own protection. More than 2000 men took part in the 'Black Line', which, after a campaign of seven weeks and at a cost of £35,000, resulted in the capture of only one elderly native and one boy. For the great round-up, the troops caried 1700 pairs of handcuffs and 30,000 rounds of ammunition.

George Augustus Robinson, a Hobart bricklayer whose sympathies had been aroused by the sufferings of the aborigines, was at length given permission to try conciliation. He had shown great tact in managing a native reserve on Bruni Island, in D'Entrecastaux Channel, and the Government agreed to his proposal to bring in the natives single-handed. He went among them unarmed; travelled through the length and breadth of the island; displayed an almost sublime courage in circumstances of extreme peril; and won the confidence and respect of the natives who had been so shockingly treated by other whites. In all, Robinson covered four thousand miles over the wildest parts of the island without shedding one drop of blood, and finally brought almost the whole native population into the sanctuary set aside for them. Unfortunately, exile did not suit these freedom-loving people and their unfortunate race was doomed. The attempt to civilize them was a complete failure, and, sunk in apathy, they soon died.

Truganini, the last of her race resident in Tasmania, had been born soon after the first white settlement there. Her sister Morrina was taken captive when she was a young girl by a party of runaway convicts. Her mother was killed by men of a sealing gang, and her uncle was shot by soldiers. With such tragic recollections for her of white settlement it is remarkable that Truganini did not become a bitter enemy of all white people. But this wonderful woman, despite such fearful treatment of her race, did splendid work in trying to help the Government understand her people.

CHAPTER 17

White Australia

HAVING usurped the aborigines' hunting-grounds and driven them from their primeval tribal country, the newcomers decided henceforth to make this country a White Australia. As evidence of the feeling against the introduction of Asiatic labour, the most important item on the agenda of Melbourne's first Town Council meeting in 1842 was the oddly-worded resolution to 'stop the importation of Cannibals and Coolies'. The previous year the New South Wales Legislative Council also opposed coloured immigration on the grounds that the introduction of such people would make difficult the maintenance of 'a social and political state corresponding with that of the country to which Australia owes its origin'.

Robert Towns, after whom Townsville was named, was one of the first to bring in 'cannibals' to this country. They were South Sea Islanders known by the Polynesian name of 'kanakas' and their introduction was to supply cheap labour for work on the Queensland cotton fields and sugar plantations. Ben Boyd, founder of the ill-fated Boydtown in New South Wales, was another importer of kanakas. In 1847 and the following year he brought in some 140 'boys' to work on his sheep property near Twofold Bay, but the experiment was unsuccessful. Kanakas were also used for pearl-diving in Torres Strait.

The story of the kanakas is a sorry tale of abuse and often tragedy which has largely been forgotten. 'Blackbirding' vessels operated on a wide scale in the Pacific, and between the years 1847 and 1904 approximately 57,000 natives from the Solomon Islands, the New Hebrides, the islands of New Guinea and the Torres Strait were taken from their homes, often in circumstances of brutality, violence and deception. The blackbirders raided villages, cap-

185

tured the islanders at sea in their canoes, or maybe enticed them aboard the luggers with gifts of tobacco and trinkets. They would be battened down in the hold to be sorted out—the old and the very young natives sometimes thrown overboard—on the way to the mainland. In theory, the islanders were engaged of their own free will for a term of three years, 'recruited' by the skippers of luggers and supposedly under 'contract'. Instead, they were brought to this country virtually as slaves.

Commander A. H. Markham, R.N., reporting on blackbirding activities in February, 1872, said that a nefarious system of kidnapping was practised 'to an almost inconceivable extent'. It amounted, he said, to slavery; in many cases, to murder. Even twenty years earlier official circles were made aware of the many abuses in the trade. Earl Grey, the Colonial Secretary, wrote to Governor Fitzroy referring to reports of outrages committed by labour recruiters and expressing the anxious desire of the Government that natives should not be ill-treated by British subjects.

Henry Lewin, one of many blackbirders who scoured the islands for cheap labour and made a fortune out of the infamous business, put the following advertisement in a Brisbane newspaper of April 26, 1867:

'SUGAR PLANTERS, COTTON GROWERS,
AND OTHERS.

Henry Ross Lewin, for many years engaged in trade in the South Sea Islands, and well acquainted with the language and habits of the natives, begs to inform the public that he will be happy to receive orders for the importation of South Sea natives. For the past four years he has been in the employment of Captain Towns, having brought the natives now on Townsville plantation.

Parties favouring Henry Ross Lewin with orders may rely on having the best and most serviceable natives to be had amongst the islands.

TERMS. £7 each'.

(Henry Ross Lewin's claimed knowledge of the habits of

the natives was not sufficient to avoid retribution at their hands; the man-stealer was subsequently put to death by Islanders in the New Hebrides.)

Another disreputable blackbirder was a former medico, Dr. Carl Murray, who was later arrested for ordering the massacre of seventy kanakas on his brig, *Carl*. Dr. Murray's father publicly disowned his notorious son. In a letter to the *Sydney Morning Herald* he said '. . . As regards Dr. Murray, whom I have for years cut off as a disgrace to creed, country and family, your editorial condemnation of that cruel unhappy being I fully endorse. May I add that although opposed to capital punishment on principle, if any of the *Carl* crew murderers ever ascend the gibbet for the seventy kidnapped and cruelly slaughtered poor Polynesians, Dr. Murray should be the first'.

But the former Melbourne medico escaped punishment. Nine of those on board his 256-ton brig were eventually charged with murder, but only two were convicted. Even these were not executed, while Murray himself turned Queen's evidence and so defeated justice.

Most notorious of the blackbirders was William Henry Hayes, better known as 'Bully' Hayes. He also engaged in gun-running and piracy, ranging the Pacific from San Francisco to the China Coast. His career was a much longer one than most of his contemporaries, hence his exploits have become legendary. Hayes was a tall, powerfully-built man endowed with good looks, a full beard giving him a picturesque, swashbuckling appearance. He was always well-dressed and, unlike most of his fellows, was a strict tee-totaller. An American Encyclopaedia has this entry concerning him:

'Born William Henry Hayes. His father was a bargeman on the Mississippi, and young William Henry worked with him until he was about 18, when he ran away to sea taking with him 4,000 dollars belonging to Hayes senior. Married when he was 20, but deserted his wife after a few weeks and went to San Francisco with a second "wife". Here he was caught cheating at cards, and in the brawl that followed one of the gamblers cut off Hayes' ears. Leaving his "wife" Hayes embarked on a career of piracy, outwitting the British, American, French, Spanish, Dutch and German law. By audacious swindling and trickery he got command of various trading vessels which he later sold in many ports to unsuspecting buyers. He looted cargoes, and for many years was engaged in the slave traffic, becoming the most notorious "blackbirder" in the Pacific'.

No mention is made of his Australian activities, which were many and highly colourful. In 1857 Hayes landed in Adelaide, where he met a rich and pretty widow, Amelia Littleton, who fell for his charms. He led her to the altar and, after obtaining considerable money from her, disappeared shortly afterwards. Knowing that the Australian police authorities were on his trail, the buccaneer made for New Zealand where he 'married' Rona Buckingham. Soon afterwards in company with Bully on a voyage to Nelson she disappeared overboard.

A favourite trick of his was to vanish for a few months and spread rumours about the islands that he was dead. Then he would come to light afar off and begin his piracy all over again. The *Sydney Morning Herald* of January 6, 1860, published an article entitled 'The Story of a Scoundrel' in which the author described Hayes as 'one of the greatest rascals that ever went unhung'. Later Bully sent this quaint, sanctimonious letter to the editor protesting that he was not as bad as he had been pictured:

Sir,

In the *Sydney Morning Herald* of January 6, 1860, you have published an article representing myself.

Much as I am pained by the perusal of the libel, I feel some satisfaction in the reflection that I have friends in many places who can, on oath, if necessary, contradict the gravest charges. This fact, coupled with my own conscious innocence, supports me in my trying adversities.

It is easy to string together a pack of lies, or innocent truths worked up into odious fiction, to gratify the morbid tastes of a depraved public.

The article said I would not dare to show my face

in Australia, the Far East and elsewhere. This prediction would be fulfilled if the numerous charges so ruthlessly levelled against me were true. I have nothing to dare. However, I freely confess that had even half those lying tales been true I would not dare to face Australia again, or indeed any of my former scenes.

Yours, etc.,

WILLIAM HENRY HAYES

The old sinner met his death in 1876 while navigating a stolen vessel (he also stole the owner's wife and took her on a Pacific cruise) through the Line Islands. In an argument with his cook, Hayes kicked him severely and—according to the cook—rushed below to get a revolver to finish him off. When he came on deck again the cook was waiting for him at the companion-way with the iron handle of the tiller. He struck hard—so hard that the redoubtable Bully ceased to exist. The cook couldn't believe that he was truly defunct. When careful investigation assured him that such was really the case, he tied the body to a small anchor and committed it to the deep, remarking thankfully, but a little fearfully, 'For sure he's dead this time!'

In 1868 the Queensland Government passed an act to control the recruiting of kanakas for labour in Queensland and to supervise the conditions of their employment. Natives could not be brought to Australia except under licence, and bonds were required of all persons wishing to import labourers and of the masters of recruiting vessels. The fallacy of the Act was shown when the captain of the *Daphne* and his supercargo were charged with having double the number of natives the vessel was licensed to carry. No conviction was obtained and the court held that according to law the natives were not slaves.

Of the thousands of kanakas brought to Queensland for working in the sugar plantations and cotton fields, very many succumbed to tuberculosis, influenza, dysentery and fever. Average age of those islanders who died in this country was the early twenties, but included were boys of sixteen and seventeen, young women and children. No records exist of the numbers of islanders who died aboard the slave ships—victims of the dysentery outbreaks which swept the overcrowded holds.

Missionary influence stirred up considerable agitation to suppress the blackbirders and British pressure was brought to bear on the Queensland Government. The British Navy at one time had five men-o'-war patrolling the Pacific to try to clean up the slave trade. A Royal Commission decided that all native recruiting should cease in 1891, but the following year the order was rescinded on the grounds that no substitute labour was available. The blackbirders were quickly back in the business.

In 1901, when the Commonwealth came into being, the Federal Parliament passed an Act authorizing the deportation of any kanakas found in Australia after 1906. After December of that year about 3600 natives were returned to their island homes. Any who had married here or who had been in Australia for 20 years and wished to remain were allowed to stay. The final chapter of the ugly story had been written. Descendants of kanakas can be found working as fishermen or on cane farms in Queensland and the Tweed River district of New South Wales. Indeed, there are still a very few old kanakas in Australia who in their youth were clubbed into insensibility on island beaches and dragged aboard blackbirding luggers for this atrocious trade.

Turning to 'Coolies' in Australia we find that there was an influx of Chinese into the country as a direct result of the cessation of the transportation of convicts to New South Wales in 1840. As the supply of cheap labour began to dwindle anxious employers brought in labourers from China, a practice that was continued until the discovery of gold in 1851 made the undertaking unprofitable, since the Chinese decamped to the fields almost as soon as they were landed.

Trouble broke out at an early stage on the goldfields of Victoria between the white miners and the swarming Chinese. (An indication of the rapid growth of the Chinese population is revealed by the figures for the 1850s. There were 2341 Chinese in Victoria in 1854; over 30,000 in 1857, and 42,000 in 1858-9.) A disturbance occurred on the Bendigo field in June, 1854, when a public meeting of Europeans decided that 'a general and unanimous rising should take place in the various gullies of Bendigo on 4th July next for the purpose of driving the Chinese population off the Bendigo goldfields'. Prompt action by the authorities prevented serious trouble but it had become obvious that drastic measures must be introduced.

In 1855 an Act designed to restrict Chinese immigration was passed, but the only effect of that legislation was to make the masters of incoming vessels unload their unwanted human cargoes in adjoining colonies, whence they very soon made their way into Victoria. Many Chinese were dumped on the jetty at the South Australian port of Robe, from where they were overlanded like cattle in the charge of self-appointed drovers who offered to put them on the track. The Chinese had to pay up to £5 each for this service, but once across the Victorian border they were usually left to fend for themselves—the guides clearing off with their money. Sixteen thousand Chinese came ashore at Robe in the first five months of the immigration restrictions.

At a rising at the Buckland River goldfield in northeastern Victoria, white miners attacked the Chinese camps, burning and destroying property and chasing the occupants into the bush, where several died from exposure before police succeeded in restoring order. Public feeling on the Chinese question was so strong that the ringleaders of the riot were found not guilty at their trial.

The discovery of gold in New South Wales brought thousands of Chinese from other colonies hurrying to the fields with the inevitable clashes with European miners. A large number of Chinese settled on the gold diggings at Tambaroora, where their law-abiding community had its own theatre, stores and joss-houses. Many European diggers resented the presence of the hard-working Orientals, baiting and assaulting them, cutting their dams, destroying their sluices and wrecking their homes. The rallying cry of these hoodlums was the parody:

Rule Britannia, Britannia rules
the waves,
No more Chinamen shall enter
New South Wales.

Official records of the Lambing Flat riots—diggers versus Chinese—in New South Wales treat the affray rather lightly. In the records it would not appear to have been very serious—mostly one of sticks and stones, a few broken bones and plenty of Chinese pigtails cut off. But it was far from that. It was a harsh, sordid demonstration of wild cruelty and unrestrained brutality, the true story of which was told by Dean Pownall from the pulpit of St. John's Church, Young, just four years after the riots.

A beautiful church of bluestone, St. John's is not the original one of that name at Young, but it was built on the same site, and it may be said to have been built as the result of the riots. In the 1860s, when Young was known as Lambing Flat, the area was the scene of extensive goldfields. Most of the miners were a mixed European population who resented the influx of Chinese. The latter were diligent workers and they made a success of their gold seeking, but their success only angered the Europeans. Action was decided upon, and about 3000 men, headed by a brass band, held a meeting in which the question was put, 'Is this to be a European diggings or a Mongol territory?'

In his sermon at the opening of the church, Dean Pownall had this to say on the events that followed:

'My dear brethren, we must remember that we are all one in the sight of God—no matter what our race or colour. The Chinese who came to these goldfields had equal right with our own and other nationalities. But they were treated with shocking violence.

'Mob rule is a terrible thing. Those Chinese were seized and thrown down their mine shafts; their pigtails were torn from their scalps[1]; wounded and bleeding Chinese were trampled on and left unconscious where they fell; their

---

1 The trophies were used by bullock-drivers for whip lashes, and for years afterwards many coach-drivers in the district utilized the pigtails for their whips.

tents, together with their humble possessions, were burnt in a giant bon-fire.

'When the police force was outnumbered and compelled to withdraw to Yass the mob released prisoners from the jail and burnt the police station to the ground. There was no authority to say them nay. The mob surged through the township, raiding the hotels and stores. The evening closed on that day of madness with miners, wild with drink, filling the air with hideous din. Please God, never again will this lovely land witness such a calamity'.

Dean Pownall told of the Chinese hiding where they could during the riots and how more than 1200 were saved from starvation by James Robert, a station-owner, who supplied them with food for some weeks, and who was afterwards indemnified by the Government. Continuing his address, which was reported in the *Sydney Morning Herald*, he said:

'It is fitting that we pay tribute to the wonderful work of a former resident of this district, now in England, Captain John Wilkie and his wife were living here during the time of the riots. On the death of her husband, Mrs. Wilkie returned to England. But she did not lose interest in this far-away part of the globe; her heart was sad at the thought that this was a large, restless community, with little respect for God or the laws of the land.

'This good woman set herself the task of interesting church people in the Mother Country, and as a result a missionary was sent here and the necessary money was raised to build this church.

'Out of evil—the evil of the riots—has come good . . .'

* * *

Dame Mary Gilmore's vivid poem, 'Fourteen Men', was inspired by a Lambing Flat lynching incident she witnessed as a child. In notes on the poem, which is included in her book of verses under the same title, she has this to say:

'Very foolishly, we have pretended that Australia had no lynchings in her primitive years . . . In regard to the fourteen Chinamen I saw hanging on the trees, raking memory for exactness I find it was twelve we passed when

going out, but there were two more on our return a day
or two later . . . It was bright moonlight; most of the bodies
had fallen, each one a little heap under its tree. As we drove
on, father suddenly pulled up with a jerk. There were two
more hanging beside us, one in shadow, one in the clear
white light of the moon. My mother said of the latter, "This
one must have been dead before being hanged, as the face
is so peaceful and calm!" There was no distortion. All the
others had been dressed in coarse blue nankeen trousers and
no shirts. This one wore a heavily embroidered, quilted,
pale yellow silk coat, and long, wide, ivory-white trousers.
The little head with the smooth hair was slightly on one
side; the face was enamelled; and the toes of the tiny blue
slippers on the "golden lily" feet just showed as they pointed
straight down to the ground. It was a woman, and she was
very young'.

CHAPTER 18

Spoilers of the Forest

SINCE the beginning of the 19th century, the Hawkesbury, the Hunter, the Illawarra, and the Shoalhaven districts of New South Wales had been continuously exploited for the splendid red cedar (*Cedrela australis*) abounding in the river valleys and the ranges thereabout. By the 1850s this valuable timber was wiped out, but with the discovery of the magnificent red cedar country of the Northern Rivers the spoilers of the forest turned their attention to the rich new field. It must be admitted, however, that the cedar-getters played an important part in the development of New South Wales; they were pioneers of pioneers, preceding the settlers. Though most were wild and irresponsible they had a rough code of law governing their operations, one of which was that no pair of sawyers could claim a right to more trees than they could saw at one pit.

The first export of cedar was made in 1795 when the *Experiment* took some of the wood to India. David Smith, one of the early cedar-getters of the Illawarra district, stated that there was scarcely a valley, ravine or gorge between Bulli and Broughton's Creek that was not dotted with cedar trees. Governor Macquarie during his visit to the district in 1820 had one noble tree measured; it was 100 feet high and 21 feet in circumference 10 feet from the base. (The red cedar, which is indigenous to Australia, reaches a height of about 150 feet.)

In July, 1799, Captain Flinders was sent in the *Norfolk* to examine the coast of New South Wales, north of Sydney, particularly those parts passed by Captain Cook in the night time. He was also on the lookout for some large river which might lead into the heart of Australia. He discovered and named Shoal Bay but was disappointed to find no indication of the big river of which he was in search. Had he made a closer examination of the country which, according to his journal, did not seem to show 'anything of particular interest' he would have glimpsed the wonderful cedar forests that enriched the Northern Rivers districts.

The first white men to see the cedar forests of the North were seven convicts, escapees from the Moreton Bay penal settlement who had wandered for six years with the aborigines. In 1834 one of these convicts, a man named Craig, learned that a free pardon was offered to any convict who discovered some bullocks that had strayed from the settlement at Moreton Bay. Craig found them, delivered them to the authorities, and claimed and got his freedom. He reported that during his walkabouts with the natives he had seen a big river, a mile wide, around which there was much land suited for pasturage, while all about were 'beautiful cedar trees'.

A century ago the Clarence, Richmond, Tweed, Dorrigo and Brunswick rivers of the North had their banks lined with towering trees in areas of hundreds of square miles of great hardwood forest. There was a remarkable variety of timbers, including red cedar, beech, pine, rosewood, teak, bean and cudgery. The forests, too, were the haunts of many species of birds such as the regent birds, satin birds, rifle birds, the wonga and bronzewing pigeons, and the brush turkeys. Especially beautiful was the regent bird with its brilliant orange and black plumage, but even more gorgeous was the rifle bird with its shot plumage of purple and black and scale-like head feathers of green and gold.

Until 1836 Sydney timber merchants were getting all their cedar supplies from the Illawarra and other south coastal areas, but now there was a great demand for the red cedar of the North. Soon after Craig's disclosure of the cedar country of the northern rivers, both cedar-getters and squatters made haste to get there. The squatters could occupy the land on payment of a license fee of £10 a year, and timber-getters were allowed to cut timber on payment of a license of £6 a year for cedar and £2 a year for hardwood. If a man held the two licenses he could cut any timber.

View of Brisbane

The first sawyers to enter the red cedar trade were sent in a schooner from Sydney, and they established their camp on a site which is now part of the town of Maclean. Here was a wonderful growth of red cedar growing right on the river banks. After felling trees, all the cedar-getters had to do was to make cross cuts and roll the logs into the river, float them alongside, and have them hoisted aboard by the schooner's own tackle.

News of the new cedar land spread rapidly and soon bands of sawyers from the Illawarra and other districts made their way north to seek their fortunes, and a fleet of schooners was employed to carry the red cedar to Sydney. The cedar-getters were like prospectors in search of goldfields. In one find after another they discovered abundance of cedar, and a new rush would set in along the Richmond, the Clarence, the Brunswick and the Tweed districts. They always worked in groups and, while working on the river-banks, they found it convenient to live in their whale boats, moving these homes up and down the river as required. Their licenses permitted them to build huts but not to cultivate land or buy any. This was one of the reasons why the sawyers lived a wild, irresponsible existence.

Alexander Harris, an emigrant mechanic who wrote the story of his colonial experiences under the title of *Settlers and Convicts,* relates an experience with the cedar-getters about 1825 when he and his mate were camped near them:

'. . . At first we did not much heed the shouting and shrieking in every tone and dialect, from that of cockney-ism to that of the Irish province which is said to be a mile beyond his Satanic Majesty's residence; but it came nearer and nearer. At last it crossed the river, and came up the road through the bush; and by the time we were out at the fire in our shirts, the whole corps debouched before us. Some wore check shirts, some wore woollen; some were in red ones and some in blue, and some in none at all; some had straw hats, some Scotch caps, some old working skull-caps, some nothing but their own shock heads of hair; some had sticks in their hands, some the ration-bags they had been to get filled; some the axe they had been sharpening at the grindstone and some three or four ribs of salted beef for tomorrow's dinner; some sang, some yelled, some said nothing, but the one unanimous demand was the remainder of our stock of rum.

'All remonstrances were ineffectual. I was told at last that if I did not give it they would take it, and put me on the fire for a back-log. Of course, further parley was useless; I brought it out, and they set to at it with all the pannikins they could muster . . .' Elsewhere he says, 'a more unlicensed and reckless mob . . . prolonging day into night in their carousal until all the liquor was gone, it would be impossible to find anywhere'.

John Henderson (*Excursions and Adventures in New South Wales,* 1851) describes the cedar-getters as in general a strange set; they were mostly desperate ruffians, often ticket-of-leave men or emancipists, and sometimes runaways. 'They labour very hard but they are certainly the most improvident set of men in the world, often eclipsing in recklessness, misery and peculiarity of character the woodcutters of Campeachy and the lumberers of the Ohio and Mississippi'.

A newspaper report of the late 1860s refers to the sawyer as 'the roughest of rough fellows, muscular as a working bullock, hairy as a chimpanzee, obstinate as a mule, simple as a child, generous as the slave of Aladdin's lamp'. Adding that characteristics of the men included a fondness for rum-drinking and a weakness for fighting, the writer concludes: 'There is a good deal of rude honour about these fellows. Thus, if one chance to light upon a "fall" of cedar, none of the others will attempt to cut even a tree out of the group'.

The Rev. Dr. Lang, writing of conditions in Lismore in 1856, said that the cedar-getters 'were denied every opportunity of making homes for themselves and were driven perforce to spend their evenings in riotous dissipation and reduce their wives and families to misery and ruin'. He mentions one case where a cedar-getter had saved £800, and then because the squatter on whose run he had erected his hut threatened to evict him for trespass, 'had so lost heart that he spent the whole lot in one frenzied dissipation'. It became the custom of the cedar-getters to hand their money over to the store-keeper, rum seller, or later to the hotel-keeper to hold, and when it was all spent to go out and cut down more timber. No schools were built in the Northern Rivers districts for many years after the first settlement, nor were there resident clergymen or doctors. Most of the squatters' children received their education at home, but generally those of the cedar-getters grew up in ignorance. The food of these people was of the simplest kind—usually corned beef, damper and tea—but often the little schooners that brought the supplies would be bar-bound and there would be a severe shortage of foodstuffs.

A reflection of the difficulties and isolation of the cedar-getters' lives at that period can be seen in carefully preserved diaries of some of the early pioneers in the Richmond River town of Coraki. Reading these diaries one is struck by the fact that one of the problems in those days was getting married. The nearest clergyman was a hundred miles away at Grafton, and it was an impossible journey to undertake. A cedar-getter and his girl, having no means of getting there, married themselves by throwing a stone into the river and vowing to be true to each other 'till the stone floated'. Another couple got tired after months of waiting, and according to the lady's diary she proposed this solution: 'We can't go round the world looking for a clergyman. Let us begin together and get married when one turns up'. The man agreed and years later when a clergyman did arrive at the outlandish village he performed not only the marriage ceremony, but the baptism of their seven children.

The winning of the cedar was no easy task. Little difficulty was experienced with the trees on the rivers' edges, but when these were depleted the sawyers had to fight their way through the scrubs and forests to get at the prized cedars. When the trees were felled they were cross cut into logs which were branded so that the owners could distinguish them. To get the logs down to some stream which would, when flooded, carry them down to the river necessitated the cutting of a track through the scrub and the employment of bullocks. The cedar-getters continued with their cutting till the heavy rains came; then all hands set to work to put the logs into the rushing torrent. The red logs rushed down the various swollen streams till they reached the river, where they were caught in hundreds by chains stretched across their track. When the flood had abated, the logs of each owner were sorted and made into rafts. Logs which could not be sent down to the rivers were chopped into flitches and hauled to market by bullock teams.

Some of the cedar trees yielded immense quantities of timber (a good tree contained about 25,000 feet) and one such red cedar felled at Booyong yielded 33,000 feet. Even in those days cedar was worth £1 a hundred feet. As the forests and scrubs became denuded of this wealth of timber the sawyers turned their attention to the abundance of pine and other hardwoods. According to the *Report of the Intercolonial Exhibition of 1870* at Sydney, no less than 3,639,933 super feet of cedar was sent to Sydney in 1869 alone. The figure for pine and ash sent to Sydney the same year was 5,567,250 feet.

So ruthlessly were these magnificent timbers stripped that little was left at the dawn of the present century. Today the great forests are no more. Settlers seeking land for sugar-cane or dairying destroyed many millions of feet of extremely valuable timbers—the red cedar, beech, bean, rosewood and teak. The timber could not be used at anything like the rate at which it was being cut down, and so the trees had to be burned where they lay. Never again will Australia see the grandeur and beauty of the great red cedar country that was once part of her heritage. Relics of it are found in the cedar panelling and fittings of old homes in and about Windsor, Paramatta, Maitland, and the south coast districts. And what went overseas?

Epilogue

Out of the medley of his strange birth, wild youth, his trials, courage and resourcefulness emerged the Australian. He saw the subtle change come over the outlook of Britons on Australia, transforming the colonies, in their eyes, from a den of criminals to a bright land of opportunity. So he grew up with a fiercely independent character and manners—which often irked strangers—ever ready to assert that he was as good as or better than the rest of the world. This complex, probably a by-product of his earliest times, developed in an endeavour to impress those from other countries with more orthodox history, gradually diminished (if it has not entirely disappeared) with succeeding generations.

Upon the stock of the Australian colonial was engrafted as the years passed the adventurous overseas strains from Britain, other European countries and, to a small extent, America. Men and women staking new frontiers of settlement in this untamed but challenging land.

When celebrating in 1959 the centenary of responsible government in Queensland, her people rejoiced that a State which started off with 7½d. in the Treasury (and this was stolen the next night) is now the home of great herds of cattle and flocks of sheep, her sun-drenched coastlands producing vast agricultural wealth, and her mineral resources daily revealing themselves richer than the most optimistic ever imagined. It is interesting to reflect that the 18,000 who saw the Centenary Year Davis Cup match at the Milton Tennis Courts in Brisbane was about four times the total population of Brisbane when the city first became a municipality.

Similar success stories can be told of all the Australian States. Victoria's high standard of living and economic security have been built up through the strength of her industrial development. Melbourne's overcrowded University has been given relief with the completion of a second one in that city. Western Australia, the Cinderella State of former years, is no longer just a large undeveloped slice of Australia 'somewhere on the other side of the continent'. The £40 million refinery at Kwinana, the great asbestos mining at Wittenoom, and the multi-storey buildings replacing the old-fashioned structures in Perth all point to unlimited development.

Tasmania, that once pitiful convict outpost, is now the Mecca of holidaymakers, but its flourishing tourist trade is not its only important asset. Soundly-based heavy industries, the harnessing of the State's water resources for electric power, greater land settlement, all indicate the prosperity of one of the world's greatest fruit-producing countries. South Australia, too, has developed on an unprecedented scale with mammoth industrial plants, an ever-expanding shipbuilding industry, and shrewd long-range projects.

When one considers that from the thousand unhappy souls who landed at Sydney Cove on January 26, 1788, and subsequent days, there has grown a nation of more than ten million people, and that the sad and sombre little penal settlement is now one of the world's greatest cities, second only to London in the British Commonwealth, one must salute such astonishing progress. And salute the pioneers, those of British stock and all other nationalities and races who have come to Australia and made it their home and the richer for their coming.

'Australia's economy is growing so fast it is almost "exploding" ', said the vice-president of a world famous international motor company group, on his arrival in Sydney recently with plans for the manufacture of a new Australian-made car. 'This country is one of the soundest in which we think we can operate', he added, 'and we want to grow with it'.

In the inevitable rise and fall of older nations this so young and vigorous Australia with her enormously rich potentialities, and whose future destiny is being moulded in the Pacific, will in due time surely be a world force to reckon with.

Bibliography

Apart from the many sources of references mentioned in the text, the following works have been consulted and in some instances quoted:

Historical Records of Australia.

The Australian Encyclopaedia.

Alexander Maconochie of Norfolk Island. (Barry.)

Governor Phillip. (Milford.)

Macquarie's World. (Barnard.)

150 Years of Sydney. (Bertie.)

Old Sydney. (Bertie.)

Stories of Old Sydney. (Bertie.)

Curious Facts of Old Colonial Days. (Bonwick.)

Men and Manners in Australia. (Allan.)

Out of the Past. (Abbott.)

Blue Bloods of Botany Bay. (Mackaness.)

True Patriots All. (Ingleton.)

The Northern Rivers of New South Wales. (Cousins.)

The Newcastle Packets and the Hunter Valley. (Abbott.)

History of New South Wales. (Barton.)

Admiral Phillip. (Becke.)

Then and Now. (Valentine.)

Royal Australian Historical Society Journals.

The kindness of the Trustees of the Mitchell Library, Sydney, for permission to use prints as line drawings for reproduction in this book is greatly appreciated.

Index

208

212